THE POINT OF
CARE

How one leader took a health service from ordinary to extraordinary

A Business Fiction

The Point of Care
How one leader took a health service from ordinary to extraordinary

Published by Qualityclass Press, Melbourne, Australia.

ISBN: 978-0-646-99458-1

Editor: Susannah Noel

Proofreading: Tom Bedford

Design: meadencreative.com

SQS model graphic: Alice Edy

Further tools, training and information: www.cathybalding.com

THE POINT OF
CARE

How one leader took a health service from ordinary to extraordinary

A Business Fiction

CATHY BALDING

PROLOGUE

'You may not always have a comfortable life and you will not always be able to solve all of the world's problems at once, but don't ever underestimate the importance you can have. Because history has shown us that courage can be contagious and hope can take on a life of its own.'

- Michelle Obama -

The story of how Kinsley Valley Health Service (KVHS) transforms from ordinary to extraordinary is fiction. But it's very much based on the real world. Every health and human service organisation faces the struggles described in this story: how to create consistently high quality care, how to comply with governance requirements while staying focused on what's important, how to enable and motivate staff to lead change, how to manage the cynics and shift the boulders.

The Point of Care draws on the information in my technical books on creating great care, adds contemporary research and experience, and places it all in a tale that anyone responsible for leading and creating great care and services can relate to. You don't need to be a CEO to find the material relevant; anyone with a governance, leadership or management role in taking a service or organisation somewhere better than it is will recognise and learn from the KVHS' trials and triumphs.

The story demonstrates how a strategic quality system can tackle the myriad problems inherent in poor quality care, showcasing key tools required to create a consistently high performing organisation, including:

- Defining high quality care
- Making high quality care a strategic and operational priority
- Developing the right organisational mindset to achieve it consistently
- Equipping and empowering staff to create it with consumers every day
- Developing the quality and clinical governance structures and systems to support it.

The Point of Care also explores the human side of creating consistently great care through the lens of complexity, socialisation and resilience. If we don't integrate these into our approach to improving care, we are unlikely to make the leaps we need to get where we want to go—and where consumers need us to be.

I'd like to thank the thousands of people who've welcomed me into their organisations over the years to work with their consumers, boards, executives, and staff. This book would not have been possible without the knowledge and experience I've gained from all of you. A special thanks to Professor Sandra Leggat at La Trobe University who made it possible for me to find out what an effective quality system really does look like via the three-year research project we undertook together, and to draw on that material for aspects of the KVHS story.

Finally, to all the quality leaders out there: set your goals and go after them! Some days you'll make progress in giant leaps. Others, you'll be lucky to take a step. But keep going! Persistence with purpose adds up. Never doubt that consistent effort, channelled through a realistic and positive mindset and focused on supporting people to be great, will result in great care.

I hope that engaging with the KVHS Team's struggles and successes will help you shape your own quality leadership path—and that you a enjoy a good read in the process!

Note: *The Point of Care* is neither documentary, nor autobiography. The characters, health service and improvement initiatives depicted in this book are drawn from an amalgam of my experience, research, the relevant literature and the many organisations and people I've worked with over a long career. None of the issues or improvement ideas in this book is a direct copy from any organisation. Any story line, initiative or character closely resembling a real person or place is unintentional and purely coincidental.

Where key points are derived specifically from another source, this is noted in the Sources and Influences list. When my models and tools referred to in the text are included in the appendices, this is indicated by a superscript A# corresponding to the appendix number. While I encourage you to draw on the material in this book, it is important to remember that all ideas and tools must be assessed for, and adapted to, an organisation's specific context and circumstances. Ultimately, it's the quality of your implementation process that determines the results you achieve.

More complete lists of references that I've drawn on over my career are found in my technical books: The Strategic Quality Manager Handbook and Create a Great Quality System in Six Months Blueprint.

For my sister-in-law and friend, Denise, who made excellence look effortless.

CHAPTER ONE

• •

The Minister for Health sat stony faced. This was clearly not a social call.

"Last. Last! You should be ashamed, Carol. You're the CEO but you don't seem to know what's happening in your own health service!" The minister pointed past Carol. "Look at what's going on under your very nose!"

Carol Mathewson stared out the window of her office at the sparkling new inpatient building opposite. Hundreds of doctors, wearing identical white coats, poured out of the sliding-glass doors and down the street in military formation. Like the water-carrying brooms in Disney's *The Sorcerer's Apprentice*, their march was relentless and apparently endless.

The minister gazed at her severely. "So, what are you going to do about it? Don't give me excuses. I'm looking for a solution!"

Carol woke with a jump from the dream—or nightmare—that had disturbed her every morning that week, feeling a mix of relief and frustration. Relief, because who wants to be stuck in a dream like that? And frustration, because she wished she could hear her own answer. The minister may have been a dream, but her concerns reflected stark reality. She did need solutions, and fast. In fact, a little sorcery wouldn't go astray right now. Carol had worked in healthcare all her professional life, and disgruntled doctors were not unusual. But her health service being on the bottom of the state "league ladder" for both consumer and staff satisfaction? That was a new experience and she had no intention of getting used to it.

Carol glanced at the clock and summoned her willpower for an early-morning workout. She would need all the strength she could muster to face the challenges of the new week. As she approached her fiftieth birthday, she was working hard to get her health act together after a few years of hit and miss, and she enjoyed feeling strong and fit again. But she did not enjoy getting out of bed before dawn. She dressed quickly in the gym clothes she'd left out last night to nudge her good intentions into action, pulling her shoulder-length grey-blond hair into a ponytail as she descended the stairs.

As always, the silence of an empty apartment caught her by surprise. She hadn't lived on her own for fifteen years, until a few months ago when she and her partner ended their relationship, and she hadn't yet fully adapted to the change. Not that she didn't have more than enough going on in her working life to keep her occupied. Carol had been the Chief Executive Officer of Kinsley Valley Health Service (KVHS) for only a few weeks, and it was already clear that the hours in the day didn't quite match the demands of the role. But the mornings and evenings on her own were still tough.

She shook her head impatiently. No time to wallow. She filled her water bottle, grabbed an apple, and headed out the door. Her neighbour across the street greeted her with a happy "Morning!" as Carol threw her gym bag in the boot of the car. He smiled broadly and pointed to the front page of the local paper he held in his hand. Carol couldn't quite make out what he was saying. It sounded like "bad day at the office," but it couldn't be that, could it? She waved cheerily at him as she drove away.

*****

A couple of hours later, Carol was typing furiously on her computer when her Executive Assistant, Rosie, poked her head around the door. Rosie had looked after five Kinsley Valley CEOs, and had mastered fierce protection down to a fine art, albeit camouflaged in a sweet demeanour. Although planning her retirement, she showed no signs of slowing down. Her back was as ramrod straight, her wit as sharp, and her dedication to her job as strong as ever.

"Professor Yang would like to see you—now. I told her you were busy, but she won't take no for an answer."

Carol looked up from the Board Quality and Clinical Governance Committee papers. Although Rosie's tone was light, she was shaking her head decisively. Carol smiled inwardly. If Rosie was saying no to this meeting, she was probably right, and Carol's initial reaction was to protect her quarantined committee preparation time. But a quick mental application of her consumer rule of thumb made the decision for her.

"Ask her to come in please, Rosie."

Professor Yang was the hugely influential Surgical Unit Head. Short, feisty, and endlessly on the move, she talked in short, sharp dot points that often left her listeners breathless. Encounters with Professor Yang were more like speed dates than conversations, and she was commonly known around the health service as the "pocket rocket." Carol braced herself and stood up.

"Nice to see you, Lian," was the last complete sentence she managed to get out as the professor charged past Rosie and into her office.

Fifteen long minutes later, she stalked out. Rosie's head appeared around the door again, this time accompanied by her hand holding a mug of coffee.

"Thanks, Rosie, you're a lifesaver." Carol smiled gratefully.

"I don't know why you agreed to see her." Rosie picked up a pile of papers from Carol's out-tray as she scolded. "She didn't have an appointment, and you know she's on the war path."

"Well, in these situations I apply a little consumer rule of thumb I've developed over the years of dealing with healthcare egos—including mine!" Carol laughed at Rosie's polite confusion. "Yes, I'm happy to admit that my ego is healthy. It's hard to get to be a CEO without it! It's *managing* my ego that's the issue. I apply the same rule for others as I do for myself: what's best for the consumers affected by this situation? In fact, to be honest, what I really think is, what would be best if my mother were affected by this situation? When I look at it that way, it's better to see Prof now when she's between surgery and clinic rather than later in the afternoon when it suits me but will make her patients wait. If my mum were one of those patients, I wouldn't want her waiting longer than she needed to because the CEO pulled rank on a doctor."

"Challenges are what make life interesting and overcoming them is what makes life meaningful,"[1] Rosie recited, as she refreshed the water in the vase of wildflowers she brought in for Carol every week.

Carol nodded. "Yes! Something like that. And some challenges are best addressed head-on and then done with. As you well know, there are some pretty damaged bridges with the doctors here that I need to repair. Prof Yang had a point today, even if I didn't enjoy her delivery. It seems that lots of decisions have been made over the past couple of years without involving the doctors. She's particularly cross about the new operating room booking system that was implemented without her input, which she now says doesn't work the way the surgeons need it to and is reducing patient flow and throughput rather than increasing it. I'll talk to Kristen about it."

"Did she threaten to defect to the new private hospital and take all the other surgeons with her?"

Carol's eyebrows shot up.

"Oh, yes, that's the word around town," Rosie continued. "The docs are saying that if 'management' doesn't start listening to them, they'll all walk out, and then you won't have a hospital. Of course, they said that when Seb was the CEO, too, but he didn't take any notice. As far as he was concerned, the clinical staff did their job and he did his and never the twain shall meet. Unless they wanted to spend money, of course. Then he couldn't wait to meet with them to tell them they couldn't. That was before there was a shiny new private hospital, though. Now if they walk out, they only have to go five hundred metres down the road to a new job!"

Carol had a mental flash of marching lines of white coats. She shuddered.

"Are you okay?" Rosie peered at her. "You look like someone just walked over your grave. You've certainly had a good old-fashioned Kinsley Valley baptism of fire. Not helped by this, I expect." She laid today's edition of the *Kinsley Valley Leader* newspaper on the desk in front of Carol. The headline yelled, NEW CEO NOT UP TO FIXING KVHS.

Carol was momentarily speechless. Her neighbour had not been kidding.

"They've been at us ever since the deaths on the medical ward were made public," Rosie explained with a grimace. "But this is the most personal rubbish I've seen so far." She paused while Carol scanned the article, which was a collection of unnamed "sources" criticising Carol's leadership style. "Still think you made the right decision?"

Carol swallowed. "I can't deny that there have been moments. I do love a challenge —and I've certainly got one." She took a sip of coffee, staring at the headline, and clenched her jaw into a determined line. "But we can't let this sort of thing distract us. I'll have more trouble than this if we don't get these Board Quality and Clinical Governance Committee papers to the Chair today. I'll have them done by lunchtime."

Rosie left, closing the door behind her, and Carol attempted to refocus on the committee agenda with little success. She glanced at the article again, then sat back and looked around her office. Administration was in the "old" hospital, and although the CEO's office was the largest in the block, with enough room for a small meeting table and whiteboard, it was hardly palatial. However, a fresh coat of cream paint, Rosie's wildflowers, and bookcases filled with leadership and healthcare management books, topped with some photos, created a pleasant space. Her PhD certificate sat on the wall alongside a couple of leadership awards and enlarged aerial before-and-after photos of the KVHS building works. As in her dream, Carol's windows looked across the road to the new inpatient building. There was a corner office available there, with commanding views over Kinsley Valley township, but Carol had decided that its current function as a meeting room made more sense.

Rosie was right: her first few weeks had been a baptism of fire, with Prof Yang just the latest in a succession of angry people who'd confronted her since she'd started as CEO. Although unpleasant, the reaction to her as a new CEO wasn't surprising. Carol had worked in healthcare all her life and she knew the ups and downs. And Kinsley Valley Health Service had been in a long "down" over the past couple of years. A damning accreditation result and an external review of long-standing poor patient care on the medical ward had attracted both bad press and community anger. A major move into the new building and an organisational restructure, not to mention a new CEO and Board Chair, had left the staff and community anxious, frustrated and unsettled. Carol wouldn't admit to Rosie, or anyone else, that she was struggling to find her feet under the weight of the problems, not to mention the staff hostility. She was feeling it all more than she had expected to.

She stood, walked over to the window, and looked out at the busy comings and goings. *Overcoming challenges does make life meaningful. But how much meaning can I handle?*

Carol had spent most of her time so far observing and listening. She was in the fortunate position of not having to make any immediate decisions as the urgent medical ward and accreditation "rescue" work had been addressed, and the hospital move completed, before she started. But the memories lingered on, and there were many issues to sort through. Coroners' cases on some of the patient deaths were proceeding and likely to drag on for years. Staff morale was low, patient complaints were high and KVHS was at the bottom of the state-wide results for both. Internal quality and safety metrics also indicated that suboptimal patient care wasn't confined to the medical ward, with problems scattered across the organisation. Besides that, the community trust in their health service had plummeted over the past couple of years, and there had been little consumer input into improving KVHS services. As demonstrated that morning, the local newspaper loved to fill column inches with the latest KVHS bad news story; supplied, Carol suspected, by disgruntled staff, as well as unhappy patients and families. She hadn't expected it to be a picnic; she'd done her due diligence on KVHS and knew the story. But the depth of the negative culture had taken her by surprise.

Carol picked up the photo of her farewell from the city hospital she'd left for KVHS. How she missed it! If she could have, she would have brought them all with her. How much easier this role would be with her old team around.

As always when she felt herself slipping into nostalgia for her old job, she reminded herself that she was there for a positive reason that outweighed the negatives. When Carol's father died just over a year ago, she'd had some big decisions to make. Her mother was too unwell to remain living alone in Carol's rural hometown, and she soon moved to the local aged-care facility. After a few months of driving or flying the eight hundred kilometre round trip to visit her every second weekend, Carol knew it was time for a decision. Her mother needed her to be closer and Carol realised that she wanted to be. She loved her job as the Chief Operating Officer of a large metropolitan hospital, though, and wasn't ready to give up her healthcare career just yet. So she kept an eye out for jobs coming up in the major regional centres around her hometown.

Carol couldn't believe her luck when the position of CEO of KVHS was advertised and, after a rigorous selection process, she got the job. Kinsley Valley was a beautiful area about forty minutes' drive from her mother's aged care facility. Carol knew it well as she had attended high school there and worked her way up to Chief Physiotherapist at KVHS before leaving for the city. Twenty years had elapsed since then and Kinsley Valley town and health service were unrecognisable. A new university and research precinct ensured there was plenty going on in a growing population of mixed cultures and ages. The coffee was as good as she needed it to be, local wineries produced very drinkable drops and provided great places for a good meal, and the agricultural sector had found some lucrative niches which kept employment ticking along.

Carol sat back down at her computer and drank a long gulp from her coffee cup, frowning at the amount of work it was taking to craft a Board Quality Committee agenda and papers that actually warranted a meeting. Her eye was drawn to a report from aged care showing significant improvement in dementia care, and she smiled. It wasn't all doom and gloom! Despite its problems, KVHS had a lot going for it. The new and impressive two-hundred-bed inpatient building had opened six months ago without too many disasters, the finances were stable thanks to the previous CEO's focus—not perfect, but manageable—and the Board had turned over several members and was now equipped with what looked like a useful set of skills. The

KVHS residential aged care and community services seemed to be running well and gave Carol hope that all was not lost.

From her first few weeks' observations, she could see that, like most organisations, there were pockets of brilliance, some things that desperately needed fixing, and some solid mediocrity in between. The CEO she'd replaced had been an infrastructure and numbers man, and, whilst he had produced a new building on time and budget, he'd ignored the creeping decline in staff morale and standard of patient care while his attention was "up and out." Not long after the new building opened, he was gone, along with the Board Chair, as the enormity of patient harm in the medical service and accreditation failure became apparent. The publication of the first set of state-wide results for staff and consumer satisfaction—showing KVHS languishing at the bottom of both lists—was the final straw.

Clinical governance warning bells had rung in Carol's head since her first walk around the health service, as obvious risks (some of which had two legs, two arms, and a head) stared her in the face. One of those risks was her Executive Team, who bore the scars of the past year and clearly hadn't quite recovered from their previous CEO's sudden departure. Carol believed there was a lot of potential to be unleashed if she could just pull the right levers. She secretly relished the workout her skills and experience would get.

Little did she realise she'd be flexing her leadership muscles in earnest the very next day.

*****

"I'm sorry, but I don't get it." Anton Voronin, the Chief Finance and Information Officer, shook his head. In his early forties, Anton had recently switched careers from banking to health, and although he was enjoying the change, he was not yet fully conversant in the mysterious ways of healthcare management. He adjusted his glasses and leaned forward as he always did when making a point. His sportsman's powerful shoulders hunched over the table. "You may not fully appreciate yet, Carol, that under the previous CEO we invested heavily in state-of-the-art reporting platforms. I'd say we have one of the most sophisticated information systems of any regional health service in the country. And now you're telling us that it's not up to scratch?"

"I suppose you're comparing it to your big-city health service information system,"

Dr Anne Bixton, the Chief Medical Officer, drawled, speaking slowly as if to give Carol time to keep up. She patted a stray silver-grey hair into place, straightened the pearl bracelet on her wrist, and glanced at her phone as if distracted by other, more important things.

Carol looked around the table at her Executive Team. They were barely an hour into the first day of their two-day off-site planning workshop, and already she could feel the wheels spinning. Despite the pleasant surrounds of the wood-panelled conference room, with the morning sun pouring through floor-to-ceiling windows, the atmosphere was dark. Some of them had obviously saved up their negativity for this event and were now letting it flow. *They're probably overdue a bit of catharsis.* The trick would be to get the balance right, so they also accomplished what they came here to do. She summoned up her positivity.

"Actually, it's a far better data system than the one I used to work with," Carol responded pleasantly, rising from her chair and picking up a whiteboard pen. "It's what goes into it and comes out of it that's the problem."

This stirred the normally quiet and reserved Quality and Risk Executive Director, William, into speech. "Um, but Carol, the Board is happy with our reports. And we didn't come unstuck with accreditation on the basis of our reporting."

Everyone looked at William with surprise. Since the massive failure a few months ago, they hadn't heard him utter the word "accreditation." Despite the fact that the problems had been with clinical care, William Hayes had been silently blamed by the others around the table for the poor result, and he knew it. His contribution had subsequently decreased to the point where he could sit through a whole meeting without saying anything at all. His health also appeared to have deteriorated with his confidence. His shirt buttons strained against his stomach, and his suit, which had fitted him perfectly six months ago, now looked a size too small. His pleasant face was puffy below a thatch of sandy hair that he ruffled when agitated, and thus was in a state of constant disarray. He was slowly but surely demolishing a plate of croissants that began the meeting in the middle of the table but had made their way to a convenient space in front of him. Traces of pastry could be seen around the corners of his mouth.

The fact that William had continued to be blamed for problems outside his control told Carol a lot about her Executive Team. They may have called themselves a team, but she didn't think of them as one. They lacked every building block: common goals, shared commitment, agreed ways of working and communicating, role clarity, accountability, and trust.[2] This lack of real teamwork was impacting the broader organisation and was likely the root of much of the mess the health service found itself in. Not that the people in front of her seemed to realise this. Carol had noticed that some members of the group liked to attribute KVHS' woes to anyone but themselves; with the accreditation result placed squarely on Williams' shoulders. She was hoping that by the end of the workshop, the group would be on the way to gelling as a team and, in the process, that this would solve another problem that needed to be addressed as a priority: their lack of focus on core business.

"Let's look at it this way," Carol said, writing a question on the whiteboard. "How good is KVHS clinical care?"

"The best, of course," Kristen Aldenberg, the Chief Operating Officer, answered confidently, tossing her ponytail. Kristen's sun-bleached hair, sturdy build and healthy glow reflected the hard work she put in on the olive farm that had been in her family for fifty years, much of it every morning before leaving for her KVHS day job. She had worked her way up from her first role as a ward clerk and loved KVHS and—nearly—everyone in it. Carol liked her; she was naturally street smart and had acquired some useful formal qualifications over the years. Although seemingly casual in her approach, no one knew better than Kristen how KVHS worked, and no one was more disappointed at the year they'd had and where they found themselves. She had experienced the issues close-up, acting as CEO while the search was on to replace the previous incumbent, and in that role had been secretly shocked at the myriad unaddressed problems she'd found on the CEO's desk.

"What does 'best' mean?" scoffed Anne. "It's impossible to know, isn't it? Probably really good in some places and not so good in others, like any hospital."

Elena Taverna, the Chief Nursing and Midwifery Officer (CNMO) and Executive Director of Clinical Services, spoke up for the first time, shifting self-consciously in her chair. She was a striking woman her early sixties, with short, stylishly cut hair that remained remarkably dark for her age. She was third-generation Kinsley Valley; her grandfather had established one of the first vineyards in the district after emigrating from Italy. Elena had nursed all around the world to escape her strict parents, eventually and unexpectedly meeting and marrying a local farmer. That was many years ago, and her children were now adults. "I'd say 'excellent,' thanks in no small part to our nursing staff." She glanced at Anne as she spoke; they'd been comrades in arms on this Executive Team for years and understood each other's thoughts.

"We compare alright on national indicators." William pointed to some graphs on the table in front of him. "I'd say that, overall, we're about average."

"So, what shall I write?" asked Carol, underwhelmed but not surprised by the response. "Pretty good? About average? Best, but poor in places? Excellent where the nurses are involved?" She wrote on the whiteboard as she spoke.

The group chuckled uncomfortably.

Carol turned to face the group. "Complacency is the enemy of quality care. It's easy to become complacent about care in human services because we don't know enough about how good it really is. And, interestingly, no one really asks us to. Apart from some specific measures and accreditation, there's limited external expectation that we'll draw a line in the sand about how good we want our care to be. Or that we'll know at any given time where we sit in relation to that. It's all a bit hit and miss. Think of your favourite professional sports team. If someone asked their coach or CEO on national television to rate their standard of play, and they gave the answers you just gave, how impressed would the fans and sponsors be? Or the players, for that matter? 'Oh well, we're pretty good; we're excellent depending on who's playing; brilliant in patches; impossible to tell; about average....' "

Carol stopped. There were wry smiles around the executive group, except for Elena, who sat impassively. Anne was similarly stony-faced and tapped the table rapidly with an impressive gold pen.

"Don't tell me you're one of those CEOs who insists we be more like an airline or a sports team or a hotel," she snapped. "Because we're none of those things. And measuring the quality of our care is much harder than measuring the performance of a sports team."

"No," reassured Carol, noting Elena nodding in agreement with Anne. "I'm not one of 'those' CEOs. I know exactly how hard it is to create and maintain consistently high quality care in the complex healthcare environment. I've lived it as a clinician and manager, and I've studied it. I'm the last person to underestimate the degree of difficulty. But that doesn't mean we can't learn and adapt helpful things from other industries. Right now, I do want to pursue the sports team analogy just a little. You make a good point, by the way, Anne. Why is it easy for a sports team to measure their performance?"

Before Anne could answer, sports-mad Anton cut in. "That's easy," he said. "Because the results tell the story. A team can't hide from the scoreboard. It's there for all to see. And we …" He trailed off, realising the hole he'd dug and leapt into. "Oh, I see." He grinned at Carol.

"What am I missing?" Elena looked put out that Anton and Carol seemed to be sharing a private joke.

"Yeah, come on you two, you've left the rest of us behind," complained Kristen. "Anton, would you like to do the honours?" Carol sat down.

"Well," Anton began slowly, unused to leading discussions on topics other than budgets and IT, "I think I get where Carol's coming from. Sports teams have results that show how they compare to others and therefore how good they are. In fact, they measure lots of things, from players' individual performance to training and game stats. All of these metrics help them to reflect and improve. But in the end, the only results that really tell you how you compare are the game-day results and where you are on the ladder."

"Oh!" exclaimed Kristen, who was a football fanatic. "I get it, too. Here at KVHS, we also measure lots of things in our beautiful reporting system. But it's mostly process. We don't have any 'final scores' to show how good we really are—or not. And without knowing that, I guess the easiest path is to believe that we are good until something happens that says we're not."

Elena glared at Kristen. "That's all very well, but where would we get that information? There's hardly any decent data around, except for what we already have on our clinical risks and what we report to the Department of Health. And you're telling us that's no good!"

"Not exactly, Elena," Carol said. She walked over to a window and opened it, letting in a slight breeze as the room warmed up. "Anton just did a nice job of describing that it's important to have all sorts of measures. So I do value those we currently look at. And thanks to the Department of Health, we know where we sit on the league ladder with a couple of really important measures."

"What, staff and consumer satisfaction? What do they have to do with the quality of care? Just when I thought I was getting it …" Anton shook his head in confusion.

"Come on, Anton, you do get it. Think about it." Carol was keen not to lose Anton just as he'd been showing signs of progress.

But Anne wasn't having any of it. She sighed in exasperation. "Don't give us that touchy-feely stuff. I don't know if you've noticed, but we work in a health service, not at Disneyland. Patient satisfaction! You can't expect patients to be happy. They're sick. I suppose there's room for improvement with food and parking. They've been problems forever, along with communication. But what can you do about that? And if staff aren't satisfied, well, as long as they're doing the job we're paying them to do, is that something that should take up our time here, when we have so many urgent clinical issues to discuss?" She sat back and crossed her arms.

Carol resisted a strong urge to point out how *not* discussing staff and patient satisfaction had landed the health service in the situation it was in. "I know you're a fan of research and evidence, Anne, so you'll be interested to know that many studies suggest that staff well-being and morale are strongly linked to patient satisfaction, as well as to the standard of clinical care provided. The fact that KVHS is thirty-fifth out of thirty-five health services in this state for both is no coincidence. So if you want to discuss important issues, these are some we should start with. This is embarrassing for us as executives. Yes, we should be embarrassed"—Carol looked directly at Anne and Elena as they exchanged outraged looks—"because we've allowed things to slip to the point where patient care is compromised, and the consumer experience at KVHS is suboptimal. Not to mention the way we've let the Board and the Kinsley Valley community down. So in response to your question, I guess the short answer is … these are urgent clinical issues."

No one spoke for a minute. Carol hadn't intended to wade into this minefield so early in the session, but opportunities had to be grabbed when they appeared. She waited.

Kristen turned an unbecoming shade of crimson. "I suppose we deserve this. We haven't really discussed it properly since those state-wide results first came out from the Department of Health just before Seb left. We basically handballed the staff satisfaction issue to the People and Culture Service and patient satisfaction to William and his team. We … we haven't really owned it…"

Carol gave Kristen a supportive nod, hoping her appraisal would open the others to greater honesty about the situation. She looked enquiringly around the table, but the rest of the group was tight-lipped. This was not the sort of conversation they were used to having and there appeared to be little appetite for change. Carol decided she'd pushed hard enough for now.

"We've scheduled these issues to be addressed tomorrow, so let's stick to that. The data we have don't tell us the whole story about how good our care is. It's a bit like thinking the Milky Way is the whole sky. It's easier to see than other galaxies, but that doesn't mean the others aren't there, or that they're unimportant. William is right. KVHS didn't come unstuck with accreditation because of the reporting system. It came unstuck because the measures didn't pick up where things were falling down. Incorrect diagnoses. Treatment not based on evidence. Patients sent home too soon. Uncoordinated care that allowed patients to slip through the cracks. Clinical deterioration not picked up. Basic neglect. Unfortunately, too many patients in the medical ward fell through those gaps and suffered unnecessarily for too long before the problems were identified. Even though we're plugging those holes now, is anyone willing to promise me there aren't similar care and reporting gaps elsewhere in the organisation?"

"I'd like to promise you that, because I think you're overreacting," Anne began, twirling her gold pen rapidly. "But I can't. I don't think we should continue to rake over old problems. Oh, I know those things shouldn't have happened"—she responded to Carol's frown—"and particularly not over such a long period. But the medical patients are getting more complex every year. And they don't all make it easy. If they'd follow instructions and look after themselves, half of them wouldn't need to come to hospital and expose themselves to our heartless clinicians and bad care."

The rest of the group glanced nervously from Anne to Carol. It seemed that Anne was on for an argument. But Carol had heard these sentiments many times before and refused to take the bait. "I understand why you'd say that. It must be frustrating as a clinician to see your good work and effort ignored by some patients. Care is hard to get right for many reasons. Our responsibility is to help clinicians give the very best care they can and to help patients do the things that will support their own health. And to foster partnerships between both to get the best results. But we can't know how we're doing with any of this if we don't have some decent measures from both the consumer and staff perspectives."

Anne put her pen down and sat back. "So, what are these magical measures you have in mind? And where will we get this amazing information?"

Carol looked around and saw all eyes on her. The energy in the room had escalated from half an hour ago, even if it had taken an agitated CMO to achieve it.

"Million-dollar questions. But before we get to that, bear with me for a few more minutes while I play out the sports story." She sipped some water and looked around the table. "What's the ultimate goal of any professional sports team?"

"To win a championship," the group chorused.

"So they have one huge advantage over healthcare, because they have an unequivocal, and shared, definition of success—or high performance—that we don't have."

"But isn't ours 'high quality care for our community', as it says in our vision statement? And … let me see," Kristen said, swiping her phone screen rapidly, "that includes: 'satisfied consumers and a happy, healthy staff and community.' "

"Yes," broke in Elena, "but we're back to the measurement problem again. A championship or premiership, or whatever you want to call it, is easy to measure. You either win it or you don't. 'High quality care' is hard."

"Almost impossible," said Carol with a smile, "if you don't define it."

"You can't define 'high quality care.'" Anne rapped the table with her pen again and scowled at Carol. "It's different for everyone. Every patient is unique and every clinician has their ideas about what excellent care is for their own patients. Don't give us some jargonistic definition that no one understands and say we've defined quality care."

"No, I'm not going to give you anything," said Carol. "You're going to define 'high quality care' yourselves. Yes, Anne, I get what you're saying about individual patients and clinicians. We want clinicians to think about the needs of each person, not colour by numbers. But there are some basics that we must get right for every consumer and some care that must be standardised—no excuses, no exceptions." Elena opened her mouth to speak but Carol held up her hand and kept going. "Our definition of 'high quality care' is our definition of success. Like a sports premiership, it's something we can all agree on and work towards together. If we don't define it, the default definition in healthcare is usually 'compliance and staying out of trouble,' which isn't very motivating for our staff—or consumers—and anchors us firmly in complacency and mediocrity."

"Oh!" exclaimed Kristen, brow furrowed. "That's not very good is it? You're right. I just hadn't thought about it that way."

"Yep, it seems that compliance has definitely been our default definition of success. But it didn't keep us out of trouble, did it?" Anton pushed his chair back, stretched his long legs out in front of him and looked quizzically around the table.

"I'll let you be the judge of that." Carol noticed Anne's scowl and nodded briskly, anxious to avoid more diversionary outrage. "And to go back to your lightbulb moment, Anton, once we're clear on what high quality care is, we'll have a better idea of the results we're trying to achieve, and therefore what we'll need to measure to tell us if we're achieving them. Rather than having a conversation about 'what we should measure' in a kind of vacuum, we have that conversation based on 'what will tell us we're achieving our definition of success?' Then we work out how to get the information."

"You've lost me." Anne stood up. "This is too much like the mumbo jumbo I heard at that quality conference I had to go to last year so Seb could show the accreditation assessors I was a 'clinical leader.' It sounds to me like you intend to interfere in clinicians' work. If that's what this is about, I'm not interested. Look, I know you've got a job to do, Carol, but count me out of this conversation. I'll be downstairs catching up on my phone calls." And with that, she picked up her bag and left.

As if choreographed, William, Kristen, Elena and Anton stared at the door, each other, and, finally, at Carol.

"This would seem to be a good time for a break. I'll see you back here in fifteen minutes."

CHAPTER TWO

Carol breathed deeply as she descended the stairs in search of Anne. She found her sitting in a corner of the deserted lobby, looking at her phone.

"May I?" Carol indicated the chair opposite Anne.

"Of course." Anne's reply was "yes" but her slight turn away from Carol's chair signalled "if you must."

Carol opened her mouth to speak, but Anne beat her to it.

"No one who saw us in action this morning would know we have a busy hospital to run," she began. "Why we had to come all the way out here to talk rubbish is beyond me. Seb was perfectly happy with a hotel in town if we needed to get away from the hospital to discuss something. He didn't feel the need to splurge on wineries and overnight stays."

Carol couldn't help but smile—on the inside. It was hardly a splurge given that the decisions they made in the next two days would directly influence the health service's direction, progress, and success over the next three years. She was convinced of the value of getting people away from the workplace to refocus and reframe and had deliberately chosen a small winery far enough away from Kinsley Valley to necessitate an overnight stay. It was a lovely old place. The recently refurbished conference room boasted balcony views over the vineyard, and comfortably contained twelve people around a large wooden table, two whiteboards, and a screen. Basic but comfortable accommodation rounded out the package. Rosie had recommended it because of the moderate cost and also because the winery frequently supported KVHS by donating wine and hampers for fundraising events.

But it was useless trying to explain any of this and she suspected that Anne's complaint about the venue was just a preamble to the real issue, anyway. She didn't have to suspect for long.

"I'll be honest with you, Carol," Anne sighed. "If this is what you're going to be about as a CEO, I'm not going to like it."

Carol rather thought that she already featured on Anne's "things to dislike" list and that the morning's discussions had merely cemented her place in the top ten.

"I'm sorry you feel that way," Carol said. "But let's cut to the nub of the issue. The safety and quality of care at Kinsley Valley are not close to where they should be."

Anne rolled her eyes as if to say, "here we go again." But Carol continued, unfazed.

"There's a lot of work to be done. But none of that can happen unless and until we take responsibility for the problems and commit as a team to fix them. What we need is a whole-of-organisation approach to creating Great Care for every single patient. And that's impossible to achieve without a whole-of-Executive-Team approach to leading it."

Anne's voice rose. "Why should we take responsibility for the poor care in one service? What happened to people being responsible for their own actions? All this 'no blame' business lets people get away with whatever they like. And somehow that's our problem!" She leaned forward and rapped the table between them with her knuckles. "Look, Carol, I don't think you really understand rural hospitals. You're not a doctor, and you've been working in the city for a long time. We do things differently here. We don't need all these formal processes and rules and compliance. We all just get on and do our best. We did it like that before you, and we'll keep doing it after you're gone."

Carol paused before responding. "It doesn't matter if we're the biggest or the smallest health service in the country—those doctors on the medical ward should not have been allowed to work outside their scope for so long. Patients were harmed unnecessarily because no one was game to take them on. It took the patients' and families' complaints to the Minister to get anyone to pay attention! Yes, the people involved in what went on over the past couple of years are answering for their actions in various ways. But ultimately, it's the executives' job to not get into that situation in the first place. That's our role on behalf of the Board and our community."

She waited for the expected counterattack from Anne, but there was silence.

"And for the record," Carol continued, "no, I'm not a doctor, and I don't pretend to be. Not a *medical* doctor, anyway. But I do know how clinical care works as a physiotherapist, and I do know how to lead and manage a health service to make it successful as a health service manager. This is what I'm here to do at KVHS, where, by the way, I started my career as a junior physio and worked my way up to managing the department before leaving. I know how important this health service is to this community. I love rural health. I wouldn't be back here if I didn't."

"That's all very well," Anne responded, crossing her legs and arms simultaneously, "but that's no guarantee that you won't make a mess of things. No doubt you've got some big restructure planned that will throw the place into turmoil. Every new CEO does. I don't want any part of it."

Carol nodded slowly. "Yes, the temptation for a new CEO to restructure is strong, I agree! But, no, not now. I'd rather put all that time and effort into helping people to better enact their current roles. I can't promise not to tweak here and there, but there won't be a major restructure."

Anne raised her chin at this unexpected parry from Carol but said nothing.

"We might as well be clear about our relative positions," Carol continued. "If you want to be part of the work this Executive Team has in front of it over the next few years, and if you're prepared to make some tough decisions and drive some big changes among the medical staff, I'm more than happy to support you. I know how much the doctors respect you and that's a precious asset. However, if you can't fully commit to the new direction and priorities that we're here to develop over the next two days, then we'll have to have a difficult conversation."

The corners of Anne's mouth twitched. "Oh—a *difficult* conversation! Not like the delightful chat we're having now?"

Carol was grateful for the icebreaker. "I can't do what needs to be done without every one of us rowing in the same direction. I've tried it before in other organisations and it just doesn't work. Turning a health service around needs more than half-hearted lip service." She glanced at her watch. "Time to get back. Are you coming? Or would you like some time to think about it?"

Anne gazed out the glass doors in silence. Carol took some deep breaths as she waited. The ball was firmly in Anne's court, now. A minute passed before Anne turned back to Carol, her mouth set. "No, I don't need time to think about it," she said quietly. "I've thought about it. Finding the right time to retire is usually tricky, but in this instance, you've done me a favour and made it easy. I've been watching you this past month and I can see you mean business. Oh, I know KVHS needs to change; I'm not blind to its faults. But I'm not interested in investing my time in more management work. I have many friends among the medical staff and I'm not going to jeopardise that for a CEO who may not last very long anyway. You'll have my formal resignation on your desk when you get back to work on Monday. Goodbye, Carol." She rose, picked up her bag, and hunted for her car keys.

"I'm sorry to hear that." Carol's response was genuine. In a funny sort of way she had grown to like the feisty, straight-shooting CMO. But at the same time, she had reservations about Anne's ability to lead the clinical practice changes required to support the quality of care she wanted KVHS to be known for. "I'll respect your decision, whatever it is. But sleep on it before you write that letter, just in case you change your mind."

"I will," said Anne, "and don't worry, I won't go back to the hospital now and cause a stir. Hillary and I have a weekender about an hour from here. I'll go there and prepare my reports for the Board Quality and Clinical Governance Committee; yes, I know they're late, Rosie has been at me for days. But at least this way she'll have them tomorrow instead of Monday. And no"—Anne caught Carol's sceptical glance—"this is not a ruse to find time for writing committee reports! Having said that, it's worked out rather well, hasn't it?"

Carol felt a stab of annoyance as she watched her CMO walk out with what looked suspiciously like a spring in her step. Had Anne picked a fight to get this precise result? She shook her head. No point being paranoid. She'd take Anne at her word and see what happened on Monday. She sighed and turned to climb the stairs back to the conference room.

Great start. What will I do for an encore?

*****

All heads turned as Carol walked in. "Where's Anne?" asked Kristen.

Carol sat and surveyed her team. "Anne isn't coming back to the workshop."

Everyone spoke at once. "What happened?" "Was she really that angry?" "Should we still have the workshop?"

Elena had the last word. "We came here to develop our KVHS quality care strategy as a team. That's going to be a bit of a challenge without the key medical person in the organisation, isn't it?"

Heads nodded around the table.

"Anne isn't comfortable with the direction we're heading in, nor with my leadership style," Carol began.

She paused as she noticed a distinct shift in atmosphere. Everyone was looking at her with startled eyes. Was she being too open? *Is this the first time they've heard a CEO admit to anything other than being universally respected?*

Carol decided to ignore the reaction and keep going. "Anne is entitled to her opinion and she expressed it loud and clear. She sees that I'm taking the Executive Team and the health service in a new direction, one that she said she's not interested in. So, she's taking the weekend to consider her next steps." Carol didn't want to pre-empt Anne's formal resignation, so she stopped there. But her team smelled blood.

"Did you ask her to resign?" demanded Elena, eyes wide.

"No," responded Carol, "but I made it clear that I need everyone equally committed to the changes that have to be made."

Elena's face dropped. "Anne's been the Chief Medical Officer at Kinsley Valley for twelve years. The doctors love her. If she leaves, the problems you have now will look like nothing. This is not good."

Elena's stress was contagious, and it ran around the table like a turbocharged virus. Even Carol felt it, though she didn't show it. She looked around the room. The remaining members of her team looked downcast, shoulders slumped. Carol steadied herself.

"I hear you, Elena. But it's Anne's choice. And I'd like you to respect her confidentiality please." She leaned forward. "I need an Executive Team that pulls together in the same direction. No exceptions. Whatever happens, we'll work through it together. And"— she paused and looked at each of them in turn, her gaze lingering a little longer on Elena—"I don't have problems. *We* do."

"I'm glad you mentioned that." Anton folded his arms on the table and pushed his glasses up his nose. "We were talking at the break and, sorry to say this Carol, but it seems as if we're in agreement with Anne. There are so many clinical and operational problems we need to solve, but you insist on making 'quality' the focus of discussion for this whole first day. We're not sure that you fully appreciate some of the issues we're facing. Can't we leave quality to William? It is his job, after all."

A wave of fatigue ran through Carol, and she suddenly remembered that she'd missed her break. She realised there was no use pursuing her agenda until the rest of the group had pursued theirs. "Alright," she said. "I was going to leave this until later, but I'm happy to do it now. I'm taking a short break and will be back in around ten minutes. Why don't you use the time to list and prioritise the top five issues you feel we should discuss over the next two days?"

She was aware of four pairs of eyes boring into her back as she left the room.

*****

When Carol returned, she noted with surprised that the group was putting the finishing touches on their priorities list. *People support what they help to create*, she thought wryly, noting the improved energy level and mood. "Okay, what have we got?"

Kristen turned from the whiteboard. "I'm not sure we're all in absolute agreement that this is the right priority order," she said. Carol, noting thedownward turn of Elena's mouth, was inclined to agree. "But this is what we came up with:

1. Pharmacy service.
2. Private hospital.
3. Operating room throughput.
4. Nurse numbers.
5. New catering contract.
6. Medical ward quality issues.

"Yes, there are six," acknowledged Anton before Carol could say it. "We had five, but that was without the medical ward issues. We didn't think you'd be too impressed if we left it off."

"I guess that's true," said Carol, suppressing a chuckle. "I won't die in a ditch about it.

Who wants to explain why these are the priority problems?"

"Well," Elena remarked irritably, "it's obvious, isn't it? We can't run a hospital without a pharmacy service. Seb made the decision to contract it out as part of the move to the new building, but negotiations with the preferred provider broke down months ago, and we don't have a plan B." She paused and took a sip of water. "That brings us to issue number two. We're bleeding doctor time to the private hospital. If it keeps up, we'll have to consider closing one of the new operating rooms, which won't help with issue three, which appears to be related to new building teething problems that no one anticipated. And if the waiting list falls over, we'll be in more trouble with the Department of Health, not to mention the community, especially if the local newspaper gets a hold of it." Elena's volume increased as she moved through the list, and she emphasised each point with a knock on the table.

"Issue four, nurse numbers—which I think should be issue one—is also a problem partly also related to the new private hospital which is madly recruiting all my staff, and partly to the internal KVHS upheaval of the past twelve months. I have a very touchy workforce at the moment."

"Which issue five isn't helping," broke in Kristen. "The new catering suppliers do not seem to be able to deliver an accurate meal, let alone a hot one. We have reports of patients choking, losing weight, and even a severe allergic reaction, all because the caterers aren't doing their job."

"And of course it's the nurses who pick up the pieces," snapped Elena. "As if they don't have enough to do!"

The room fell silent. "And issue six?" asked Carol, looking at Elena. "Don't ask me, ask William!" she retorted.

Carol's irritation levels rose. If things kept going in this vein, she'd be having the same conversation with Elena as she'd had with Anne. But she could see that Elena's stress was very real and decided to let it go for now.

Everyone looked at William. "Um," he began slowly, "there's still a lot of work to be done on the medical ward. The big problems were fixed post accreditation, of course, and the care issues that contributed to the deaths have been resolved—we hope. I know that Elena and Kristen, and even Anne," he glanced nervously at Carol, "have been helping them. But the data still indicate lots of incidents and complaints, and the last internal staff survey demonstrated pretty clearly how unhappy they are. I've instigated some clinical improvement activities with the Nurse Unit Manager, but progress is slow and staff morale doesn't seem to be improving much."

Carol, feeling the tension creep into her shoulders, glanced around the table and decided it was time to challenge the group. "The medical ward issues are not William's problem. They're our problem. I should be hearing from each of you, not only him. William has a role to play in helping to monitor, improve and manage risk and meet the accreditation standards, of course. But what happens at point of care is the result of policy decisions made by us and interpreted and implemented by line managers and staff. William might be a nurse, but he has no line management authority over any of the clinicians he's working with. He can't dictate to them how to deliver their care, and it's unfair to put him in that position. Have you considered that making William responsible for things he can't control might have contributed to both the poor accreditation result and the poor care?"

The group digested this in silence, which was eventually broken by Elena. "But isn't accreditation William's job?"

Carol sighed, louder than she meant to. "Anton, what happens when one of our departments or services has a budget blowout? Do you decide how to prioritise their spending?"

"No, of course not." Anton grinned. I'd like to see me try. As if Kristen or Elena or Anne would want me to tell their staff how to run their services. What do I know about clinical care? Of course, one of my staff will help them analyse where the spending is and how to structure their budget. And I pitch in if things are really bad. We give them strategies for deciding on savings. But the real content work has to be done by those who understand the business."

"Nailed it Anton—thanks." Carol threw her CFIO a big smile, grateful for such clarity of thought. She could see he naturally understood that the KVHS core business should be about the quality of care delivered to and experienced by patients, but it was likely that no one had ever asked for his input on this. They would make little progress unless she could change their thinking and decided to reinforce the point.

"Think of it in terms of accreditation. William and his team have a role in accreditation coordination and preparation. They must make sure that the organisation has every opportunity to meet the standards. But it's not their responsibility if we receive a 'non-compliance' because one of our services didn't implement a standard or provide evidence of their compliance with a standard. That's a line management responsibility that flows right from the people around this table. William can't be held to account for things he has no control over any more than Anton can in his role. He and his team provide the tools and systems and knowledge that people need to do the right thing. But they can't make people do the right thing. As the Executive Team, we have authority, but even we can't make someone do something they really don't want to do. We can't rely solely on hierarchy; we must work with our managers and staff to make engagement so useful for them that they want to be part of it."

Both Kristen and Elena frowned but didn't voice disagreement.

"We'll discuss roles and responsibilities for point of care later. Back to your issues list. You've told me why these are your key concerns, and I'm certainly not disputing that they are. But why are they the priority issues?"

"Oh, that was me." Anton raised both hands as if to say "guilty." "I suggested we do what Seb would have done and base it on financial and business sustainability impact. It's not perfect, but I think we did a pretty good job in ten minutes." He sat back, looking satisfied.

"Great. Thanks everyone. That gives me a really clear picture of how you're thinking and what's worrying you. Now, let me show you how I'm thinking and what's worrying me." She went to the whiteboard and started writing next to Kristen's neat list:

- No definition or goals for the KVHS care quality.
- Unhappy and disenfranchised consumers and staff.
- A siloed Executive Team.
- Staff disconnected from the Board and senior managers.
- Weak line management.
- Board and senior management lack of knowledge about what's really going on.

Carol then drew an arrow from her list to Kristen's and wrote "Which leads to …"

Elena expressed what the others were thinking. "Are you serious? Your list is all quality and human resources, I mean, 'people and culture' "—she glanced at Kristen—"apart from the last one, and I don't know what you mean by that anyway. We don't know what's going on? And we report reams of stuff to the Board."

Carol met her gaze. "Never more serious. And if you give me until the end of today,

I hope you'll see why, and that by then we'll all consider my list the more important. I'm not saying your list isn't; of course those are all critical issues—although I would have liked to see them ranked according to patient risk before financial risk—and some are definitely urgent." She paused and glanced at each of her team in turn. "I promise we won't leave here without an action plan for each one. But if we don't address my strategic issues list, we're destined to grapple with operational problems like these at every planning workshop. We might stop the ship sinking, but we'll still be lost at sea, springing new leaks. I'd like to take our ship somewhere better than where we are. Would you?"

Four heads nodded, somewhat uncertainly.

"Let's take a five-minute stretch and bathroom break and then we'll get going," Carol spoke more confidently than she felt. She understood the group's preoccupation with operational matters. She had been a COO herself, after all. But she hadn't realised they were as far away from thinking like a strategic and high-performing team as they had shown themselves to be so far.

Chairs scraped and papers shuffled as the group dispersed.

"Coffee, I need coffee. And a little doughnut wouldn't go astray, either," Carol heard Kristen moan to no one in particular as she hurried from the room. Her early-morning farm duties left her perpetually hungry. Carol's mouth twitched as she sat down to compose herself, revelling in the silence. She summoned her strength for what she knew would be a demanding few hours ahead. Could she get the group from where they were to where she needed them to go?

CHAPTER THREE

"'Consistent quality' is impossible to achieve if we don't define it," Carol said, barely concealing her frustration as she introduced the first group exercise. Fifteen minutes had passed since they reconvened after their break and already many niggly disagreements had sprung up to slow progress. But Carol was determined to complete a couple of interactive exercises before lunch to get the thinking and conversation into a more positive frame and forged on.

"We'll hit high quality here and there when staff have a good day and everything clicks. But it won't be consistent. If you aim at nothing, that's probably what you'll hit. From my experience, the only way to even out the ups and downs that patients and staff—and you—have experienced over the past few years is to focus like a laser beam on point of care, using something I call 'The Strategic Quality System Model[A1]'". She moved to the whiteboard and began drawing the model with practised ease. "We're going to start by identifying exactly what we want everyone of our patients to experience: our Purpose. Then we're going to discuss what we need from our People to create that experience with consumers every day. Finally, we'll identify the Pillars of governance needed to support our people to achieve the Purpose. This is basically all we need to create consistently high quality care. As you can see, conceptually it's not complicated, but sometimes we make it more complicated than it needs to be. When we get into implementation, things do get a little complicated. But more of that later."

The group studied the whiteboard with furrowed brows.

"How is that different to what we already do?" asked Anton. "We already seem to spend a lot of time worrying about quality."

"Or worrying about accreditation and compliance?" asked Carol in return. "From what I've observed so far, you have some of the building blocks of an effective quality system in place, but not all. Your quality system should be working hard for you to drive three actions: defining the quality of care you want to provide and be known for; describing the people and their characteristics required to achieve quality care as you've defined it; and identifying and embedding the governance and systems required to support the people to provide the defined high quality care."

"So accreditation isn't even part of it?" Anton grinned at William. "Looks like you've been wasting your time! Don't come Monday!"

"Of course it's part of it, but it's not the point of it. Accreditation provides some of the 'governance and systems' building blocks and point of care guidance. But it's not enough on its own to guarantee consistently high quality care. Basically, no one ever jumped out of bed in the morning, excited to go to work to comply with standards." Carol looked around to see if anyone was as engaged as she wished them to be. "But they will jump out of bed to provide amazing care, if they think they'll be supported to do that when they get to work."

Despite her misgivings about all the 'quality talk' Kristen was leaning forward with her head on one side, listening hard. "I've been wondering, though: why doesn't accreditation do all this for us? I used to think that if we were accredited, that high quality care was a given. That belief has gone the way of the dinosaurs, of course, thanks to recent events. And I see that it's not always inspiring for staff. But I don't really get why."

"It wouldn't assure high quality anything if it works the same way in health as it does in the bank." Anton laughed. "We had 'bank' accreditation, and it was basically a check that we had all the proper accounting and governance systems in place and that all the forms were being filled in. They never looked at the outcomes of those systems or the impact on customers. And we did have a few scandals about mismanagement of customers' money and bad financial advice. Accreditation didn't stop that from happening."

"Sounds familiar," Carol nodded. "Accreditation tells us if we have the right things in place to give ourselves a good chance of providing high quality care. But it doesn't tell us how well those components are working and if we're using them correctly to create good care. The standards are like the recipe and ingredients for a basic 'care' cake. But - there's a big problem. Can anyone tell me what it is?"

"We're not very good cooks?" ventured Anton.

"Closer than you might think!" Carol grinned at the chuckles around the table. "Accreditation doesn't provide us with a picture of the finished cake, or even try to explain what it should look or taste like. There's an assumption that if we use the recipe, we'll get a good cake. So we mix and we cook and we hope that something good comes out in the end. But the reality is that without a shared picture of what we're trying to create, we end up with as many different types of cake as there are cooks. Even following the recipe and using those ingredients, we may not combine it with the intent, care and skill required to make a decent cake. Some will be great, because the manager 'cooks' are naturally good at it, and some will be ordinary because the manager can't be bothered."

"Mmmm, cake." Kristen sighed loudly.

"Come accreditation visit time," Carol continued, with an amused glance at Kristen, "the assessors want to know if we've used all the ingredients and followed the recipe. But they generally don't view or taste the cake to see if it's turned out correctly or determine whether it's edible. They'd really have to live with us for a while to be able to realistically assess that. So, accreditation gives us some of the ingredients for good care. But without defining what good care looks, feels and tastes like, we never know if we're producing it. Our care might be average, but not great, even if we follow the accreditation standards' 'recipe.' Or, more likely, it might be great in some parts of KVHS, where the managers make the recipe work well, but not so great in others."

Carol paused to let the group take in her analogy. A fly buzzed against one of the windows, and she took a minute to help it find its way out before continuing. "Our job is to paint a vivid picture of the care 'cake' we want to provide with every consumer and use the accreditation requirements to help us create it. Accreditation makes a helpful contribution because it provides ingredients and a recipe. But it takes more than accreditation to get where we want to go."

"And without a decent set of measures," Anton said, "it's hard for us to know how good—or consistent—our cake is." He smiled. "That's been a problem for me ever since I joined the health service. All this talk about accreditation and we don't even know if it makes a difference to care? I know we measure many things that go wrong, but that's like knowing which bits of our care cake are burnt. Important, obviously, but not the whole picture. We also need to know about taste, texture, filling, icing, how it all holds together. And where the really good cakes are."

"Is that why it's hard to get honest consumer feedback in human services? Because they're so dependent on the 'care cake' we serve them?" William looked like a light had gone on in his brain. "I heard a fantastic talk at a conference once about having to use a range of different and clever ways to find out what consumers and their families really think. Asking them in a survey, or face to face, may not be a true representation. Many are worried that if they say they don't like our 'care cake,' they won't get anything."

"That's all good, but this food talk is making me hungry," groaned Kristen. "Pass those delicious cacao protein balls!"

Carol worked them hard for the rest of the morning. They started by defining high quality care, as the cornerstone of what they'd be working towards over the next three years. The group considered a scenario that placed someone near and dear to everyone in the room in a hospital on the other side of the world. In half an hour, they were able to identify what they hoped was happening with their loved one in that hospital—and what they hoped did not happen. Carol knew what the results would be, because she had been through the exercise many times and the variation was minimal. But that wasn't the point. The act of identifying and naming the core components of a high quality experience for someone they loved was critical, both for the "aha!" moments and for the commitment to the definition.

The exercise elicited much conversation and emotion, as the group thought about the people they loved all alone in a faraway hospital. Carol couldn't be sure, but she thought she saw Elena discretely wipe away a tear as she pictured her beloved daughter in that situation. The trick was to keep the discussion focused on concrete specifics. Broad statements like "good communication" or "high standards" were unpacked for their component parts. And the focus was on the "what" they wanted for their loved one, without getting side-tracked by the "how." When they had exhausted their suggestions, Carol did a quick consolidation of the key themes and wrote:

"High-quality care for the person we love in 'Mt. Marvellous' foreign hospital is[A2]

- **Personal:** responsive to and focused on the individual.
- **Effective:** the right care with the best possible result.
- **Connected:** a smooth and integrated pathway.
- **Safe:** free from harm.

"And, of course, it's no use the foreign hospital having a quality system in place to make these things happen for every third person, is it?" Carol asked.

"No way," said Elena with feeling. "Not if my daughter misses out!"

"Exactly." The weight slipped from Carol's shoulders as she enjoyed the energetic contribution from around the table. There was certainly a lot more smiling and banter amongst the group than earlier. Maybe high performance wasn't as far away as she thought. It wasn't as if they didn't want to think this way, more that they had never been asked to.

"So to achieve high quality care," she continued, "we design a clear, jargon-free definition of what that looks like in practice, based on specific actions we can observe and measure, grouped into goals. Achieving these goals for every KVHS consumer is now our collective definition of success: what I call Great Care. But I don't mind what you call it. As long as we're all agreed on what it is!"

Kristen crossed and uncrossed her legs as she considered the whiteboard. " 'Great Care' is good for now. But what you're saying sounds a little unrealistic." Elena nodded vigorously. "It's all very well to say, 'every person, every time.' But really?"

Much to Carol's surprise, William straightened in his seat and spoke up confidently. "I get it! Nothing on that list is new, is it? We already know we should be providing these things for every consumer, wherever they meet our organisation. It's providing them *consistently* well across all services that's the challenge. And we must try for every person, every time; we can't say we're providing high quality care if some people get it and some don't. Let's face it, that's what we've got now, and it doesn't exactly make for happy patients—or staff, for that matter. You should see some of the complaints I see!"

"Better you than me," Anton chuckled.

"Hold on." Carol's eyebrows shot up. "Are you telling me that you don't all see the serious complaints?"

"Well, Elena and Anne do—and Seb used to—because they come to the Board Quality and Clinical Governance Committee." William sounded quite animated now. "Why would Kristen and Anton need to? They're not clinical."

Carol felt a shot of electricity go through her. She spoke firmly. "From now on, this Executive Team takes collective responsibility for the quality of consumer experience at KVHS. What happens to consumers at point of care is our core business. We all have individual roles in it, but we're equally responsible, as a team, to work together to make it the best it can be. And on that note, the strategic goals of this organisation are the strategic goals of this team and must come before the operational goals of your divisions. It's the only way to progress things as a whole health service rather than a series of silos all going their own way. And we can't do it without KVHS consumers and community, either. Without them we only see one side of the care coin. Great Care can only be created and sustained if we approach it as a partnership—between us, consumers, the community and the Board. I take it this hasn't been the case previously."

Anton opened his mouth to comment, but seeing Carol's determined look, he realised it was a statement, not a question, and thought better of it.

"We're not only an acute service, remember," Elena remarked, eyebrows arched. "What about aged, community and mental health services? Do they get their own definitions? Or do we not worry about them?" She smiled as she pointed out what appeared to be a flaw in Carol's approach.

But Carol had heard it all before. "You tell me." She smiled back. "Do we need separate definitions?"

Kristen peered at the whiteboard. "I think she's got you there, Elena. The actions in each goal apply to every service, don't they?"

"Yes, that's right," William interjected. "They might be differently applied; for example, 'evidence-based treatment' under the 'Effective' goal will require different actions in a mental health service than in an operating room. But it's an equally important goal in both settings."

"Makes sense. The goals don't change, but some actions within the goals will, depending on the setting." Kristen could see by Elena's pursed lips that she was irritated with the neat response to her objection, so she moved the conversation on. "What's next? My stomach insists it's lunch, but the clock doesn't quite agree, I see."

Carol laughed. "If you hang in for another forty-five minutes, we'll complete this exercise and have the first draft of our very own strategic quality system framework."[A3]

"Why a 'strategic' quality system?" William asked. "I guess I should know, but …"

"Not necessarily." Carol searched amongst her papers for a graphic and held it up. "This is my own strategic quality system model[3] based on my PhD a few years back. Yes, I know, as sad as it sounds, developing and testing this was my hobby for five years, on top of my day job. It's a strategic system because it's designed to support us and our staff to take the quality of our care somewhere better than where it is now— beyond the things we must do for compliance to the things we want to do to care for our consumers. Basically, it's designing and creating our signature 'care cake.' It's the purpose, people, and pillars of governance we need to operationalise the statements in our strategic plan that set the aspiration for how good we want to be." She handed the model graphic to Elena to pass around the table. "Does anyone know what else the KVHS strategic plan says about the quality of care we want to provide? Without looking it up?" She added this as Anton picked up his phone.

William was not going to miss this opportunity. This one he knew. "It's strategic goal four, which comes after financial sustainability, community partnerships, and recruiting and retaining the best staff: 'continuously improve the quality and safety of our care.' And, of course, our vision is to provide 'high quality care for our community,' as Kristen said."

"And *do we*?" Carol looked around expectantly. Silence.

"Do you mean do we enact the KVHS values?" asked Elena, with an impatient wave of her hand.

"No, although that's an interesting issue. As you know, we're in the middle of refreshing the values with the Board and staff to develop something a bit more actionable, so we won't discuss those today. Yes, we need the values to underpin how we go about things as a health service. But that's not my question."

Elena sighed loudly. "Really, Carol, are we back to this ridiculous conversation about results again?"

"I don't ask trick questions," responded Carol evenly. "Does KVHS provide high quality care for the community?"

"How are we supposed to know that?" retorted Elena again.

"How can you afford not to know that," Carol shot back, "if the strategic plan says that's the purpose of our organisation?"

"But … but …" began Elena. "We have operational plans, including a quality plan, that flow from the strategic plan goals. That's how we implement the strategic plan, and—"

Anton sat forward, clicking his pen. "That's not what Carol means. That's the 'how'. She's asking about the 'what'. Are we achieving high quality care for every consumer? We have no idea. Until today, we'd never defined it and therefore never measured it. We do all the stuff in our plans and hope that consumers get high quality care as a result. But—we don't know if they do. We don't know where we are on the championship ladder."

Kristen sat back, looking deflated. "He's right. If we were in any other industry, we'd be out of business for not knowing if we're achieving our vision or not. And I guess that goes for our culture, too. We talk about it, but what have we really done to improve it? Remember we adopted the 'just' culture before the accreditation survey? It was flavour of the month for about two weeks—didn't even make a month—before Seb decided it wasn't right for KVHS, even though it was definitely better than a 'no blame' culture, which seemed to mean that everyone could do what they liked with no accountability. Only Seb could argue with a culture based on the principles of natural justice."

"We will resurrect the 'just' culture. We need to be able to determine and respond differently to the causes of harm, depending on the source: human error or deliberate rule flouting," agreed Carol.

She looked around the table and saw relief replace concentration on the faces of a couple of her executives. "Oh, I see," Kristen exclaimed, her eyes lighting up with understanding. "I never really got that before."

All right! "There are many good initiatives in our plans, Elena," Carol went on, throwing Kristen an encouraging look. "I'm not suggesting otherwise. But the absolute focus required to achieve the KVHS vision for high quality care is just not there. 'Hope' is not a strategy, and healthcare is too complex to rely solely on staff getting it right. And without consumers and the community and our staff telling us what this means to them in practice, the strategic plan vision becomes a bit meaningless: nice words, but no real commitment to making them a reality. You know that staff hate lovely words in a glossy document if they don't help them to provide better care day to day. Well, from today on, that changes. Let's have a quick stretch break before we see how all this fits together to propel our health service to greatness."

*****

Kristen handed around a bowl of almonds as they resumed their seats. "Eat, keep your strength up!" she urged, taking her own advice.

"How is everyone feeling?" asked Carol. "Ready to tackle the rest of the model?"

Four heads nodded.

"So, look at the high quality-care components you've identified that you want for someone you love. We have four goals: Personal, Connected, Safe, and Effective, and a number of key actions within each one that must happen every day to achieve the goal. Who is your loved one dependent on in that foreign hospital to strive for each of these goals for her or him?"

A minute passed while they stared at the whiteboard.

"I guess that would be the hospital Executive Team," Kristen said confidently. "And they better hope that they're as fabulous as we are!"

Everyone grinned—except Elena. Carol watched her with interest. The defining care exercise seemed to have had quite an effect on her. Elena was seriously considering the question. After a few seconds, she spoke.

"Noooo, not the Executive Team, Kristen. It's the frontline staff. These are the people our loved one in that bed or chair, or on that trolley, depend on every day. I know it; I just haven't thought about it for a while. I realise that there have been other issues taking my attention."

"Okay, what have you done with Elena?" Anton joked.

"You can stop looking as if the aliens have got me, thanks," retorted Elena, pushing her dark hair behind her ears as she glared at Anton. "I've just worked out what we're doing here and why. A bit like you and the sports results this morning." She turned to Carol. "We've been hitting the target and missing the point, haven't we?"

Carol smiled. "To be honest, we haven't always hit the target over the past year, either. But yes, Elena, you've pretty much summed it up. Still think it's all 'quality and HR'?"

"Well, yes, it is. But now I can see how quality and HR can shape the KVHS future."

"Righto, can we stop with the 'quality and HR' love-in?" said Anton irritably. "This time it's me that's lost."

Carol shot Elena a grateful glance. "Let's keep going and all will become clear."

They worked steadily for the next half hour, identifying the desired characteristics of the frontline staff looking after their loved one, and then up the organisational chain, discussing attributes and responsibilities of middle managers, senior managers, and, eventually, the Executive Team and Board of that Mt. Marvellous foreign hospital.

William sat up, his eyes alight. "So everyone in the organisation really does have a role to play in what happens at point of care. I've been saying that for years, but I never really knew how to explain it properly."

Kristen's enthusiasm levels were also rising. "Yes, of course, we say it all the time: 'everyone's responsible for quality.' But that's meaningless unless we're really clear about what we want at point of care, so we can have a sensible discussion about the specific contribution everyone needs to make for it to be a reality every day. I'm the Chief Operating Officer, and suddenly I feel as if point-of-care quality is all my responsibility. It's weird."

"Still lost, Anton?" asked Carol, turning to Anton.

"No. I think I've put it together. We're all responsible for what happens at point of care, because that's our core business. Just like at the bank, if profits were down and our shareholders were unhappy, that was the executive and senior managers' problem, but everyone had a role to play in fixing it. I've never thought about it like that before because I don't know anything about clinical care and didn't think it was any of my business."

"I suppose Anne and I did send that message pretty strongly," admitted Elena with a shrug. "But that's what I was brought up to believe: only clinicians understand clinicians' business."

"I get that," Anton replied. "But I'm not trying to take over your business. I want to help the hospital run well, so the patients get a better deal. I don't know anything about clinical issues, but I do know about planning and resource allocation and budgets and IT. As we've discussed, it's pretty hard to create high quality care for every person without those supports. And I can see now that we have to get after high quality care every day – like fitness. It's something that's hard to build and easy to lose. From now on I'll think of Great Care as the KVHS fitness regime! "

"Love that analogy, thanks Anton. Works for me too. Speaking of budgets, we haven't even discussed how many of our precious resources are wasted on overuse, poor care and addressing fallout from adverse events." Carol looked grim. "By my back of an envelope calculations, it could be a million dollars a year. So we're pretty unfit! Got your attention, Anton?"

She smiled as Anton did a double take. "What? Impossible."

"Very possible. Let's make time to discuss it when we get back to work next week. Improving services should improve our bottom line as well as our care."

"We really all do have a responsibility, don't we?" said Kristen looking around the table. "Now I see why we should all be discussing the serious complaints. They're ours to address—as a team."

"Correct!" Carol said with a flourish of her arms. "You've got it. It's not unusual for health service executives to work in silos of course. One of the key purposes of the early modern hospital was to train doctors, and later nurses, with the older ones passing on their skills to the younger. We still see that hierarchical apprentice model today. Health services evolved around these needs, which makes consumer-centredness and interdisciplinary approaches to care a huge challenge. We've grown up within our tribes, which translates organisationally to silos. But we can choose to do it differently at KVHS."

"We can?" Elena asked, her eyes narrowed. "If we can, how come everyone else doesn't as well? We're not the only health service with problems."

"Of course not! Healthcare—and the whole of human services—has become incredibly complex and challenging for everyone. Consumers need all of us working together to achieve common goals. Not every health service chooses to do this, however. Many are happy to meet compliance requirements and avoid disasters, as I said earlier. In many ways, that's easier than working with managers and staff to make the real changes required for high quality care, so compliance becomes the default 'quality.' " She looked at her watch, conscious of the key lessons she wanted to cover before lunch.

"I hope it's now obvious that we can't achieve Great Care for every consumer unless it's our individual and collective priority. There are only two roles in Great Care: creating it, which requires frontline staff and consumers to work together to achieve high quality care; and supporting it, which is the rest of us doing our bit to support the frontline staff and consumers, whether line managers, administrators, support staff or executives. Okay, if we're all good on people and roles, I have one more exercise. Can anyone guess what it is?"

"Well, given the conversation we've just had, I'm hoping it's all about finance and quality!" Anton joked. "I'm quite enjoying my new-found responsibility!"

Carol dared to feel a kernel of hope as she observed her executive sharing a chuckle.

"Not exactly Anton. But warm! Look at the things we've identified as important to provide for every consumer at point of care, and the characteristics of line managers all the way to executive level that we want—and need—to make that happen."

All heads turned to the Great Care goals, actions, and people on the whiteboard. Carol dragged a flipchart next to the whiteboard and wrote "Governance Supports" at the top of the page.

"The staff can't make GC happen by themselves, even though that's been the clinical quality model for years: good, intelligent people, well intentioned and hardworking, doing great things. Of course these people are the cornerstone of creating Great Care, but it takes more than that to perform consistently well within the complexity of a modern health service. We found that out when we started collecting good data on consumer harm, closely followed by public inquiries into poor care. It was a shock! But one we needed." Carol brushed a strand of hair off her forehead and discovered to her surprise that she was sweating. Like most things, co-designing a quality and governance framework, particularly with a sceptical executive, was harder than it looked, and she was doing some furious paddling under the water to glide like a swan on top of it. "So, Anton, you're on a roll—what more does it take?"

"They need resources, of course, and IT systems providing really good information about how well they're doing—you know, whether or not they're providing that level of care to every patient."

"And they all need to know what the quality-of-care expectation is … and their role in it … and see it led from the top of the organisation," suggested Kristen, her chin resting on her hand as she gazed at Carol's list.

"And be empowered to create it and lead it within their own teams," chimed in William. "Not to mention all the decision-making and guidance tools they need, like policies and protocols."

"Great staff based on intelligent recruiting and retention. Supported and kept safe." Kristen was in the swing of it now.

The room fell silent.

"You're doing well for ten minutes pre-lunch," said Carol encouragingly. "But there are a couple more key system supports the managers and staff need to create Great Care for every consumer. Thoughts?"

William cleared his throat and everyone looked up expectantly. "I think I've got it. They need to be supported to change and improve when the data indicate they're not achieving Great Care. And they've got to be able to identify and manage their risks. Otherwise they won't be providing consistently Great Care. Honestly, I should have thought of these first," he said with a shake of his head.

"No problem, William. It doesn't matter what order we identify things as long as we get them all in the end!" Carol grinned as William pretended to bang his head on the table. "You're spot on; and when you mention risks, you don't only mean in the 'Safe' goal, do you?"

"No, of course not," he responded confidently. "Every one of the four goals"— he pointed at the whiteboard—"is loaded with risks to patients, and staff, too, for that matter. For instance, if care isn't 'Connected,' with everyone on the same page, consumers can fall through the cracks and get the wrong information, or conflicting information, about their care. Or the wrong care. Or too much or too little care. This sort of thing accounts for over half our patient complaints: situations where the consumer has to relate their story over and over, or everyone has a different story about the consumer's care pathway and things get confused and mistakes are made. It can also lead to duplication of tests and unnecessary treatment, and the lack of consistent messaging drives patients and their families to desperation. They get stressed and angry, and next thing we have a complaint on our hands that probably could have been avoided with better coordination."

"And that beautifully brings me to the final key system that managers and staff need to provide Great Care." Carol turned to the flipchart and wrote "Consumer Partnerships."

"You're lucky Anne isn't here," chuckled Elena. "If she hadn't left already, she would now!"

"Healthcare is in transition around consumer partnerships, trying to balance consumer focus with our traditional staff focus," said Carol, choosing to ignore Elena's comment. "There's a broad spectrum of opinions on how to do this, of course. But basically, we can't create sustained Great Care without the people we want to experience it! So, we need an effective system to support and promote consumer participation in their care, and to help us define and create Great Care, in the same way we need quotas to encourage and help women take on more Board roles."

"Mm-hmm—makes sense," Kristen observed with feeling. "In the same way organisations need a little nudge and some formal process to get their Board gender balance right, health services need a nudge and processes to get our consumer and provider balance right. Health services are traditionally organised around the staff, and biased towards staff, so it's going to take significant changes to achieve true 'consumer-centredness.' If we don't actively drive it, it might never happen, even if we think it's a good thing to do. It's up to us to set up the systems to make it a reality."

Carol nodded and made some notes on the flipchart. "Exactly. Okay - good work. These GC supports that you've identified," she said with a flourish of her marker, "are what make up clinical—or quality—governance. I like to think of it as the systems engine room that propels the organisation towards the quality goals. Planning and Leadership, Partnering with Consumers, Positive People and Practice and Pursuing Greatness are the 'levers' we must constantly adjust, in response to our measures, to make sure the engine is purring along and providing the platform we all need— Executive Team, consumers, managers and staff—to pursue the quality goals. But in and of themselves, these things are not 'quality.' Each of these systems is only as good as it supports staff to create personal, effective, connected and safe care."

"Really?" asked Anton. "Clinical governance is an active thing? It's always seemed so—"

"Passive? Boring? Yes, I know," William finished Anton's sentence with a grin. "But it's so hard to make it interesting."

"Maybe not as hard as you think," continued Carol. "It all depends how you look at it. Sometimes governance becomes an end in itself, because much of it comprises the compliance items we must demonstrate for the Department of Health and for accreditation. If that's all quality governance is at KVHS, it becomes a tick box and 'extra work', rather than anything useful." She pointed to the list of governance systems on the whiteboard. "Many staff think of these things as 'quality'—and not fondly! To them, these are bureaucratic tasks they have to do, such as audits or attending mandatory training, or implementing a new standard. The secret is to help staff see that these processes are there to support them; that governance and systems are a means to providing Great Care, not an end in themselves." She put the whiteboard marker down and turned to the group.

"Take the Connected goal. To achieve that for every consumer requires planning and leadership, consumer input and partnership, positive people doing the right things every day, and pursuing greatness through measurement, improvement, and risk management. Quality governance is an active thing. Make sense?" To Carol's surprise, there were enthusiastic nods around the table. *Progress!*

"And now that we have some concrete goals—describing the high quality 'cake' we want to provide—making it active will be easier to do," she finished, and sat down.

"Congratulations to us!" Kristen exclaimed. "We've defined the purpose, people, and governance pillars required to create consistently high quality care. And we get it! The only thing left to do is make it happen. What will we do with all our spare time?"

The group laughed and Carol nodded. "Ha—if only! Implementation is never straightforward, but I like to keep the big picture simple before we dive into the detail. To summarise, over the next twelve months, our job is to:

- Make the case for change.
- Make the expectations clear.
- Make it as easy as possible to get started and keep going.
- Make it business as usual.
- Make it easy to see progress with good measures of success.

"Fortunately, we have a roadmap to get us where we want to go. Over the years I've learned that it takes six key pieces of work to get us to our destination: Great Care for every KVHS consumer. We need to:

1. Paint a Picture of the point-of-care quality we want to be known for. We've made a good start on that today, but we must repeat the exercise with as many staff and consumers as possible so it's their definition, not ours.

2. Plot the components of quality care into a framework, describing the Purpose (Goals), People (Roles), and Pillars (Governance).

3. Pilot the framework, practise implementation and learn how to make it work.

4. Plan to make the point-of-care Picture a reality across the whole organisation as simply and effectively as possible.

5. Put the Plan into Practice and Persist with implementation, even when challenging.

6. Promote and Promulgate Progress.

"Today we're working on the first cut of actions one and two, and we'll also engage as many consumers and staff in this process as we can over the next few months—which we'll discuss after lunch." Carol shuffled her papers into a neat pile. "Thanks everyone—time to eat! I'm a great believer in a decent break when we're doing intense work like this, so I've scheduled seventy-five minutes. Make sure you get some fresh air, take a walk, have a nap. Please don't stay glued to your devices for the whole time, or you'll find this afternoon a struggle. See you in seventy-five!"

The group rapidly dispersed and Carol stayed behind to check her messages. Nothing that couldn't wait, except a text five minutes ago from Rosie: "Nancy Murray wants to talk to you as soon as you break for lunch."

Carol sighed, her newfound cheerfulness oozing out the soles of her shoes. She didn't imagine her Board Chair was after a social chat. She stretched, sat down, took a long drink of water, and dialled Nancy's number.

*****

Carol leapt into consciousness off the back of her usual dream, which was the same as it had been every night—except this time the marching doctors all looked like Anne.

She propped herself up on her pillows and reflected on the past twenty-four hours. The planning workshop had been an unexpected mix of highs and lows. On the "highs" side, there'd been some wins. By the end of the day, the group had completed a high-level gap analysis against the strategic quality system framework and identified key implementation issues. They'd all been happy to see that the to-do list wasn't as long as they thought it might be and realised that KVHS already had most of the goal actions and governance systems in place; it's just that they weren't always consistent or effective. "It's like we do all this stuff for accreditation and the Department of Health, but we're not using it properly for us or our patients," Kristen had mused.

"Yep. A football team can be full of stars, and great equipment and facilities and sponsorship, but a weak club administration and bad politics can kill your success." Anton had sat forward in his characteristic pose as he shared his analogy. "There are lots of good ingredients, but no one's bringing it all together. Even with some individual brilliance, the team might never win a cup without shared goals and plans. Looks like that's been KVHS' problem. We'll never win a championship, either, unless we do things differently."

The group discussed how to use their quality governance systems to more directly support managers and staff to create high quality care for every consumer. They also worked out how they were going to engage the Board, and as many consumers and staff as possible, in defining high quality care and how they could achieve this through workshops, meetings, and an online survey.

This proved a bridge too far for Elena. "We know what it is now. Can't we just put it in the plan and get on with doing it?" she asked with a frown.

Before Carol could answer, Kristen had jumped in with a laugh. "Oh, you nurses! It's all about the task, isn't it? We've been down that road before, remember? Handing down quality plans like stone tablets from on high and complaining when they're not properly implemented." She paused, expecting Elena to jump in, but all was quiet.

"No wonder," she continued. "Now I see that our plans weren't about the things staff come to work for. Most of it was boring compliance. That's what got us into the quality mess we ended up in. Oh, sorry William, I didn't mean you."

William's face had turned a blotchy red. Kristen sent him a sympathetic look as she enthusiastically continued. "Come to think of it, this morning I would have dumped this on you. But this afternoon I see that the problem belongs to all of us. What a difference half a day makes! So, no, we're not doing that again and expecting a different result. We've got an opportunity with Carol to implement something that's meaningful, so let's do it."

The afternoon had been full of similarly spirited discussion, which continued into dinner. Apart from a brief awkward moment when Carol realised she'd forgotten to inform the restaurant there would be five instead of six at dinner, and they'd all stared at the empty chair in unison, they'd had an enjoyable evening. The restaurant was next to the conference room on the top floor of the hotel, and the setting sun over the nearby hills provided the perfect backdrop for their dinner on the balcony. Carol learned a little about what made each of them tick over the course of the evening, including that Elena's daughter had been in exactly the situation they'd discussed in the defining quality scenario that morning.

'Yes," Elena had admitted, "I did get a bit emotional. It brought back memories of my girl having her appendix out in a regional South American hospital. She got sick while backpacking. I got there as soon as I could, of course, but it was around forty-eight hours before I made it to her bedside. Much to my relief, I couldn't have been happier—or more surprised—with what I found. Excellent surgery, caring and competent staff, even good food! They had also allocated a volunteer who spoke English to make sure she understood what was going on. I get emotional every time I think about that lovely woman sitting by my daughter's bed when I arrived." She paused to wipe her eyes.

Anton had regaled them with hilarious tales of the daily banking grind and how, in the end, he couldn't face another day of every conversation being about money and how to get more of it. "I turned forty," he'd said, grimacing, "and realised I didn't want to retire from a lifetime of making other people rich. So when the hospital job came up, I jumped at it. And guess what: I still spend my days talking about money and how to get more of it! But for a better cause."

Kristen had told them about working her way up from a ward clerk to her current role. "I did have a few years in the city," she'd joked, "so I have seen how other places work. I moved to the city for a man—and within three months the man moved on to another city for someone else. It's fine"—she'd smiled at Carol's sympathetic look—"it wasn't working out anyway, obviously. And if I hadn't moved to the city, I wouldn't have met Scott, who turned out to be the love of my life! But I also took the opportunity to do some study and worked for a few years in human resources and project management for a national aged-care provider, which was interesting, to say the least. But I won't pretend I wasn't glad to get back to good ol' KVHS. I'm just lucky that Scott wanted to come back with me!"

William had been his customary quiet self. Carol wondered what he was thinking. He occasionally joined in the conversation but didn't seem completely comfortable. She'd tried to draw him out, asking him how he got to his current position. "Well," he'd said, "we had an accreditation recommendation a few years back to add a quality role to the Executive Team. Seb appointed me before our last accreditation to fulfil that recommendation."

"And he didn't go through any sort of due process that I could see." Elena had recovered now and was back to her blunt self. "No offence, William, but he didn't give anyone else a chance at the job."

"I know, I know." William shifted uneasily in his chair. "I was promoted from Quality and Risk Manager to Executive Director of Quality and Risk overnight. To be honest, I didn't think it would last much longer than the accreditation survey. I knew Seb wasn't convinced; you know he wasn't interested in safety and quality unless we had a problem with the Department of Health. But then the accreditation survey went belly up and next thing, Seb was gone."

Carol was glad that William had been able to relate his story over dinner rather than in her office. She had intended to ask how he'd got the job and now she knew. None of the other executives looked surprised at the story, so this obviously wasn't the first time they'd discussed it, but clearly Kristen hadn't wanted to tackle it during her time as acting CEO. Having the backstory was going to make it a little easier to have the conversation with William she knew she had to have, sooner rather than later.

So that was all good, and if she were honest with herself, she hadn't expected the day to go so well. However, despite the positive note the day had ended on and the good progress they'd made, the "lows" side of the equation had preoccupied her somewhat throughout the afternoon. As expected, the conversation with Board Chair Nancy Murray had been tense. It seemed that Anne had used her hands-free phone to good effect on the trip to her weekender, as within an hour every senior doctor at KVHS knew Anne's version of the workshop and her conversation with Carol. It wasn't long before news of Anne's impending resignation reached Nancy's ears, via Professor Yang.

"Carol," Nancy had said, sounding worried, "I have to ask. Are you sure you know what you're doing?"

Carol, trying not to show her exasperation with Anne's gleeful news spreading, explained her side of the story.

"Right-o," Nancy had said. "I've known Anne a long time, and what you're describing sounds true to form. She's always trodden her own path and we've never before had a CEO who challenged her. I'll back you on this." Nancy's voice was firm, and Carol knew she meant it. "But, you know that not everyone on the Board thought you were the best candidate for the job. I went out on a limb for you, because as far as I'm concerned, you're just what we need to take Kinsley Valley back to focusing on providing high quality care. A couple of vocal members were keen on appointing another external candidate. One was adamant that Kristen would provide consistency. And there was a push to recruit a medico for the role as well. If you set the doctors off, it's going to be very hard for me to keep the Board on your side."

"I know." Carol sounded more reassuring than she felt. Inwardly, the lead in the pit of her stomach indicated she was less than confident. "As you know, I told the Board when I started that there would be some hard decisions to make to turn the health service around, and I guess those decisions are upon us a little earlier than expected. I'll call the Unit Heads and Senior Medical Staff Chair this afternoon to answer any questions they have, and I'll meet with them next week. And I'll have the lay of the land ready to discuss at our next catch-up."

"Thanks, Carol." Nancy sounded relieved to hear that her CEO had a plan. "By the way, how did today's workshop go, apart from that 'slight' glitch?"

"It was the best day I've had at KVHS so far."

After the workshop and before dinner, Carol had called the KVHS senior medical staff to discuss Anne's departure. To say they were unimpressed with Anne's imminent retirement was an understatement and Carol experienced the full force of their disdain. Anne was a useful ally in the executive office for the senior doctors and they were none too pleased to be losing this leverage and influence. Carol weathered the storm. She'd worked in healthcare all her life, and, although unpleasant, the response was unsurprising. She listened, took notes, and arranged to see them all in person the following week.

She saved her call to the Senior Medical Staff Committee Chair until last. Dr Jeff Zammit was in his mid-forties, which made him a youngster by KVHS senior medical staff standards. Both his crew-cut hair and beard were on the way to grey, and his quiet demeanour gave no indication of his brilliance as an emergency physician. He also had an MBA and PhD to his name and had nearly finished his medical administration qualification. He'd moved to Kinsley Valley two years ago with his wife, who'd been appointed head of a new agricultural research organisation attached to the university. Carol had spotted him in her first week when he gave an impressive presentation to the Board on the first few months in the new hospital emergency department, which he had taken the lead on designing and commissioning. She wondered how a regional hospital like KVHS was going to keep a smart, ambitious guy like this now that the new ED design, setup and move were completed and the wrinkles nearly ironed out.

Jeff had listened attentively to Carol's side of the story. "I'm not surprised," he'd said with a chuckle. "These docs haven't been challenged for a long time, if ever, and some of them need to be. As I've only been here five minutes in KVHS years, I'm not wedded to the status quo. If KVHS is to fulfil its potential, a few fundamentals must change on the medical side of things. I can help you with that if you like. To be honest, I wouldn't mind a new role."

Carol had accepted his offer gratefully and they'd had a constructive conversation about managing Anne's departure.

"Thanks so much," Carol said sincerely, preparing to hang up.

"You're welcome," he said, "but—this all rests on one very important condition." Carol resisted the urge to say "anything!" "What's that?"

"If the doctors have to change, so does the Executive Team. It's time they got out of their offices and out and about a little more. And more open to hearing the staff point of view. This is not going to work if it's all one way."

Carol had breathed a silent sigh of relief. "I promise," she said with a smile. "We need to work together to develop some sensational clinical leaders at KVHS, and I'm willing to do whatever it takes."

Carol pushed herself up onto her elbows to check the clock. All in all, yesterday hadn't been a bad day at the office. At least things were moving! Whether it was in the right direction remained to be seen. She'd lost a key executive, but it might have saved her having to initiate this herself later on. *Better not lose another one. One is careless, but two ...!*

She swung out of bed for her morning walk, never guessing how soon that thought would come back to haunt her.

CHAPTER FOUR

On the Monday morning after the Executive Team planning session, Rosie hurried into Carol's office and dropped a pile of messages in Carol's tray. "How did it all go?" she asked. As usual, she didn't stop while Carol replied, but busied herself with changing the flowers.

"Surprisingly well, thanks, Rosie," said Carol watching Rosie's deft flower arranging admiringly. "We've got a ways to go, but there's definite progress. We committed to some good decisions. Now the hard work continues." She decided against discussing the bit that hadn't gone so well until Anne's final decision was confirmed. The message on top of the pile caught her eye. "What's this one from the National Rural Health Association?"

"Oh!" Rosie stopped what she was doing, flower in hand. "That's good news. Just after you left for the executive planning workshop, the association called and—wait for it—asked if you'd be willing to be the closing speaker for the annual conference, to talk about how you've turned KVHS around. No one from Kinsley Valley has ever been asked to give a keynote address at the conference, so it's a real honour!"

Carol opened her mouth to respond, but Rosie continued hurriedly. "Of course I said I'd check with you but that I was sure you'd say yes. You'll have so many good stories about KVHS with everything that's going on. We haven't seen this much action for years!" She stopped and peered at Carol. "You don't look as pleased as I thought you would. Is something wrong? I thought I was doing the right thing."

Carol immediately assembled a smile.

"I am pleased—that you are so proud of Kinsley Valley, Rosie. And of all the hard work everyone is doing. I'm just not sure there will be enough good news stories by the time the conference is on. Isn't it before the state election?"

"Yes, in a few months. And you will have good stories to tell, I'm sure of it." Rosie suddenly noticed she had stopped moving and continued with the flowers. "The staff will be so proud that the whole country will hear about Kinsley Valley. Lots of them will be able to attend as this year it's being held at the Woodside conference centre, only three hours away. Just down the road! Year after year, we've had to hear CEOs from other rural health services blow their trumpets. The Mountain Health Care CEO has done that closing address three times in the past seven years. Their care may be average, but their self-promotion is outstanding. If I never have to hear that man speak again, it will be too soon."

Carol regarded the normally positive Rosie with interest, surprised at her intensity.

"The staff really need something to brighten them up," Rosie said in response to Carol's raised eyebrows. "This past year has been such a grind. If you can't do it, no one can."

Carol rolled the idea around in her mind and felt the familiar lead in the pit of her stomach. She did not entirely share Rosie's optimism. As nice as it was to be asked, and to hear Rosie's enthusiastic endorsement, Carol knew that concrete improvements might not have emerged by then. After everything the health service had been through, they didn't need to add public embarrassment at a national conference to their list. And did the minister attend the conference? She imagined her sitting in the front row. No—it was too big a reputational risk.

She shook her head, sat down, and picked up her phone. "Sorry Rosie."

"Carol. We need this." To Carol's surprise, Rosie's normally cheery voice wavered.

Carol looked up at Rosie and saw tears in her eyes. She was beaten, and they both knew it. "Okay," she sighed as she put down the phone. "Tell them I'm confirmed."

She may have imagined it, but she could have sworn Rosie skipped a little as she left the office. *It's all right for her, she doesn't have to stand up in front of a thousand people.* Carol took a deep breath as she imagined this worst-case scenario, feeling the lead in her stomach grow heavier. Then she squared her shoulders. Whatever happened, she'd deal with it. She picked up her phone to start returning calls.

*****

Ten days later, the Executive Team met for the second time since the workshop. The first had been to discuss Anne's resignation, and it had been tense, to say the least. With that behind them, Carol dared to feel optimistic as they gathered in the boardroom. Kristen had volunteered to coordinate the core operational problem plans they had made on day two of the workshop and Carol was looking forward to hearing about their progress and moving things along.

"Let's get started," Carol began briskly. She looked around the table and noticed everyone squinting in the morning sun pouring through the large boardroom windows. Anton's glasses had turned so dark, she couldn't see his eyes. Kristen noticed and got up to close the blinds, laughing as she said, "Anton, is that you? Or has a KV Leader spy infiltrated our top secret planning session?"

"Thanks, Kristen," Carol continued. "Just in case you need a reminder, some of today's issues will be discussed at my first quarterly progress meeting with the Department of Health tomorrow, so I need to be absolutely clear about where we are and where we're going. Elena let's start with you. What's happening with pharmacy?"

"Well, nothing yet." Elena looked defensive. "But, you know I only got that one because Anne left. I've been flat out with other things since the planning workshop and haven't got around to reopening negotiations with the preferred provider."

Carol suppressed her frustration. "Elena, you did volunteer to take this over. If you're too busy, is there anyone else we can ask? We've got to get this process moving again ASAP."

Kristen raised her hand. "My procurement manager would love to have a bigger role in this. I didn't suggest it at the workshop because it seemed like such a 'clinical' thing, and in the past, we've stayed out of each other's territory. But I've been thinking since then: that's not necessarily the best thing for the patients, is it? That approach is more about us than them. We should be finding the best people for these important tasks, regardless of which division 'owns' the service or issue."

Anton nodded. "Yep, and there's someone in my office who has significant contract experience. With the right clinical input, they'd be really useful to have on the team."

"I'm sure Jeff Zammit would help with that as well. He's been really good about managing Anne's departure and reassuring the senior doctors that the sky isn't falling." Carol made notes on the whiteboard. "In fact, most of them have been reasonable, once I had a conversation with them. Even Professor Yang heroically restrained herself last time we met. I could see all the critical things she wanted to say, but didn't, jumping up and down in her throat."

Kristen laughed. "Ha—you got off lightly! But, you know, I'm not surprised. Most of them hardly ever got to have a one-on-one conversation with the CEO before you came along. Seb was an accountant and generally tried to stay as far away from clinical staff as he could. I tried to meet with them regularly when I was acting, but that fell by the wayside as there were so many other things to do. I heard through the grapevine that even Dr Walters is saying you're 'not the average CEO.' "

Carol wasn't so sure that was intended as a compliment. She recalled how she'd dreaded her meeting with the crusty Head of the Mental Health Service. A distinguished seventy years of age, with a flowing mane of white hair and a bow tie, he carried himself like the revered mental health expert he was. He rarely met Carol's eye, but talked over her head, as if dealing with her face-to-face was beneath him. The first ten minutes had been distinctly unpleasant as he reeled off everything that was wrong with senior management generally, and Carol in particular. But having unburdened himself, he'd become slightly less combative. As he got up to leave, he'd flashed her a broad smile, showing brilliant white teeth, and said, "I'll give you six months."

Carol related his parting shot with a shrug. "Six months for what? To succeed? Or before he disposes of me? Or I crawl out of here on my knees with my career in tatters? Or before all the doctors march out the front door?" *In their white coats.* "And he's not the only one. Every time I see Ken Jezlowski, the Social Work Head, he looks around as if he's being followed and mutters, 'Let me know if I can help you *out.*' It's a little creepy."

Rosie knocked and entered the room with a jug of iced water and a plate of fresh biscuits from the KVHS Volunteers' Group fundraising stall just in time to catch Carol's comment. She chuckled as she placed them on the table. "As you know, the CEO before Seb was a lovely man called Peter," she said. "I don't think he'd had much management training as he pretty much worked his way up to the top. But he was a good manager because he understood people. Staff would storm into his office and come out looking like they'd had a photo opportunity with John F. Kennedy." She handed the biscuits around the table. "One day I asked him his secret. 'Four little letters,' he said. 'SWTA: Start Where They Are. Then I explain where I am, and we try to meet in the middle. It doesn't work every time, nor with everyone. But if it doesn't, I just give them a week's extra holiday leave and that generally brings them around.' He was joking, I thought, but I was never quite sure …"

"Ha! Four little letters that I also believe in," Carol said, taking a biscuit. "Great minds think alike. That reminds me: Is there a KVHS change management process? I haven't noticed much SWTA in how things are done. I think I might know the answer, but I thought I'd check."

"Well, yes, there is," replied Elena with an expressive flourish of her hands. "In nursing we have a process for changing the policy and procedure and training the staff in the new way and communicating the change."

"But we don't all use that process." William shook his head. "I'd say the answer is no." Kristen and Anton looked blank.

"Most health services don't pay enough attention to good change management," Carol said. She took a sip of water, ready for some push back. "We tend to change the policy and procedure, pass it down the hierarchy, and expect that people will do what they're told. I know, Elena, we might think that's how it should work," she said with a glance at her CNMO's pursed lips, "except that people are working in a complex environment where introducing and embedding something new is incredibly difficult. There are things we can do that make it easier, though. Kristen, part of the reason that Prof Yang is unhappy is the way the operating room scheduling changes were made, not that the changes themselves are wrong. She doesn't feel any ownership of the process, and that's a serious threat to full implementation."

"Can't she see that we're trying to help?" asked Kristen in an irritated tone. "She won't have a surgical service if we don't get that throughput up and stabilised. The Department of Health won't hesitate to take the funding from us and give it to a health service that meets its targets."

"Facts support understanding, but feelings drive action, " Carol recited. "That's one of the truest of truisms. The facts might say that there are many good reasons for the changes you want to make, but Prof Yang's feelings say that her role and input have been overlooked. Which do you think is uppermost in her mind?"

Kristen paused. "Okay, okay, I get it. You're right, if we don't work together on this, it will never happen. I'll go and see her tomorrow." She glanced at the clock. "Look at the time! Let's get going on this list or we'll be here until midnight. And yes, Carol, I am interested to hear about a good change process when we have time. To be frank, I'm sick of wasting time on half-implemented strategies, or hosing down spot fires from badly managed change. I've got better things to do, like getting this list fixed."

"Of course," continued Carol. "But before we continue, that reminds me: I wanted to share some 'leading Great Care' actions[A4] I've developed over the years. I keep them with me as a reminder." She pulled a small laminated card out of her wallet and read:

1. Start Where You Really Are—not where you'd like to be.
2. Then—Start Where They Are.
3. Develop a set of shared, non-negotiable goals for Great Care.
4. Embrace the hard yards together.
5. Make it as easy as possible to win.
6. Model the behaviour you want to see in the team.

The group listened politely and then turned back to the job at hand without comment. *There's obviously a limit to how many inspirational lists people can take in at once!* Carol smiled to herself. *Especially when there are operational matters to discuss.* "Right! We'll revisit it at another time." She nodded at Kristen. "Keep going."

Kristen continued to work them through the list of core problems and plans. Progress had been made on some issues and not on others. For the first time, though, they tackled the discussion as a team, each contributing resources and ideas.

"Now for the strategic list." Carol went to the whiteboard where her issues from the workshop were written:

1. No definition or goals for KVHS quality care.
2. Unhappy consumers and staff.
3. Silos in the executive and senior management group.
4. Staff disconnected from the Board and senior managers.
5. Weak line management.
6. Board and Executive Team's lack of knowledge about what's really going on.

"We've identified KVHS Great Care goals and actions, and we're working on the siloed executive group," she began. "That reminds me: How is it going running the workshop scenario with your staff?"

Silence.

"Come on, people," Carol pleaded.

Anton shrugged as he got up to take a phone call he'd been waiting on out in the hall.

Kristen waded in. "We've been up to our ears with the core problem list, and don't forget we've had reports to prepare for your quarterly check-up visit with the Department of Health. There's a lot going on around this place since you arrived!" She looked down and fiddled with the whiteboard pens on the table, looking flustered.

"I guess I'm impatient to get things moving," Carol admitted. "Have any of you at least made a time to meet with your managers to discuss it?"

Much to her surprise, Elena was the only one who nodded. "Oh, I know you're surprised, Carol. You think I'm going to be the laggard to be coaxed along. I admit I'm wary of some of the things you're proposing. But your quality system really does seem to focus on the patients and staff, and, heaven knows, we need to try something different to engage staff in improving things. Nothing else has worked, and we mostly appear to have driven them away from being involved during Seb's period as CEO." She looked up as Anton re-entered the room. "If I'm completely honest, I'm worried that if we don't do something to improve morale and job satisfaction, we're going to lose good nurses to the private hospital, not only the disgruntled ones. So, I'm prepared to give it a go. I've added an hour to the senior nurses' monthly meeting next week to define high quality care and their roles in it. I'll let you know how we go."

Kristen looked at her admiringly. "Good on you, Elena."

"Thanks, Elena," Carol said. "I look forward to hearing about it. Let me know if you'd like any help preparing for the meeting. Now, where were we?" She looked at the whiteboard and down at her notes. "Number six. I'm going to run the defining-quality scenario with the Board and have the discussion about the KVHS vision and strategic plan. Once they've defined good care and set the quality goals they want us to achieve, we'll be on the same page. It will be easier for us to work together on identifying where we are in relation to where we want to be and to be honest about what's really going on."

"Really?" William was wide-eyed. "With the Board members? Will they really want to waste—I mean spend—their time on that?"

Carol sighed inwardly, but before she could respond, Anton leaned forward and pushed his glasses up his nose. Everyone looked at him expectantly. "William, do you have any idea how much time we spend at the Board Finance Committee— and the full Board meeting—strategizing about the budget? That phone call was the Finance Committee Chair querying if we'll have enough time on the next meeting agenda to fully discuss the new budget. The quality of care we provide is our core business. Remember the workshop discussion? The budget is only a means to supporting that end: high quality care for every consumer. The Board should probably spend more time on strategizing for high quality care than they do on the budget."

"Thanks, Anton, couldn't have said it better myself." Carol smiled. "The Board is accountable for the quality of KVHS care in exactly the same way they're accountable for responsible financial governance and organisational sustainability. Look at what happened to the Board after the Medical Unit Review. I don't imagine it was pretty."

"No, pretty ugly actually," sighed Kristen. "We don't want to go through that again. The whole community got in on the act. Everyone had an opinion, and you couldn't go to the supermarket without someone giving you theirs at full volume. I was trapped in the cereal aisle for fifteen minutes one day while the Volunteers' President gave me her detailed analysis of what went wrong and how to fix it. I'm sure that's where the local paper got the next day's headline from. I thought I spotted the editor lurking near the muesli." She winced at the memory. "Half the Board left under pressure from the media and the Minister for Health and the other half are still upset."

Carol nodded. "All the more reason for us to get on and repair some of this as soon as we can. Numbers two, four, and five we have yet to start dealing with. But they're all connected. We haven't a hope of achieving our Great Care goals for every consumer without our directors and managers absolutely on board. Some key people aren't performing in their roles and we need to put some processes in place to resolve this. Finally, I want to agree on the KVHS values that have come out of the staff forums over the past few weeks." Carol handed out sheets of paper. "This is what we've narrowed it down to." The paper read: "KVHS Values in Action. We are:

- Proactive.
- Thoughtful.
- Aware.
- Collaborative.
- Respectful.

"What about things like 'trustworthy'?" asked William.

"We've tried to identify values that prompt behaviours," Carol responded. "Of course we want people to be trustworthy, but it's hard to translate what that means every day. These values will provide the 'cement' to bind the Great Care goals to behaviours we all value. We'll keep working on it; I just wanted to show you how it's panning out." Carol shut her laptop as she drew the meeting to a close. "Before we finish, there's one more, extremely important, thing to discuss."

"Not sure I can take too many more extremely important issues," said Kristen warily.

Everyone looked expectantly at Carol.

"Now that we've got to know each other and worked through some of our problems, let's take a little time to appreciate our strengths. It mightn't feel like it right now, but we have a lot going for us and I want us to keep this in mind. A real commitment to KVHS. Practical skills that will be invaluable as we work through these challenges. Deep corporate knowledge balanced by some new thinking. A recognition that we can be better. We're going to rely heavily on these assets over the next few months, as well as new ones we'll discover as we go. Let's talk more about this in future exec meetings. For now I wanted to say, thanks, everyone. That was a real team effort."

Carol was pleased to see that everyone had stopped packing up. Some looked a little embarrassed, unused to positive recognition.

"Did you say *team*?" asked Elena, eyebrows raised.

"I do believe I did!" Carol said, smiling. "Didn't mean to—it just slipped out! It appears that you are starting to exhibit the behaviours of the *Greatus Teamus* in its natural environment, starting with sharing responsibility for identifying and fixing problems. Who knows what you might do next!"

"Don't get too excited," Elena warned. "This Executive Team can go backwards at speed. I've seen it plenty of times. And while we're thinking about teams, shouldn't we add 'no CMO' to our operational problems list?"

Carol felt the wind drain from her sails but worked hard not to show it.

"You're right, Elena. If we stop moving forward, it's easy to go backwards. It's no mean feat to make consistent progress in this environment. And we will make mistakes –

lots of them! We're all only human after all. But we won't let that stop us. My aim is to learn from our mis-steps and draw on what we're good at and what our organisation is good at as the basis of what we can become. And don't worry about the CMO. I've asked Jeff Zammit from ED to act in the role until we can recruit and he's indicated that he'd like to do it. It's not formalised yet but I'm hopeful it will fall into place. He's looking for a new challenge, and I was afraid he'd find one at the private hospital. Hopefully our problems will be big enough to keep him here!"

"Well, that's the first time I've heard a CEO hoping for big problems," laughed Kristen as she left. "Come on, Anton, let's get our diaries together and make a time for our staff to talk about this pharmacy business."

William lingered behind as the others dispersed. "Carol…" he began.

"William!" Carol smiled. "I've been wanting to talk to you, too."

William sat down, looking far from comfortable. Carol shut the door.

"Now," she began, as she sat.

William held up his hand. "Carol, please let me go first. I've been trying to get a time with you for the past two days to tell you … I'm leaving."

Carol was momentarily surprised into silence.

William continued, "I'm going to the private hospital. I'm sorry, Carol, but I think we both know I'm not what you need in this role. I'm not strategic and I've always preferred risk to improvement. I should never have accepted this role in the first place, but Seb was not the kind of CEO you said no to. I've wanted to focus on risk management ever since we found out a couple of years ago that we were only reporting around thirty per cent of our adverse events, compared to the numbers identified by audit and coding data. I realised then that my true interest lies in doing something about it. The private hospital wants a senior risk manager and that's what I want to do."

Carol noted the sheen of perspiration on his forehead and realised how difficult this conversation was for him. It was no picnic for her, either. She didn't know whether to feel relieved or disappointed. She knew he wasn't quite up to the role yet, but thought he had the potential to blossom with some support and mentoring. "I was going to suggest some coaching and professional development for you. Sure you don't want to think it over a little more?"

William shook his head. "No, thanks. I feel really good about my decision. I love risk management and it's what I'm good at. I think I'll enjoy the challenge of a new health service. I've been here eight years. If that's long enough for US presidents, it's long enough for me! But thanks for the offer."

For the next few minutes, they discussed William's new position and his exit strategy. He left the office with a smile on his face, looking five years younger than when he'd entered.

Phew. Carol exhaled as the door closed behind him. *There's my second Executive Team member gone in as many weeks.* She frowned. Just as things seemed to be picking up, this was a blow. Now she had to find someone else who could help her with a major strategic quality system implementation—and fast. *Someone to help me turn the whole organisation around. No biggie.* She rested her head on her hand and gazed out the window at the gleaming new hospital building. No doctors with Anne's face streaming out the doors, just the usual coming and going of patients and staff.

Her frown deepened as she remembered she'd be seeing Nancy, her Board Chair, first thing in the morning for their trip to the Department of Health. Nancy had already warned her that not all Board members were happy with Carol as the CEO. *What will they make of this?*

She wouldn't have to wait long to find out.

CHAPTER FIVE

The next day, Carol met Nancy at 7:00 A.M. sharp for the ninety-minute drive to the large town where the Department of Health regional office was located. Nancy was a red-haired, large-girthed force of nature, and the Mayor of Kinsley Valley. She was generally easy going—until someone came between her and her goal to make Kinsley Valley the best rural town in the country, when the full force of her determination was unleashed. "Happy for me to drive?" she offered. "You can run me through your presentation for today if you like." She twisted her hair into a bun and secured it with a clasp as she spoke.

Carol pulled the printed slides out of her bag. They told the story of her impressions and analysis so far and plans for tackling them. "But first I need to talk to you about something, Nancy."

"Uh-oh." Nancy glanced at Carol as she swung out of the hospital carpark. "I imagine you're not about to warm my heart with tales of an unexpected financial windfall. Let's see if I can guess. You haven't gone and lost another executive, have you?"

Carol shot her a look.

"You're kidding. Well, I was kidding, but I can see you're not. Who?"

"William." Carol briefly filled her in on the conversation she'd had with William the previous afternoon. "I know this isn't ideal ..." She trailed off.

Nancy smiled at Carol as she pulled up at a red light. "You don't need to be sorry, Carol, unless you're bullying your executives into leaving! I spoke to Anne, and although you two clearly didn't see eye to eye, she said you were never anything but respectful. Clearly that didn't stop you having a few robust discussions! No, I'm not worried that William is leaving because of you. I will want to see his exit interview, of course."

"Of course." Despite the reassurance from her Board Chair, Carol was nervous about what would come next.

Nancy drove on in silence, so Carol asked the question. "How do you think the rest of the Board will react?"

"I'd say they'll feel the same as me." Nancy paused while she overtook an enormous truck. "Relieved."

Carol blinked and shook her head. "Relieved? What do you mean? You've already told me that half the Board members aren't convinced I'm right for the job. Surely this can't do anything but further persuade them."

"Well, if it were any of the other executives, that would be true," agreed Nancy. "But not William. We all knew he shouldn't have been made an Executive Director. Seb was a great money manager, and he got that new building built, but he wasn't very smart with people—staff *or* patients. We all knew William was the wrong choice and put there for the wrong reasons."

Carol, unusually, was at a loss for words. She had spent half the night worrying about Nancy's response and bracing herself for a showdown with the Board.

Nancy grinned at Carol's bafflement. "Not what you were expecting, was it? Didn't get much sleep last night? You should have called me! Although, of course, I was in a council meeting, and wrangling those councillors takes all my brain space, so I wouldn't have been able to discuss it sensibly with you anyway. As I said, the Board won't be sorry. Don't get me wrong: we like William as a person. He's been a solid contributor to KVHS. But he hasn't been able to give the Board or the Board Quality Committee—or the senior managers, for that matter—the technical support and guidance we've needed to turn things around. And the staff aren't that fond of him because they associate him with the poor accreditation result. The Board thinks he was promoted beyond his capability, which, I must say, does not seem to be an uncommon occurrence in healthcare. Any idea why that is?"

Carol recovered her powers of speech. "There are many theories. From my experience, we don't always value management roles in health services; let's face it, it's hard to compare a manager to a clinician who saves lives. But this attitude has caused many of the problems we have in healthcare organisations, in my opinion." She adjusted her sun visor to block the glare as the sun climbed higher into the sky, then went on.

"Managers largely determine how an organisation operates on the ground, and the high performers are worth their weight in gold. These are the ones who don't just manage the day-to-day operations well but are strategic about where their service is going and how it will get there. They don't want to keep a service ticking over; they want to provide a good service. They see the bigger picture and the contribution they make to the broader organisation, and they know that striving to make things better is part of their job, not some extra 'thing' they do on Tuesdays. They're good with planning and decision-making and delegation and providing useful guidance to their staff, without expecting clinical governance to be someone else's job."

Nancy turned up the air-conditioning to counter the outside warmth. "How can we get more of these marvellous beings into healthcare?"

"It's a constant issue. We don't always put the right people in management roles. And often, we drive good people away because we don't support them. Just because someone is a good clinician doesn't mean they'll be a good manager. And even if they do have potential, we're not very good at systematic skills development and support." She pushed her sunglasses up her nose and took a sip from her water bottle before continuing.

"Healthcare culture can be brutal, and there's a fair bit of 'sink or swim' thinking. That's fine for the swimmers. But many people sink without a trace and take their services down with them. We often blame the manager, learn nothing, and go on to rinse and repeat. If I could wave a wand, I'd create skilled, supported managers from bedside to executive, and many of our problems would disappear. Oh, that's right, that is what I'm trying to do, but without the wand, unfortunately." Carol sighed. "I think William was treading water," she added. "But he could have been a swimmer with some focused development and proper guidance and support."

"Alright. We won't blame William." Nancy nodded. She tapped her perfectly manicured, bright red nails on the steering wheel for a moment. "But from what you've said, I'm wondering if we even need an Executive Team member with a specific 'quality' responsibility. Jeff Zammit has a good grasp of clinical governance; couldn't we employ another quality and risk operational manager to report to him? It would save a few dollars; maybe we could invest those in developing the line managers, so they could look after quality themselves."

Carol gathered her thoughts for the second time that morning. "It would save a few dollars and give me one less direct report, which would be helpful." She gazed out the window at the bright yellow canola crops stretching to the blue horizon, wondering how best not to lose an executive position she knew would be almost impossible to get back. "Let me ask you a question. Would you replace Anton if he left?"

"Of course," Nancy answered without hesitation. "Can't run an organisation without a Finance Director. Or IT! I thank my lucky stars at every Finance Committee that he defected from the bank."

"Sooo …" Carol began.

"Don't tell me you're trying to equate William with Anton."

"Not his skill level, no. But the positions? Yes." Carol took a deep breath and launched in. "Anton runs the finance system that keeps us viable: planning, funding, resource management, tracking and tweaking in response to our results. He supports the managers to manage their budgets, but he doesn't manage those budgets day to day. Anton and his team provide the systems and intelligence and tools—and help when required—for managers to use their allocated resources to run their service. And the Executive Team and Board take ultimate responsibility for how resources are managed, with the technical help Anton's team provides. These roles are not mutually exclusive, they're complementary. It should be exactly the same with the quality system."

Nancy pursed her lips. "Really? I get what you're saying, but it seems kind of … far-fetched. I don't expect clinical managers to be expert budget managers. That's why they need a Finance Department to help them. But shouldn't they be experts in the quality of care their service provides?"

Carol looked out the window again while she considered how best to convey the complexity of managing a health service. "Yes! You're absolutely right, Nancy, they should. The thing is, they are experts in how care is delivered, but not in how to make sure that care is delivered consistently well. William has made his role about 'quality control': basically he administers a risk and compliance system. That's important, of course, but to achieve high quality care for every consumer, that role must evolve to become like Anton's: a mix of strategy, planning, skilful improvement support for managers, and reporting—that loop back into the strategy and planning. Healthcare cherry-picked quality systems from other industries; they're meant to be a mix of control and improvement, with a view to achieving strategic quality goals. But many people just dabble in quality compliance and in improvement to achieve compliance."

"Really? I suppose I've never thought of a quality role that way because I've only ever seen the compliance and administration version. But shouldn't everyone be out there every day providing high quality care? Isn't that why they get into healthcare in the first place? Oh, I'm sure this is my niece coming the other way!" Nancy wound the window down and waved wildly at the oncoming car. The driver responded in identical fashion.

Carol enjoyed the temporary rush of warm air from the open window and waited until Nancy's arm was safely back in the car before responding. "If I had a dollar for every clinician, executive, and Board member who'd said that to me over the years …! Yes, if it worked like that, life would be a breeze! But it doesn't. Even with the best staff and the best intentions, poor care and adverse events continue. If KVHS were a factory run by robots instead of a health service, it would be a lot more straightforward; we'd set the specifications and every patient would receive identical levels of care. Even then, the robots wouldn't be responsive enough to unexpected issues. But we're not a factory run by robots—yet, at least. We're a complex system.[4] Look at these roadworks." Carol pointed out the window at a mass of earth and machinery. "Why are they building a new bridge?"

"The old one was falling down, and sooner or later someone was going to end up in the river." Nancy shrugged. "I know all about this project as it's been on the agenda of our council meetings for five years. We had so many problems getting started that I never thought I'd see actual construction. The new bridge will be wider, of course, to take more traffic as our population grows, and higher, as the river floods more often these days. And stronger to withstand larger trucks. The engineers also have to build it while protecting a rare water bird that lives nearby."

"Think of all the things you had to take into account to build one bridge," Carol said, watching a bulldozer cross the road in front of them as they waited behind a stop sign. "You're making it safer, more effective, more efficient, and considering the surrounding environment while you're doing it. And when it's finished, you'll monitor and maintain it. The road system is also a complex system, just like healthcare."

"I'm not sure if I follow you." Nancy smiled at the road worker who waved them through.

"Many components of our drive today need to go well for us to have a successful journey." Carol held up her fingers to count them off. "Weather that we can't control, but bad weather would make our drive less safe and slower. The car has to be in good condition, which we can control, but even then, we could get a flat tyre."

"Don't tempt fate," Nancy warned.

"Or a sinkhole might open up in front of us," Carol teased. "So what else? The road must be well designed and maintained. We want all drivers that we encounter, including you, to be competent and alert and ready to deal with an unexpected event, and not under the influence of substances that will limit their judgment or ability. There are rules"—she pointed to a police car coming in the opposite direction—"which people variously obey. And if there were a problem on the road, we'd want it cleared as soon as possible so we could be on our way. When we get close to the Department of Health, we'll rely on someone, somewhere, monitoring and tweaking the traffic signals and signage to keep everything flowing smoothly through the busy centre of town."

Nancy was quiet for a minute. "That's a heap of variables. Some we can control and some we can't."

Carol nodded. "It's like an enormous jigsaw puzzle with thousands of pieces. And our trip back to Kinsley Valley could be quite different if those pieces combine differently. We'll have the afternoon sun in our eyes, for a start."

"Unless it's raining. Either way—you'll be driving," Nancy laughed.

"Yes, despite all those variables and challenges, we set a target of 'zero road toll,' because what's the alternative? But to achieve that, all those components must come together and be managed in a planned and systematic way to achieve that target, while allowing enough flexibility to cope with the unexpected."

"So what you're trying to say"—Nancy nodded thoughtfully   "is that KVHS is a big road system in disguise?"

"That's one way of putting it," Carol answered. "They are both complex systems, which means they're dynamic, with many moving parts and interdependencies, which makes them unpredictable. We rely on a lot of things to go right for a journey to go smoothly, be it a road trip or a healthcare episode. But we don't just put a few things in place and hope that all goes well. One episode of care for one consumer has more variables than a busy road journey, so it's even harder to make it go right.

And those variables combine differently on different days to pose fresh challenges all the time."

She removed her sunglasses as the sun suddenly disappeared behind a bank of clouds. "That's why providing consistently high quality care is genuinely challenging in a complex environment. It takes more than good—even great—people, trying hard. Obviously, people are a cornerstone, but those people need to be supported by great systems that are designed to help them create high quality care within that complexity. Just like the new bridge, a quality system has to be fit for purpose. What you've had at KVHS for the past few years is a compliance-based quality system. That's like investing all your road resources in making road rules and policing them. There's no doubt that that would save some lives, but eventually the road itself would fall to pieces from neglect and people would lose their driving skills."

"Yes, I see," said Nancy. "Without the other pieces, like design and maintenance and equipment safety and driver training and traffic flow, things would deteriorate, even if everyone followed the road rules; which they wouldn't, because many people would pride themselves on finding a way around that as well."

Carol nodded vigorously. "Exactly. Rules, while important, are only one piece of the complex system jigsaw. There are many other pieces. But healthcare managers struggle to understand this, even though many of them were clinicians themselves— who didn't always follow policies and protocols. Our whole system is based on good, clever people, working hard, following the rules. Yet clinicians will usually find the easiest or fastest way to do things or break the rules if that's going to meet the clinical needs of their patient. Work is not always being done as we would like to imagine and we need to embrace the reality of that. Because of this, if we don't keep on top of care quality through constant monitoring and action, it erodes, like an unmaintained road system, and then we don't know where the holes until we hit them. The 'good people trying hard' theory has another major flaw, of course."

There was silence while Nancy judged the opportunity to overtake a slow car and caravan. "Yes, indeed," Nancy declared when they were safely past. "That's the same flaw I see in my council meetings. The assumption that we in positions of power and responsibility are somehow superhuman and don't make mistakes. But even the best people make the biggest mistakes and don't always follow the rules. Including me!"

"All of us," Carol chuckled. "Somehow in healthcare we've defaulted to compliance as the cornerstone of our quality system, forgetting that a complex system needs many more levers than that. Don't get me wrong, compliance is an important part of the jigsaw, like the road rules and policing. You do need to get that bit right; of course we need staff to adhere to evidence-based practice. And to standardise care wherever possible and to implement protocols that keep patients safe and make the organisation run well. Hungry?"

Nancy reached across and took a handful of almonds from Carol's bag of snacks, prepared before dawn that morning.

"But there's more to it than that," Carol continued. " I call it 'freedom within a framework.' We need a framework of what good care is and the key levers that support that care. And within that, we need our fabulous staff to use their knowledge and judgment to make the very best decisions they can with and for patients, whether they're in direct care or a support role. Sometimes there won't be a rule or protocol for what they're faced with, and in that situation, we need them to think first, then act to the best of their ability. Just like I'd want you to act appropriately if something unexpected happened on our drive today."

"When you put it like that, it makes sense," Nancy said. "And I see now that we haven't been thinking like that, with disastrous results. People corner me all the time to complain about what happened to them or their family member or friend when they were a patient in KVHS. And they don't hold back, believe me. It's one of the downsides of this role. You'll get it, too, once they recognise you.

Carol turned to Nancy, eyebrows raised. "Did I forget to tell you? I already have. I'd only been in the job a couple of weeks when I had an encounter in the supermarket. One minute I was standing in the checkout line minding my own business, and the next the cashier was yelling and everyone was looking at me. Not a pleasant experience, to say the least." Carol's tone was light, but she felt a familiar lead weight in the pit of her stomach at the memory. Suddenly, more almonds didn't seem like such a good idea and she dropped them into her bag. She shuddered every time she thought about the encounter with the bereft daughter of a man harmed whilst a patient in KVHS, albeit long before she'd arrived—not for the embarrassment and discomfort of the situation, but for the tragic story she'd subsequently uncovered.

"Horrible. I'm sorry you had to experience that. Welcome to Kinsley Valley! Do you know who it was?" asked Nancy, eyes firmly on the road as she negotiated some fallen tree branches.

"I didn't then, but I do now. She announced to the whole supermarket that the hospital had ruined her family's life the day we gave her father an 'experimental' cocktail of drugs for a chronic heart problem. Apparently, he hasn't been the same man since and his wife has had to give up her job to look after him. The whole episode appears to have exacerbated his depression to the point where he can no longer work. One of the many sad stories to come out of the medical ward's dark days."

"Terrible," Nancy responded with feeling. "We'll be dealing with the personal and legal fallout of those cases for many years, and it will be a long time before this town forgives and forgets. The poor care on that ward touched so many families. What I find really interesting, as well as sad, is that when we investigated, it wasn't all experimental treatments that caused the problems. We found that a lot of the issues stemmed from staff not thinking. It looked like they were just going through the motions and ticking boxes."

She paused to turn on the windscreen wipers as a misty curtain of rain swept across the valley. "The place reeked of complacency," she continued. "No one acted even when one of the senior physicians started his medication 'experiments'. We found out later that he was dealing with a chronic disease that was getting worse and his decision-making deteriorated along with it. But no one wanted to deal with it, least of all the Unit Head who was busy with other 'business interests' that had nothing to do with running the service. It seems he wasn't paying enough attention to either his care or his management role. One of the issues identified in the investigation was that KVHS had no processes for detecting deteriorating patients or clinical practice. We do now of course. But it's a bit late for those patients. And we still have to do something about the thoughtlessness and lack of caring at the root of it all."

Carol grimaced. "Yep. Management gurus bang on about 'learning organisations' all the time, but I would much rather have a 'thinking' organisation first and that's what I'm trying to create. Don't worry Nancy. These problems are hard to identify and fix, no doubt about it. But there are a few things we can do."

"I'm all ears."

"Well, we develop our suite of measures to show if we're achieving the quality goals, which gives us some ability to cross reference between effectiveness and safety; which should help pick up clinical care results trending in the wrong direction. We'll keep a much closer eye on consumer satisfaction and hear first-hand from more of them more often. We need to find better ways to assess staff satisfaction and to support people to speak up for patient safety. It would also be good to hear regularly from Unit Heads and other senior clinicians and department heads about how they provide good care and what their issues are."

The misty rain turned into heavy pellets splattering across the windscreen and Nancy slowed down. "Risk management," she explained. "I know how bad the roads are around here and they immediately deteriorate in the rain. Another thing we can't control but have to adjust for." She briefly turned to Carol and smiled. "That all sounds good, Carol. I haven't heard a CEO talk like this in a while."

"Thanks. But making it all happen requires a multi-pronged approach. A Quality Executive Director with a strategic brain and focus could help us to pull the pieces together, make sure they're well designed and fit for purpose and craft them into a comprehensive approach to supporting staff to provide consistently high quality care." They crested a hill and Carol peered through the wet windscreen at the cluster of buildings on the horizon that signalled their destination.

"Line managers are not experts in how to construct a technical quality system that can do all that," she continued, "any more than they could design a finance system. We want our managers to focus on what they're good at—providing or supporting care—and to use the quality system to help them reach their potential." She turned to Nancy. "The KVHS strategic plan talks about providing high quality care for every consumer. This will never be achieved if we don't operationalise it with a mature and sophisticated quality system, and we need someone with the strategy, technical skills, and knowledge to do that."

"Do such 'quality' experts exist?" Nancy raised her eyebrows.

"They're a rare species, but I believe there are a few left in captivity." Carol grinned. "I hope I used to be one of them! I promise I'll find one for KVHS. I'm going to look internally first as I think there are some promising candidates."

"Good. My brain is full. Thanks to you, I'll never think of a road the same way again!" She looked at Carol. "By the way, how are you holding up in the middle of all this chaos?"

Carol weighed her words. She liked Nancy a lot but didn't yet feel comfortable enough with her to open up completely. "I'm okay. I won't lie—there are some things about the job that get me down. But I'm confident we'll work through them. And I really appreciate your support."

"You've got it. I believe we can do great things together for KVHS. We just have to shift the boulders in our way first! However, shifting boulders—or getting other people to shift them—is my specialty. Now, why don't you run me through your presentation for the department?"

Carol slipped on her reading glasses.

"I don't expect it to be a fun meeting," Nancy continued. "They'll need major convincing we can drag ourselves off the bottom of the staff and patient satisfaction heap, so we'd better both be on the same page. We'll be there in half an hour—unless that sinkhole opens up, of course …"

CHAPTER SIX

· ·

"It's been a roller coaster." Carol sat on her oldest friend's sofa, glass of wine in one hand, patting Nelson, a beautiful black cocker spaniel, with the other. A week had passed since the meeting with the Department of Health. "Honestly, I feel like this is the first time I've really stopped since I started the job."

"I can't believe that you've been back in town for weeks and this is the first time you could fit us into your hectic schedule! Chen will give you a hard time about it too when he gets home. He had an early game tonight and they go out for pizza afterwards. Did you know he's coached the Kinsley Valley Under 18s mixed hockey team for two years? And that last season they won the state championship? It's game one of the new season tonight. He can't wait to tell you all about it."

Carol looked fondly at her friend. She and Angela had gone to Kinsley Valley high school together and their mothers were good friends. Although they hadn't seen a lot of each other over recent years, they'd kept in touch. Angela had been a basketball player in her youth and was tall and angular, towering over both her husband, Chen, and Carol. It wasn't unusual for her relatives and friends to experience a sweep of her curly hair in their eyes when she bent over to kiss them hello and goodbye. Her wide smile and twinkling eyes made her a popular figure in Kinsley Valley, and no party was complete without her.

She and Chen had met when he came to lecture at the KV University. They were married within a year and had two children in quick succession. As the kids grew up, Angela had established a thriving company helping women start work-from-home businesses, and Chen worked his way up to managing a university department, so their roots were firmly planted in Kinsley Valley society. Carol had tried to catch up with them when she saw her mother on flying visits from the city, but there was seldom enough time on either side. It felt good to be relaxing at her friends' place on a Friday night, with no plane to catch or long drive back to the city to spoil it.

"Wow, that's impressive! I must try to get to at least some of the games this season." Carol had played hockey for her university team and loved it. "Things will settle

THE POINT OF CARE

down eventually—I hope. I know I've ignored you, but there's been so much to do. It's not like I've been hitting the Kinsley Valley night spots. I feel like I've been working eight days a week and spending time with Mum in between!"

The past week had indeed been hectic. The meeting with the Department of Health had been predictably tense. KVHS was below average across all measures except financial: access, adverse events, infection, readmissions and mortality rates, to name but a few. The report was a sea of red. And the department officials had reminded Carol and Nancy in no uncertain terms that they had six months until publication of the next state-wide staff survey and consumer results, and a significant turnaround was expected.

"They didn't quite say 'or else,' but they might as well have," Nancy had announced when they were back in the car. "My head will be on the chopping block unless we fix it. Six months' time is no random number they've plucked out of the air; it's two months before the state election. If we're still bad they might give you another six months because you won't have been CEO for even a year by then. But I've been on the Board for seven years—not Chair, mind you, that's only since Seb left. I don't think he would have coped too well with a female Board Chair; he was old school." She took a swig from her water bottle before continuing.

"He and Noel, the previous Board Chair, were thick as thieves. They ran the health service with two iron fists. The rest of us were pretty much kept in the dark and only there for decoration. But the department—and the minister—aren't concerned with the 'why.' Blame will be apportioned, and a high-profile scalp like the mayor of a regional town always plays well politically before an election. Makes the politicians look strong and decisive. However, I've decided I rather like being chair of KVHS, particularly since you came along, and I'd rather not receive a 'sorry to see you go' letter from the minister. At least now you're here we can get after these results and do something about it. Your Executive Team will have to step up, too. I know they've had their hands full putting out all the bushfires around the place, but we've got to start moving forward. Let's not blow it."

She'd spent much of the trip home on the phone, strategizing with Chris, her Deputy Chair and Chair of the Board Quality and Clinical Governance Committee. "Let's get Andy involved ASAP," Carol heard her say. Andy Bidwell was a new Board member who had recently taken over chairing the KVHS Consumer and Community Partnerships Committee. "It's too late to get today's discussion into the meeting papers, but Carol will present it …" Nancy continued, talking a mile a minute.

Carol wasn't as optimistic about her job security as her Board Chair, suspecting that length of time in the role may not be a consideration two months out from an election. However, they did agree on one thing: she had no intention of 'blowing it.' Nancy had been good to her, and she would not let her down. Nor would she let the patients and staff of KVHS—or herself—down. She was determined not to go back to the department with anything other than significantly improved results.

"No work talk tonight. Come and eat," Angela said, placing a large bowl of spaghetti on the table, shaking Carol out of her reverie. She cocked her head to one side and looked at her friend. "Have you heard from Tess?" Tess was Carol's ex-partner.

"Yes. We email of course and there's the occasional call. She's based in Geneva now, so she's not exactly down the road. And she's incredibly busy."

"And you're not! As your oldest friend, it's my duty to ask what happened to you two—although if you'd rather not …" Angela heaped spaghetti onto Carol's plate and took some for herself.

"It's fine," Carol sighed. "And it's not complicated. Tess got the top technology development job at her company around the time Dad died. Everything seemed to go off track from there. There she was, finally achieved her dream job after years of working for it, set to travel the world, and there I was with my dream job, set to travel to Kinsley Valley every second weekend and eventually to move here. She wanted me to quit and go with her and I couldn't do that. We tried, but we couldn't find a compromise. Eventually we decided to split up rather than keep fighting about it and risk losing our friendship as well as our relationship."

"I'm sorry to hear that." Angela reached across the table and took Carol's hand.

"It was sad, but our lives took different paths. It happens. I'm feeling much better now. I was in a bad place for the first few months, but to be honest, I haven't had much time to think about it since I started this job. I won't kid you, because you wouldn't believe me if I said that everything was fine. It's been tough to be alone again. But I'm gradually starting to feel more like myself. Anyway, I'd rather not wallow in it tonight! Let's talk about something more fun."

Angela knew her friend well enough not to push it. "No worries, that won't be hard. Half our high school class still lives in town, and I want to tell you as much juicy gossip about them as we can fit in!"

An hour—and satisfying amounts of juicy gossip—later, Chen arrived home. His face was boyish, even in middle age, and his black hair showed only the faintest signs of grey. His sports uniform fit his muscular frame perfectly, and he glided rather than walked across the floor to greet her. In many ways, he and Angela couldn't have been more different, and yet they were a great team. He embraced Carol warmly before attending to Nelson, who was writhing in a frenzy of welcome around his feet. "Hello stranger!" he greeted Carol in his quiet voice. "Good to see you. About time!"

"Don't you start on me. Ang has already made me feel like a naughty five-year-old. Good to see you, too. Congratulations on being a superstar coach and winning the state championship! How did you go tonight?"

"We lost four to two." Chen shook his head. "I think we might have a championship hangover! We played the team we beat in the grand final last year, but they had our measure tonight."

"How did you manage to win a state grand final only two years after you took over as coach? As I recall, Kinsley Valley usually makes the finals, but then gets knocked out in the first round." The KV team played in a highly competitive league with many strong teams and winning a championship was rare.

"If you two are going to talk sports for the next half hour—yes, I can see it coming —I'm going to check in with Mum. She's been visiting her sister in the city this week and should be home by now," said Angela, searching for her phone. "And by the time I get off the phone, I want the sports talk over!"

"You know, I would talk about it all day if I could, but Ang gets a bit sick of it," Chen said, grinning. "So I'm happy to have a fresh pair of ears to bore! The coach before me had the team super well drilled in skills. Technically they were the best team in the competition. That was enough to get them into the finals, but not much further."

"Because?" asked Carol, pouring herself a glass of red.

"It took me a while to figure that out. So many good players and so few finals games? What was going on? Eventually I realised that they'd never had a consistent game plan. The coach changed it every week in response to their last game's result, and he also made it overly complicated. If the other team had scored heavily against them, the next game they'd concentrate on defence. If they hadn't scored many goals themselves, the next week they'd concentrate on offence and attack. They were constantly reacting to the things that went wrong—" "Instead of focusing on how to make things go right." Carol finished the sentence. "That sounds like most of the health services I've known and loved!"

"That's it." He bent down and took up Nelson's offer to shake hands—or paws. "The players ran around doing their best, but without a shared understanding of strategy and tactics, they were all over the place. Some were trying to be individual stars and some were lazy. They defeated teams on the bottom half of the ladder through sheer technical skill. But the top teams with a more strategic game plan were much harder to beat. And when a game didn't pan out the way they thought it would, they couldn't adapt. All I did was help them develop shared goals for each game—what we wanted to achieve every time we played—and a set of three simple game plans that we could adapt for different teams and conditions to reach our goals."

"Only three?"

"Yep, although I had a fourth and fifth up my sleeve if we got desperate! My job was to make it all simple enough that the players had the confidence to change plans midgame if we needed to." He got up to put the kettle on. "At first, nothing went right, and we lost a few games in a row. I'm sure the players were wondering if their new coach knew anything about hockey at all! They weren't used to having to follow a plan and play at the same time. Eventually, though, it all seemed to click—luckily— and we started to play on our own terms. We could stick to the game plan, or change it if necessary, and also allow our star players to do their thing. We were resilient as individuals and as a team and playing to our strengths. We had some surprise wins against a couple of top teams, and, as you know, there's nothing more convincing than results. We made the finals and lasted two rounds before we were knocked out. Tea or coffee?"

"Tea, please. What did you do then?" Carol was riveted by the story. She loved strategy and development, whether it was a sports or a management team.

"In our second year, we built on that foundation to develop a 'big picture' plan for winning the championship. This meant we were able to develop the youngsters, rest the stars, and manage the injuries strategically through the season. That's the ultimate combination for success. But I see from tonight that we must adapt and change again!"

"Shared goals, plans, skills, flexibility, resilience, and results." Carol clapped appreciatively. "Everyone on the same page and playing to their strengths. Day-to-day strategies feeding into bigger picture plans. The ability to respond to changing circumstances. It's a neat model."

"Well, I didn't invent all of it. But my uni work certainly has helped me source lots of helpful information over the years, as well as the lessons from coaches I've played under, the sports science and high-performance literature, and a few coaching courses. I've built it over time and it gets results." Chen set a steaming cup of tea on the table in front of Carol. "I'm always surprised more coaches don't figure it out. But some of them like to win through sheer hard work: by being the most skilful, or the most athletic, or the most mentally resilient, or the most physically intimidating team. These things are all important, of course, but ultimately useless if everyone isn't working together to achieve the same things. Otherwise you end up with a bunch of different goals and game plans on the field, one for each player. That's what I inherited. Now I like to think of the team as a swarm of bees or an ant colony. Everyone knows where they're going and why, and how to get there and what role they play in the bigger picture. Tonight our ants had an off night. It happens. Sometimes the problem is obvious, and sometimes there's no logical explanation."

"'Resilience—and freedom—within a framework,' " mused Carol, sipping her tea. "Hockey and healthcare: both complex systems, both full of different permutations and combinations. Both unpredictable. And both requiring a mix of approaches and abilities to respond and adapt to achieve success."

"You're not still talking about sports—or work—are you?" Angela breezed into the room and threw herself down on the sofa.

"Definitely not sports or work." Carol wagged a finger at her friend. "Sports *and* work."

*****

Carol mused over her conversation with Chen as she navigated the fifteen-minute walk home. *One of the benefits of living in a country town!* Chen had offered to drive her or walk with her, but she was happy to have some quiet time. The evening was warm and the main street full of Friday-night liveliness, watched by a half moon in a clear, black sky. Carol noted with surprise that the restaurants and bars were full of people and noise. When she was a teenager, the town went to bed around eight thirty on weeknights and ten thirty on weekends. She much preferred the KV of today than of yesteryear.

She pondered her conversation with Chen as she walked. He had, without knowing it, given her confidence a needed boost. On Monday, she had to face the Board Quality and Clinical Governance Committee for the first time and convince them that her strategic quality system model was the right approach. Chen had provided a timely reminder that simple principles for success, mixed with solid theory and hard-won experience, were a good base to fall back on when digging an organisation out of a hole.

Even so, she wasn't looking forward to the committee meeting. Not one little bit.

*****

On Monday, Carol walked into the meeting, feeling the heavy lead of stress in the pit of her stomach. As the peak governance committee for the quality of care provided at KVHS, this was where Board and executive accountability for the KVHS consumer experience played out. Three Board members and one consumer representative sat along one side of the boardroom table, and the Executive Team, minus Anton who didn't attend this committee, sat along the other. The room was full, and although Rosie had turned on the air conditioner early, as Carol presented on the meeting with the Department of Health she noticed a trickle of perspiration down her back that may not have been entirely temperature related. She completed her analysis of the KVHS results in the Department of Health's performance report and sat down.

Rosie, who was taking the minutes, nodded at her encouragingly. Everyone else stared at Carol's final slide, which listed the measures showing KVHS in the bottom third of the state.

"How did we get into this situation?" Chris Bowman-West, the Quality Committee Chair, addressed the group. His cultured voice, expensive suits and distinguished air communicated the successful nurse-turned-lawyer he was. His round face, normally smooth and impassive, was creased with frustration. Chris took all his roles in life seriously, playing to win and expecting others to do the same. He sat perfectly still and waited for a response.

The other Board members on the Quality Committee looked at the executives, who looked down at the table.

"It's not only the consumer and staff satisfaction we need to worry about, is it?" Andy Bidwell, Chair of the Consumer and Community Partnerships Committee, pointed at the screen showing the KVHS performance results summary. "There are problems with clinical care as well."

"I meant the 'whole' situation," said Chris. "Consumers, staff, care, everything. One of the reasons I applied for a Board position here was because KVHS has always prided itself on providing excellent care. The strategic plan makes a big deal of it."

"We do provide excellent care." Elena looked up, her face flushed and eyes bright. "Every health service has its up and downs. No one expects us to be perfect. But we have very good, hardworking staff, and no one at KVHS comes to work to do a bad job. Seb always said that all the talk about quality and safety was just an excuse for the bureaucrats to keep a tighter hold over us."

Carol regarded her CNMO thoughtfully, wondering why she would make such potentially career-limiting statements in this situation. With a shock, she realised that this was no evasive smoke screen. Elena really believed what she was saying. Carol experienced a pang of stress. So much work still to do to get everyone on the same page. Elena was not going to enjoy the rest of her presentation.

"Well," continued Chris, "whilst I'd like to believe that, I think we've avoided the hard facts for too long. I know there is good work and care happening in this organisation, Elena. But it's far from reliable or consistent. So today we're facing our demons. As Carol has now had enough time in her role to get a feel for the issues, I've asked her to compile some thoughts on how we got here. I believe that we need to understand where we are and why before we work out how to get where we want to go. Our plans must be based on the reality of our circumstances or we could make the same mistakes again. Carol?"

Carol clicked to the next slide, which was headed up "Clinical Governance Warning Bells." "I've got a mental list of clinical governance warning bells that I've developed over many years in the healthcare game. Some of them are also discussed in the relevant literature. When I hear a bell ring, my antennae go up, because I know there's a fair chance there's a poor care issue lurking. Maybe not across the whole organisation, but generally one or more of these warning bells indicates that consumers may be getting a raw deal somewhere in the service. These are the bells that have been ringing in my head ever since I got here, so I thought they'd provide a good framework to look at the organisational issues that either have been and/or currently are likely contributing to our poor results. One through nine come from the literature. Ten, eleven and twelve are from my observations over the years."

The group studied the list silently. Every item had a red tick next to it.

1   Hierarchical culture with little point-of-care staff power or recognition, which can manifest as a culture of blame, fear and staff reluctance to speak up.

2.   Institutional and isolated culture, unwilling to learn from elsewhere.

3.   Board and Executive Team unwilling to hear bad news.

4.   Lack of specific clinical leadership and teamwork development.

5.   Weak reporting format and content, and lack of active response to data and feedback.

6.   Lack of robust review of clinical practice.

7.   Tolerance of long-standing problems.

8.   Lack of consumer participation in their care and little interest shown in consumers' issues.

9.   Quality system based on compliance with standards, with limited service and care improvement beyond standards' requirements and reaction to things that go wrong.[5]

10. Major organisational issues such as: capital works, long-standing budget problems, major restructure, rapid demand growth or change.

11. CEO lacks requisite safety and improvement knowledge and/or commitment to effectively lead point-of-care excellence.

12. CEO and Board Chair in conflict, or withholding information, together or separately, from the rest of the Board and Executive Team.

Chris broke the heavy quiet around the table. "This Board has been content for far too long to accept the good news stories and not probe too far into the murky stuff. Well, complacency has not been our friend. It's time to dive into the murk. Give it to us straight, Carol, and don't pull any punches."

Carol took a moment to choose her words. "In my experience, each of these 'bells' has the potential to derail the quality and safety of care. Unfortunately, KVHS rings every one of them for me, as you can see—except budget issues, for now, at least. Many CEOs would trade all the other issues on the list for that, of course. Despite all the care quality talk these days, there's still more pressure to get the dollars right."

"So, I say again, how on earth did we get here?" Chris looked around the table. "I'd like to hear from one of the other executives. William? It's your last meeting, so feel free to be candid."

William squirmed a little. "I suppose we were focused on the wrong things," he began slowly. "The new building and move were such big things and took so much of our time. And then the new private hospital opened" —he shot an embarrassed look at Carol as he mentioned his prospective employer— "and it disrupted things in ways we hadn't anticipated. We hadn't thought about it enough. And smack in the middle of all that came the external review of the medical unit, while we were preparing for accreditation. In spite of all this, Seb's focus was always ..." He paused, aware that he was about to bring his former employer into the picture as well.

"On meeting efficiency targets, balancing the finances, and completing the new building on time and budget," finished Elena. "They were the priorities, pure and simple."

Nancy broke her silence. "And to be fair to Seb and the other executives, the Board completely bought into that. We so wanted to focus on the things that made KVHS look good, like the new building and the balanced budget, that we forgot we were running a high-risk organisation full of vulnerable people. Basically, Seb asked us to trust him—and we did."

"Governance isn't a matter of trust." Chris frowned. "I know I can't comment too much on the previous incumbents as I've only been on the Board for just over a year. I do know that trust between Board and Executive is required, of course, or we wouldn't let you loose on running the hospital! But it is the Board's job to seek and receive assurance that the focus and priorities are right, that the right processes are in place, and the best possible outcomes achieved for our consumers. And while we need good staff, of course, they need good systems to support them. Good people trying hard in such a complex environment is not enough. This needn't—and shouldn't—be adversarial. We all want the same thing: high quality care for every KVHS consumer and for our community. The Board and Exec must work together to achieve it by each playing our role and respecting each other's roles. Sometimes that's going to be simple, and sometimes it'll be tricky to navigate. But if we keep what's best for KVHS patients, closely followed by KVHS staff, as our mutual goals we won't go too far wrong."

"That's so right, Chris. We accepted the executives' reassurance that the managers and staff had the day to day care under control at face value—because we wanted to believe it," Nancy continued. "You know the old governance saying: noses in, fingers out? Well we were noses and fingers out! We didn't drill into information about operations as we should have, given all that was going on. Seb certainly didn't encourage it and it did turn into a bit of a tug-of-war at times. Turns out that while we were engaged in those ridiculous games, patients were suffering. We didn't realise that while our beautiful new building was going up, our organisation was falling down. And we completely forgot that our first responsibility as a Board is to our patients—with disastrous results. I know that the Board sets the tone from the top. The way we behave and the decisions we make are eventually played out in service delivery. We didn't set much of an example, did we? " Nancy sighed quietly and her shoulders slumped. Carol noted the body language and realised that Nancy was feeling the burden of the past year more than she had admitted.

Andy sat up, pushing his wavy dark hair out of his eyes. "Oh! I've remembered a really good way of thinking about this, that I heard at the Board Directors' course last year. Governance is like an egg divided in two by a jagged horizontal line. The top half is strategy and the bottom is operations. When things are going well, the Board focuses on strategy and doesn't delve too much into what's happening operationally – so their enquiry is up on the strategy peaks of the jagged line. But when things aren't looking good, or one or more of Carol's governance warning bells are ringing, we must delve deeper into asking about operations; to satisfy our need for assurance that the executive is on top of the issues and the patients and staff are being looked after. It fits with what Chris and Nancy have been saying. If you pull the top and bottom of the egg too far apart, you'll break the egg. If you force them too close together, you'll break the egg."

"That's a great way to think about governance. Particularly as the Board didn't know much at all about what was actually going on day to day during that period–and still don't. For example, why didn't the managers and staff have everything under control?" Jodie Jones, consumer representative and member of the Consumer and Community Partnerships Committee, looked puzzled as she addressed her question to Carol. "Isn't that their job?"

Andy grinned, showing very white teeth in his tanned face. Still in his twenties, he was a respected local community leader and held himself with a maturity beyond his years. "Allow me to take this excellent question, Carol. I believe this is where I put on my psychologist hat! Healthcare isn't as straightforward as it looks to the outside world. It's what's called a 'complex adaptive system.' " He paused as Carol and Nancy exchanged glances and nodded. "A complex system has many moving parts and components that create different situations and risks every day. It's organic— always shifting and changing, making it extremely difficult for staff to do anything consistently well. Add to that the subcultures within the staff and issues like clinical independence and hierarchy, and different funding streams and incentives and penalties, and unlimited demand for limited resources—"

"Stop it!" Jodie held up both hands. She owned the largest real estate business in town and knew everything about Kinsley Valley and everyone in it. But she knew nothing about healthcare. "This is all a bit confusing to the uninitiated. I don't know how anyone runs a health service with all those headaches to deal with." She picked up a piece of paper and fanned her face with it, eyes wide. "You're giving me one just talking about it!"

Carol clicked to her next slide, headed up "KVHS Is a Complex System." "Here's one I prepared earlier which may help. You're correct when you say that it's challenging to get things to go right. Healthcare is thought to be the most complex of all complex, high-risk industries. But, as health professionals, we grow up with it and we're used to it. Most of the people who work in health and human services are prepared to deal with the hard stuff because we want to make a difference and we believe in what we're doing." Carol glanced at her team. "Unfortunately, that familiarity and commitment sometimes blind us to things we should see, but don't. We can get a bit blasé about how good we are, because we're used to things going wrong and stop seeing the opportunities for improvement. But that's no excuse. We all must be accountable for our role in what happens at point of care. And to do that we need the right mindset."

Carol put down her slide remote and picked up a marker, noting eight pairs of eyes watching her every move. She quickly sketched a two-column table and wrote titles at the top of each column. "'Providing consistently high quality care is easy' mindset" went on the left, and "Providing consistently high quality care is an ongoing challenge' mindset" was on the right.[A5] She turned back to the group. "I bet you've had the experience, Jodie, of a new real estate business setting up in town run by someone who doesn't really understand how it all works?"

Jodie nodded energetically. "Happens all the time! People see the town growing and think real estate is a quick way to make money. Ha! Some of us might make it look easy"—she tossed her perfectly waved blond hair—"but it takes strategy and hard work if you want to be successful and build a sustainable business."

"As with anything!" Nancy interjected. "Everyone thinks being the mayor is all functions and openings. If only! Trying to run this town well is the hardest job I've ever done."

"And we're the same in human services. We do know how to make things work. It's making them work consistently well that's the challenge. It's tempting to slip into a mindset that it's easy to provide high quality care: if all those highly skilled and committed people are out there doing their job, what's to worry about? And good people doing their best will get you good care some of the time, of course."

Carol quickly filled in each side of the table as she spoke, showing a series of overly simplistic statements about achieving care quality on the left side and more pragmatic statements, acknowledging the challenges of the context, on the right. She finished with "our good people always come to work to do a good job" on the left side and paused.

"But we know that's not enough to achieve great care for all of the consumers all of the time in a complex environment. There's a whole lot more to it, and that's where quality governance comes in." She turned and wrote on the right side of the table "good care is created by good people, clear about their responsibilities, supported by good systems and held accountable."

"I see. Both the active and accountable aspects have been missing in action." Chris' heavy silver cufflinks tapped the table as he drummed his fingers restlessly. "I guess what you're saying, Carol, is that the KVHS Board has had the wrong mindset. We've been sitting on the left hand side of your table, over-confident and a bit clueless about what it takes to create consistently good care. You could say we were happy to be passive governors of the quality of care. We need to migrate our mindset to the right side which is a list of inconvenient truths about the challenges of creating good care and managing risks, and work with that."

"That's right Chris. But you're not alone." Carol picked up the laser pointer and shone it at the whiteboard. "I've seen more boards—and executives too for that matter—on the left side than the right, demonstrating a lack of understanding about complexity and risk. But the mindset for success lies in the right hand column. Andy was spot on. A complex system needs to be actively and strategically monitored and managed, or it can deteriorate. Just like the road system, it's not set and forget. If you leave a health service on automatic it will organise itself. Some of those emergent properties will be useful and things might even improve in some areas. However, it's equally easy for things to slip and standards to erode, no matter how hard staff are trying." She looked around at the other executives, eyebrows raised. "I wasn't here, but I'm guessing that day-to-day operations at KVHS were largely on automatic pilot while all those other things were going on!"

"And *I'm* guessing that the divisional heads and middle managers could have used some more management training and support during that time?" Andy also gazed quizzically at the executive group. "Because in my experience, hardly any human service organisation equips their people enough considering the difficulties they face.

More silence.

Kristen cleared her throat. "I admit I took my eye off day to day operations," she said softly. "I'm sorry …"

"It was all of us." Elena's face was stiff, but her voice shook a little. "We all took our eye off the ball. It's just that there were so many balls. I really thought that my staff would continue business as usual while I was juggling everything. Some did, but many allowed things to slide."

There was another uncomfortable silence, eventually broken by Jodie. "This is all well and good, but what are we going to do about it?" Her brisk tone broke the tension and everyone looked up expectantly. "I've never seen the town so unhappy with the health service. Many people are refusing to come here, and asking their GP to refer them elsewhere, even if they drive over an hour to get there. And I understand that. The few times I've been a patient here, I always feel like I never know what I'm going to get from one day to the next. Seems like it depends on who's working that day and what sort of mood they're in!"

"I agree," said Chris. "I think we've got the picture. We're not here to blame and shame, but we do need to honestly understand where we are, so we can plan where we want to go and how to get there." He consulted his agenda and looked around the table. "Anything to add, Nancy, before we move on to strategy?"

"Looking at the list," Nancy began, turning to look at the screen, "I'd be interested to hear from the executive members—excluding Carol for now—about where we are today in terms of these clinical governance warning bells. Which ones continue to ring? Elena and Jeff, you're in charge of clinical care. I'd like to hear from you."

Jeff cleared his throat. "I think that, with the new building opened, and the changes in the Board and executive composition, items one, two, and three are definitely improving."

Elena nodded. "And ten. All those issues are either resolved or have a plan in place."

"Some aspects of items four to nine are all still real problems," Jeff continued. "I'm working on clinician leadership and clinical review, but it's early days. Everyone does their own thing—or nothing—and there's no formal information exchange or framework to hang everything together. There are two pieces of good news though. Letitia Ormond-Davies has agreed to act as the Medical Unit Head for the next six months while we continue to sort it out, so that's going to be a help. No one wanted it as it's regarded as such a poisoned chalice, but Letitia sees it as an opportunity she might not otherwise get at her age. She's a baby in doctor years! I know she's had her eye on jobs in city hospitals, so this gives her a reason to stay here, which is a huge bonus." There was a murmur of assent around the table.

"And Professor Yang has promised me she'll rally the other heads of unit to broaden their Morbidity and Mortality meetings to an interdisciplinary membership, and to lead the change with the surgical M&M meetings. She'll also help resurrect the old Clinical Review Committee, so the M&M meeting lessons can be fed into it for clinical and systems improvement, and they'll report the themes from their lessons learned to the Operational Quality Committee."

"Wow." Carol looked impressed. "If all that comes to fruition, you'll deserve a KV Board Recognition award."

"My nurses already do a lot of audit and they don't get Board Recognition awards," Elena retorted sharply. The group looked at her in surprise. "Too much audit in my opinion. Takes them away from their clinical work."

"I agree that all that auditing didn't seem to help much on the medical ward," Jeff shot back.

Chris exchanged glances with Nancy and held up his hand. "I'm happy to have a robust discussion, but bickering won't help anything. That's been a helpful summary. Except for one thing you forgot to mention." He smiled for the first time as he turned to the CEO. "Fortunately, we've also addressed numbers eleven and twelve. Let's talk strategy, Carol."

Carol felt her face grow hot as she clicked to the next slide. No pressure! She took a deep breath. "A few weeks ago, we held an off-site strategy session. Some of it was about resolving specific urgent clinical and operational issues. But we also spent a significant amount of time developing a draft strategy to bring KVHS care back to what we want to be known for. We'd now like to invite you to help us take what we're calling 'Great Care' to the next level." She paused for a sip of water. "We need a strategic quality system here at KVHS to help us get to where we need to go as an organisation. What I'm about to run through with you is reflected in this table."

She clicked to her first slide, which showed a table explaining the logic and components of a strategic quality system[A3]. The group studied it in silence.

"My first question for you," Carol continued, "is, what is the KVHS strategic vision?"

"To provide high quality care for our community," chorused the group—not surprisingly, as the strategic plan vision and goals hung over the boardroom door.

"And—do we?" posed Carol.

Chris opened his mouth to answer, but Nancy interrupted. "Don't bother," she laughed. "The short answer is 'we don't know' because we don't have a clue what we mean by 'high quality care.' She already got me on that one. In the end, I had to admit defeat. We see a fair bit of information on the things that go wrong; but, as Carol has reminded me, good care is more than the absence of bad. And we don't have the clear line of sight between Board and bedside that we flattered ourselves we did. Recent events have proved that we don't have much of an idea what point-of-care staff are doing or thinking. But the good news is, she can help us with that." She nodded at Carol. "Let's go."

For the next hour, the committee fleshed out the bones of the framework the Executive Team had developed at their workshop, using the strategic quality system model. Carol ran a fast-track "defining Great Care" session to identify their purpose, and they agreed on the key people and pillars of governance characteristics required to achieve it. The implementation roadmap was briefly discussed. Finally, Carol sat down, and the group regarded their work.

"Phew!" Jodie mopped her forehead with a tissue. "That was a whirlwind hour! But great! We talk about quality governance at the Consumer and Community Partnerships Committee, but it always seems to be about committees and data. Do you agree, Andy?" Andy nodded and Jodie continued, seemingly happy to have her observations reinforced. "I never really understood how it related to the actual care we provide. It's good to finally get it. And when the other CPC members also get it, I'm planning to start some serious discussions about our place in quality governance and what we want to offer beyond what we already do. Are you coming to the CPC to do this exercise, Carol?"

"You got in before me, Jodie!" Andy reached across to the coffee pot to top up his cup. The air-conditioning had finally won the battle with the heat of the day, and he shivered a little in his light shirt. "This will really help the committee members see how all the quality and governance jigsaw pieces fit together and relate to the care consumers receive. It's so clear that we need a shared picture of what high quality care is, or how can we all work together to achieve it? That's been part of the problem, hasn't it? Everyone has been trying to do their best and achieve good things for the KVHS consumers. But we've all gone off in different directions. Let's use this model as our consumer partnership platform."

Nancy nodded enthusiastically. "Yes! This gets the whole organisation going in the same direction. We'll also use it as our guide to monitor the systems we must have in place as well to drive the point of care results we want to achieve. It's our blueprint for developing the quality of care we want to be known for."

"The trick will be to not turn it into some faddy campaign, or you'll lose the doctors forever," Jeff said quietly.

The collective shoulders of the group slumped.

"Pouring cold water on our great ideas, Jeff?" Nancy scolded him. "Let us enjoy our smarts for a few minutes, at least!"

Everyone laughed but Jeff, who continued, looking serious. "Not cold water. Just a small dose of reality. The doctors—and all the staff for that matter—are flat out treating patients, trying their best to provide Great Care in their own way. It would be easy to lose that, either with slogans that mean nothing to them, or forcing them into a bureaucratic framework." He adjusted his glasses. "There's work to be done with the docs to engage them in the four Great Care goals in a way that's useful to them. The Safe goal has been the focus here for years, so that won't faze them. But they don't all have systematic evaluations of their care effectiveness. There's too much clinical variation out there and some of it would be doing more harm than good. The Personal and Connected goals will also challenge some of them. But let's not lose all the good things that are happening in the process of fixing the not so good."

Carol nodded. "He's right. The only reason any of us is here is to make it as easy as possible for staff to provide the best care they can for the consumers that they, and we, serve. That's what this strategy is all about. But anything to do with quality can quickly turn from this to slogans and fads; and before you know it, staff associate quality with compliance and empty words, and clinical governance with the committee structure and extra work. Not very inspiring—or helpful. It's up to us to keep the focus on point of care and make sure the governance and systems 'engine room' of supports does its job of propelling the organisation towards Great Care every day."

Chris removed his glasses and stared around the table. "We'll expect you to take care of that." Then he motioned to Nancy. "Anything else, Nancy, before we wrap this up?"

"Apart from the changes we're going to make to care, which are exciting, I'd really like this model to help this committee and the Board get better information on what's really happening at point of care. How will that work?"

"Great question, Nancy." Carol gestured to the whiteboard. "Now we know what we're trying to achieve, we'll ask better questions about what we need to know. We've committed to Great Care for every KVHS consumer: Personal, Effective, Connected, and Safe. What information will tell us if we're achieving each goal, from both subjective and objective perspectives? How will we know if the governance 'engine room' is performing well enough to support managers and staff to create Great Care? How can we report data so they help this committee monitor progress and recommend decisions to the Board that will align the whole organisation around the goals? What committees do we need to drive progress towards achieving the GC goals every day? How can we use our governance systems to better respond to data that show we're not meeting the GC goals? We'll work on these questions between now and the next Board Quality and Clinical Governance Committee."

"Thanks, Carol," Chris said. "I'd like us to start hearing regular consumer stories as well." He paused to acknowledge Andy and Jodie's enthusiastic nodding. "The good and the not so good. It's going to be a challenge to develop a stronger customer focus without hearing first-hand from the customers."

"You know, there's a wealth of knowledge on the committee about customer focus and service." Jodie sat up, looking energised. "We should tap into that more as well. We haven't had much opportunity to contribute our expertise to some of these problems—and I think we should."

"It's true, we've been kept at arm's length," responded Nancy. "Of course, we can't insist that Carol and her team do things our way. We don't run the health service operationally. But I think we should schedule more time for planning and problem solving at Board meetings, particularly when things aren't going well. We may not manage the health service, but we govern it, and it's our job to be across the issues and make sure that our governance systems are more than decoration and that our patients are getting the best care we can provide as a result. We can't expect the executives to have all the answers—no one does!" Nancy shrugged her shoulders. "And we need to hear from staff as well. Could we organise regular presentations from department heads? I'd like the Board Quality Committee to hear their perspectives on care quality as well, not to mention their ideas for solving some of the problems we're grappling with."

Chris looked at Carol, who nodded. "Yes, we'll organise that, and structure the presentations using the four Great Care goals so we build a picture of where our strengths and weaknesses are in each. It will also help the divisional and department heads to think about their care that way."

"One more thing, before we finish." Chris reached into his briefcase and pulled out the latest edition of the *Kinsley Valley Leader*. The front page featured an old photo of the Minister for Health opening the new hospital building. ROCK BOTTOM shouted the headline, followed by a recap of the performance results they'd just discussed. "This is the second time we've made the front page in two weeks. We're used to being in the paper, of course. A health service is good fodder for local media. But it's feeling more … I don't know … systematic lately. Where are they getting their information?"

Carol swallowed. "Well, Chris, you know I believe in transparency, so I shared the results with the senior managers' and clinical leaders' groups," she said, feeling a little rattled, her words not coming as easily as usual. "There was so much talk and so many rumours, I told them the real story as soon as I could. The key points are now up on the Department of Health's website, anyway."

"But the depth of information indicates that someone has briefed them in detail," said Nancy. "Did you hand out any data?"

"No, I just presented the situation to set the scene for the changes we're going to make." Carol turned to her team. "Anyone heard of any staff being approached by the *KV Leader*?"

Everyone shook their heads.

"I just get the feeling that we're making the headlines more often since you've started as CEO," said Chris, stroking his chin. "And it catches on through social media and spreads like a bushfire. When I go downtown these days, people either avoid me or can't wait to corner me to air their latest grievance." The vigorous nods around the table showed he was not alone. "I don't know what we should be more afraid of with all this bad publicity: no patients coming in, or the medical staff walking out."

Carol suppressed a shiver as ranks of white-coated doctors flashed through her mind.

"I wonder if it's because there's a new editor," Jodie said. "He started his job just before you did, Carol. Perhaps he's trying to stamp his authority on the paper by going in hard with bad news? Wherever it's coming from, I do know that the local journalists are loving it. Whenever I bump into them they act like the cat that got the cream, particularly as they know I'm on a couple of KVHS committees. I'll keep my eyes and ears open to see what I can find out."

"Thanks, Jodie. We'll get to the bottom of it—no pun intended." Despite her positive words, Carol could feel the familiar lead in the pit of her stomach. She took a big gulp of coffee and noticed that her hands were shaking slightly.

"We expect you to." Chris looked at his watch. "Time's nearly up. Where to from here?"

"Carol will run the exercise with the Board next week," said Nancy. "So those of you who've been through it today will know all the answers!"

"Does the whole Board need to do it?" Andy looked puzzled. "Isn't this committee responsible for care quality?"

"Responsible for doing the detailed monitoring and review and considering recommendations from our reporting committees on behalf of the full Board, yes," answered Nancy, looking brighter as she slipped into action mode. "And reporting to the Board on key issues and recommending high-level action. But our clinical governance accountability requires the whole Board to be across the quality of care provided to KVHS patients, in the same way we are accountable for sound financial management and viability. We have to look at the processes and the outcomes. Are we doing the right things? And are we getting the results we're aiming for?" She paused for effect and glanced around the table before continuing.

"We won't be able to enact that accountability until we share a common understanding of where we're trying to go as an organisation and how to get there. We'll integrate the definition of high quality care into the new strategic plan objectives and sketch out the strategy for achieving it at the Board and Executive planning day in a couple of weeks. Then we drive it as part of the strategic plan. We'll also agree our messages to staff at that meeting. It's about time we started presenting a united front, giving consistent information about our expectations and following up with consistent action. From now on Personal, Effective, Connected and Safe are the KVHS priorities from board to bedside."

"I forgot all about the strategic planning day!" Andy slapped his forehead. "I guess it's good timing, though, isn't it? Everything is lining up. The Consumer and Community Partnerships Committee members are looking forward to replacing those meaningless words in the strategic plan about high quality care with something concrete we can actually contribute to. I guess the work we'll do with you, Carol, will feed into the strategic plan as well and the Great Care framework?"

"That's how it's supposed to work," Carol said, "and we'll do our best to bring it all together so strategic and operational plans are aligned around KVHS consumers receiving Great Care. We can't wait for the documents, though, so we've already started. We've got another executive planning day scheduled to review our progress and plan the next stage of implementation." Carol thought she caught a brief eye roll from Elena, but she couldn't be sure. "In the meantime, we'll be working to reorganise our annual training plan, committee structure and quality data reporting into the four Great Care goals. That's the 'governance engine room' work, including making our systems into more active levers to adjust in response to results. We'll also start a Great Care pilot in a couple of services to get the goals into everyday practice. I'll report on progress at the next meeting. Oh, and we have to appoint a new Quality Systems ED, of course!"

"Is that all?" enquired Nancy with a grin. "How do you spend your spare time?"

Carol laughed and grimaced simultaneously. "That would be running the health service."

"We'd better let you get to it then! I declare the meeting closed. Good luck, team!" Chris stood up, and he and Nancy walked out together, already in earnest conversation by the time they reached the door.

Carol watched them go with a heavy heart, her optimism deserting her. So much to do and so little time. Good luck, indeed. They'd need it.

THE POINT OF CARE

CHAPTER SEVEN

* *

"Pari is well respected across the organisation." Carol looked around the table, and Kristen nodded. Carol, Jeff, Elena, and Kristen had concluded the interviews for William's job and were discussing the candidates.

Pari Kadar had moved to Kinsley Valley three years ago to take up the role as Head of the large KVHS Occupational Therapy service. She'd also chaired the Allied Health Quality and Risk Committee for two years. When William resigned, Carol had encouraged her to apply for the restructured role.

"Oh, I'd love to," Pari had responded. "But I'm not sure if I'm what you need."

Carol had assured her that they would find that out in the application and interview process. Not surprisingly, Pari shone as the preferred candidate. She held a Master of Organisational Development, including a significant quality, risk, and change management component. Combined with her demonstrated leadership and management skills as head of an OT department that provided aged care, mental health, community, and inpatient services, she had the solid theoretical and practical understanding Carol was looking for. Not everyone was convinced, however.

Jeff and Elena exchanged glances.

"It should be a nurse," Elena declared. "It was hard enough getting the nurses to listen to William, and he was a nurse. They'll never take any notice of an OT! I think Susie Brennan is the best choice. She's also got a master's and has been the surgical quality manager for years. They never have any problems with accreditation, and her risk management system there is the best at KVHS."

"Or maybe we don't appoint any of the candidates and try for a doctor?" Jeff suggested.

Kristen waded in. "I see what you're saying, Elena. I really like Susie. She is super-efficient and organised and never fails us come accreditation time. She's a great implementer as well. There's no doubt that compliance and risk management are her thing, not to mention her excellent 'Lean Method' and human factors skills. But this role is also strategic, remember—not only for the strategic plan, but for the strategic quality system. I don't think Susie is any more cut out for that than William was. Pari is a big thinker and really knows how to bring people along with her. And—it's an executive role. I'm not sure Susie is ready for that responsibility."

"There's also the small problem of no doctors having applied," added Carol. "There's no doubt that we want to develop our medical leaders. But in our current situation, I need someone who can hit the ground running and get a whole-of-organisation approach developed, pronto. Unless you can convince me otherwise, I don't think we have any medicos who fit that bill right now."

She put down her pen and leaned forward. "But here's an idea. How do you think Pari and Susie would work together? I need someone to focus on a whole-of-organisation approach to Great Care for the next few months and not be too preoccupied with routine improvement, monitoring, reporting, and compliance issues. Would Susie be prepared to take on a director role as Pari's deputy to take care of those components— and also help with Great Care implementation? I heard today that one of William's staff is leaving to join him at the private hospital, so we have an opportunity to do a minor restructure and redesign with the quality team to make it work."

"I'm not sure how she'd go reporting to an OT." Elena's thin lips belied her scepticism. "And we'd have to advertise that new deputy role and go through another recruitment round, which would slow down progress. I don't know."

There was silence while everyone calculated how long another recruitment process would take. Then Kristen looked up, eyes wide with a sudden thought. "How about we ask Susie if she'd like to act in the role for six months? That would give her a chance to see if she likes it and how well she and Pari work together, and then when we decide to advertise it, she can throw her hat in the ring if she wants to."

"Great idea, Kristen." Jeff looked relieved as he shut his computer. "We've got so much to do and so little time to do it if we're going to shift our results by the next departmental performance meeting. I say let's go with that."

"Okay?" Carol looked expectantly at Elena. "If you have no other objections, Elena, let's appoint Pari to the ED role and ask Susie if she'd like to step into an acting role as Pari's deputy."

Elena twirled a strand of hair around her finger for a minute. "All right. But if Pari doesn't work out for some reason, and Susie is keen, she gets her chance."

Carol nodded. "Agreed. Thanks, everyone. I'll call Pari first, then Susie."

And so, it had come to pass. Now Pari sat across the desk from Jeff and pushed her long, dark hair behind her shoulders. She was tall enough that her brown eyes met Jeff's blue ones at almost the same level. Her slim hands worked restlessly in her lap as she wondered where to begin. Finally, she launched in. "I hate to tell you this, but after a week of trying to source the 'lessons learned' notes from the new interdisciplinary surgical Morbidity and Mortality meetings, I've concluded that … there aren't any."

"No notes?"

"No *meetings*. And not just interdisciplinary meetings. No surgical M&M meetings at all."

"What?" The normally laid-back Jeff sat up abruptly, sending a pile of papers flying off his desk. "That can't be right, Pari. You probably don't know who to ask because you're new. Let me check." He pulled out his phone and made a call.

Not really new, she mentally corrected him. *Just new in this role*. Pari had been excited to start her new job as Executive Director of Strategy, Quality, and Governance Systems, and she'd been flat-out busy since day one with a squillion things on her to-do list. Carol was providing some initial mentoring and had added to Pari's load by insisting she also complete an online training course on strategic quality systems.

"I did it five years ago when it first became available," Carol had said enthusiastically, bringing the "Introduction to *The Quality System Kit* online course" video up on her computer screen to show Pari. "Although I'd been working in a quality role for a few years by then, before I moved into the COO role, I still learned heaps and found it really useful. It helps get your head around the pieces of a strategic quality system and how they fit together to create Great Care. Not to mention lots of useful tips for leading a strategic quality system such as socialising Great Care, influencing, public speaking, and creating change and improvement in complex organisations like ours. Enjoy!"

If she was being honest, Pari wasn't as enthusiastic as she'd tried to look as she promised Carol she'd start on it that week. But having done two of the modules, she had to admit she now better understood what she was charged with getting done.

"Competence breeds confidence" her university leadership lecturer had always said, and he was right. The importance of socialising Great Care had particularly resonated. Pari knew only too well that if you couldn't get a change into staff tearoom conversations, it may never become business as usual. But she certainly didn't feel anywhere near competent enough in the role yet to be confident. In fact, Susie, who had started in her new deputy job a couple of weeks later, appeared much more on top of the situation than Pari felt. She was worried about creating a disaster, and every time she thought about the next Board Quality and Clinical Governance Committee meeting, her stomach lurched. Being on the Executive Team was also a step up, and she was learning those ropes as well. For the first time in her career, she was out of her depth—but trying hard not to show it.

Jeff finished his second call and put down the phone. He stroked his beard. "I think you might be right," he said, looking at her, head on one side. "I spoke to two people who should have those notes if they exist, and neither of them has ever seen any."

"I might be new to this role, but I'm not new to the health service," Pari stated matter-of-factly, resisting the urge to say, "I told you so." "I've also asked everyone I can think of. If these meetings are happening, they're being held in a secret underground vault. No one wants to admit it, but it looks to me like there's been no surgical M&M meetings since accreditation."

"Since *accreditation*!" Jeff sat back and took off his glasses. "I can't believe it. Looks like I fell for Prof Yang's 'trust me, I'll take care of it' routine."

"Routine?" asked Pari, startled. "She's done this before?"

Jeff smiled grimly. "I haven't been here long enough to know. I'm only guessing, but I'd be surprised if I'm wrong. I've seen it so many times in other places. It's one of the oldest tricks in the senior doctors' book. If they really don't like a proposed change, they stall, figuring that healthcare administrators come and go. If they can slow down the change enough, the administrator might leave before anything happens. If all behaviour is rewarded, we know that this is probably a successful strategy often enough that it's worth a try." He looked at his watch. "Prof should be finished with her morning OR session about now, so there's no time like the present. Don't worry—it's all part of the fun of being a healthcare executive. Let's reschedule our meeting, and I'll go and have a conversation."

Pari followed him out and watched him stride determinedly down the hallway. As there hadn't been any M&M lessons to discuss with Jeff, she had an hour to spare until her next meeting. *Just enough time to grab an early lunch and whizz through module three*, she thought. This video course module was about change and influence, and she'd been looking forward to it, even though she'd studied it at uni, and it had been a part of every role she'd had in the past few years. She was struggling to get traction with the medical ward staff, however, who so far had done precisely none of the things she'd asked them to do, so she was looking forward to some refresher tips. She knew they weren't in her "circle of control," so she'd been working hard to influence them, with little success. She winced as she remembered the meeting she'd had with them that morning.

"I think this is the ideal time to get a Great Care pilot going here in the medical ward," she'd started brightly as they sat down for their meeting.

"This is not an ideal time for anything." Phil Blake, the Medical Ward Nurse Unit Manager, had crossed his arms defiantly. "We can't take any more change here. Unless you're going to give us more staff, of course. Come back with two warm bodies ready to do a shift and we'll talk."

"What's that about warm bodies? Have you found some?" Catriona, the Medical Unit Business Manager, rushed into the room and collapsed in a chair, followed by Meilin, the ward Clinical Nurse Specialist, and Deb, the Occupational Therapist. "I can't believe it's only 0900 and I've already put out three fires! Figuratively, of course."

Catriona smiled at Phil, but his expression didn't change. She picked up the conversation. "Pari, you've come to the wrong place. We're trying to run a ward and fix a pile of problems. We haven't got time to do our real work, let alone more paperwork for quality. Besides, we do quality on Tuesday. Isn't today Thursday?"

Pari ignored the doing-quality-one-day-per-week thunderbolt and smiled through gritted teeth. "But that's exactly why I'm here. You need to fix some problems. We need to pilot Great Care. We want to help you fix your problems in the process and improve things for patients." As soon as the words left her lips, Pari knew she had played it the wrong way.

"And what about us?" Phil had said coldly. "Just once, I'd like someone from the executive office to come down here with a project to improve things for us, rather than for the good of the patients and the good of KVHS."

Pari, who was now part of that executive office, suppressed the urge to fight back. She couldn't quite keep the irritation out of her tone, however. "Phil, I know that Carol has met with you once a week since she started and that you've had more resources allocated over the past month."

"Yes, but it's always about the patients, never us," retorted Meilin. "Isn't that right, Deb?"

Deb froze with fear, her eyes darting from Meilin to Pari, who had been her boss only a few short weeks ago.

Pari felt sorry for Deb and shot her a look that said, "Don't answer that."

Meilin continued. "Do they think we're robots that take on more and more? After everything we've been through since the review?"

Pari took a breath and centred herself. Her yoga teacher would be proud. "I know you've been through a lot over the past year. And you've done so much work to improve things. But there are still some issues, as you say, for staff and for patients. It's not either/or. I want to help."

But Phil wasn't budging. "When we get 'help' from executives, it usually ends up in more work that helps them, not us. We're not interested. Now, we've got a ward to run, and not enough people to do it."

With that, he stood up and walked out with Deb and Meilin. Catriona stayed behind. "Don't take it personally," she said to Pari. "They've had a hard time of it. Most of the problems came from poor medical leadership and practice over many years and the staff felt powerless. The Medical Unit Head left, but everyone left behind lives with the consequences. Phil obviously allowed the poor medical care to go unchallenged and he's been called to account for that. It's really got him down. There has been quite a big investment in staff development here since the review, but recovery will be slow. It's all they can do to manage the glaring problems they've been stuck with and keep the ward running. I'd say that, overall, this group doesn't feel loved enough to be able to give you much."

Pari had pondered Catriona's words as she trudged back to her office, her brain a whirl of anger and disappointment. Carol had made it clear that she expected Pari to engage the medical ward in the organisation's push for Great Care, knowing there were still many patients experiencing much less than Great Care. The organisation's results were never going to improve significantly if they didn't get the medical ward moving in a more positive direction; they were dragging the whole organisation down. "Not enough love"! She wasn't exactly feeling the love herself right now.

She sensed her enthusiasm flowing out the soles of her shoes and wondered, not for the first time, if she'd done the right thing in taking this job. Even the non-clinical staff were wary of her now that she was in a senior quality role. Last week, three cleaners had hidden in a cupboard to get away from her. Was she so much more terrifying— or annoying—as the Executive Director of Strategy, Quality, and Governance Systems than she had been as Head of OT? And now she'd confirmed that all surgical Morbidity and Mortality meetings had ceased, rather than the promised expansion to include an interdisciplinary team approach and to share the lessons learned. She supposed that Professor Yang wasn't going to be too thrilled about Pari revealing this to Jeff.

Normally positive and energetic, Pari had flagged as she sat at her desk and read a long list of new emails from around the health service, each asking her to take on another task. *Maybe I'll just give the job six months. I can always go back to OT.*

Now unexpectedly freed from her meeting with Jeff, Pari hurried into the cafeteria looking for a quick sandwich to take back to her desk. *Love a challenge, love a challenge, love a challenge* she recited to herself as she waited for her fresh juice.

"Talking to yourself? Welcome to the KVHS Executive!" said an amused voice behind her. Pari turned, embarrassed.

"Caught you!" laughed Kristen. "I think that qualifies you as a fully-fledged member of the team! Don't worry, we all do it." She stopped and examined Pari closely. "You don't look quite yourself."

Pari blushed. "Oh, it's nothing. Had a rough morning, that's all."

"Want to talk about it?" asked Kristen as she paid for her lunch.

"Well, I *should* go and watch a training video …"

"Nonsense," countered Kristen, steering Pari to a table. "I'm all for training, but debriefing comes first. So, come and sit over here in this conveniently quiet corner— and spill."

Pari sat down opposite Kristen and unwrapped her sandwich. "I don't want to sound like a whinger."

Kristen nodded. "I know. But you're not whingeing. You look sad and stressed, and I don't often see you look like that. In fact, I don't think I've ever seen you look anything other than positive or determined. I'm asking you why."

"It's just that … well, I'm used to being competent. And now I'm not." Pari looked surprised at her own statement. "I didn't mean to say that—it just came out! But … that's how I feel."

"Go on," encouraged Kristen, drizzling dressing on her salad.

"I'm used to being pretty good at what I do and having other people listen to me. But since I took this job, that's changed." She quickly filled Kristen in on the past few weeks, finishing with that morning's meeting with the medical ward.

Kristen frowned. "Yes, even though it was the Medical Services Head that caused ninety per cent of the problems, because he was allowed to run the medical service like it was his own personal fiefdom—and a 1950s fiefdom at that—things don't suddenly resolve because he's gone. There are many pieces to pick up. We've done a lot of support work with the staff, quite apart from the clinical improvement work that Elena led to improve patient safety. Even Anne chipped in to help modernise some of the medical processes."

Pari was momentarily distracted. "Led by Elena? I thought you instigated most of the changes?"

Kristen smiled. "As acting CEO, of course I had oversight and accountability. But Elena led most of the on-the-ground response. Don't be too hard on Elena. Underneath that 'matron' exterior beats a heart …"

Pari waited for the rest of the sentence that never came. "Of gold?" she eventually finished, laughing.

"Hmmm—not sure. But there's definitely a heart there. Elena really does care about the patients, you know. But she sure has a funny way of showing it sometimes. Now, back to you. What did you say to the medical ward about why you wanted to run a pilot there?"

"Um, I think I said something about 'needing to pilot Great Care and improve things for patients.' Didn't go down too well."

"About as well as my approach to the new OR booking system went with Prof Yang, I guess?" Kristen shook her head in frustration. "Two things I've learned the hard way about change: first, no one cares how much you know until they know how much you care. People need to feel that some of your need for change aligns with what they want, not with what you want. I didn't do that with Prof Yang, and now she's leading a medical resistance movement!" She paused for a drink before continuing. "Boy, have I learned *that* lesson. There's not enough love to go around in health services, I've decided. Maybe it's the science base. Maybe it's the apprenticeship system. Maybe it's that there's never enough resources to cover the relentless demand. I don't know. But I do know that we need to at least try to make changes benefit both patients *and* staff."

"That's the second time today someone has mentioned love—or lack of it—in this organisation."

Kristen sighed. "Yes, I do think it's a real issue. Not only here—right across healthcare. And probably beyond to all human services. I certainly saw it in my time running the People and Culture Service. But it seems to be too 'soft' for the hard-headed healthcare types to give much credence, in my experience, anyway. Or maybe they don't get how important it is for people to feel appreciated and involved, no matter how high performing they are. I'm really hoping that Carol will be different. Fortunately, the early signs are encouraging."

"Second?" asked Pari, sipping her juice.

"Start Where They Are, not where you are. It was a favourite saying of Peter, a previous KVHS CEO, and he used it well. When we had a problem getting people on board with something new, he'd ask us: Do you really understand how those staff feel about their current situation before you stomp in with your plans to improve it? Are you starting with how they really get their work done—and not how you'd like it to be done? Have you built a common understanding of the change that has meaning for them? If they're not convinced there's merit in the change, you're going to be eternally pushing that project uphill. In the end, you may not get the outcome you want."

"You're right. I should know all this stuff. I've just forgotten it in the middle of everything else that's going on."

"Easy to do." Kristen chewed thoughtfully for a few seconds. "I came back to KVHS when Peter was CEO, not long before he retired and Seb took the job. He was genuinely interested in the staff and they knew it. He understood that people really like meaningful connection and contribution in their work, and he wanted everyone who worked at KVHS to experience that, no matter what job they had. He also expected them to be accountable—and he supported them so they could be. Peter wasn't clinical, but we didn't have too many care problems then. People were proud to say they worked at KVHS. We all went into shock when Seb started."

"What happened?"

"Nothing! That was the problem. Seb implemented a more traditional command and control hierarchy. A lot of staff who had shone in their roles stopped doing the things that made them shine. No one wanted to attract attention, because it never ended well. I know! I had a few close encounters with Seb when trying to promote innovation." The memory showed itself in her pursed lips. She continued, brows furrowed. "Seb liked people to follow the rules and not bother him. That killed much of the enthusiasm and goodwill Peter had fostered. In six months, KVHS was a different place. I guess Peter loved his staff and his health service. When Seb started, that love disappeared and everyone could feel it. He got the budget back in the black, of course. And the new inpatient building was completed on time and budget. Both very important things! What we needed was a mix of both of them. Or for Seb to delegate the human side of his job to someone else to look after it for him."

Kristen leaned in. "Speaking of love, how are you feeling? Are you getting enough support?"

To Pari's surprise, she suddenly felt a lump at the back of her throat and swallowed hard. "Don't be nice to me, Kristen. I might cry. I don't know why I'm like this. I usually just get on with it." She took a long drink of her juice while she regained her composure. "I don't want to complain. Carol has been great. She's got so much faith in me, and when we meet, she teaches me so much. And she's paid for an online course and says she'll organise me a coach. But she's so busy. I can't expect to land on her doorstep every time I have a problem."

"No, you can't," Kristen agreed. "She is too busy, and she'd expect you to solve many of your own problems anyway. But when the going gets tough, she'd want you to talk to her. And so do I, for that matter. If I were you, I'd sort that out at your next one-on-one meeting with Carol. She would hate to think you felt like this and didn't tell her. She won't think any less of you. I'm sure she's felt like this many times herself, in her career, and probably once a day since she started this job. I sure do!" Kristen emphasised the point by stabbing her fork in the air as she spoke.

"Health professionals are used to being experts in their field," she went on, "and sometimes find it hard to cope when they take on a new job and start all over again. Particularly in a quality role where, from what I've observed, the reality is that you get most of your work done by influencing. Apart from your own team, you can't direct anyone to do anything and don't have much control. And yet you're dependent on people to do the things you need them to do, to achieve what you need to get done. It's not an easy gig. Don't expect to win everyone over at once. I always try to find the 'first third' first and work from there. I figure that about a third of all people are willing to give something a go, so I find them and start there!"

Pari's spirits lifted. She wasn't incompetent! She had a lot to learn in a challenging role. "That's so true! Thanks, Kristen. You've made me feel better. And you're right, I'm judging my success by whether everyone is on board with my agenda, instead of starting with the people who are interested in doing things differently. Time for a re-set!"

Kristen shook her head as she wiped her mouth with a napkin. "No need for thanks. I'm relieved to have someone on the Exec Team to take care of some of these long-standing issues, so if I can help, that's good for me as well as you. And while you're discussing your role with Carol, get your accountability framework well and truly agreed on."

"Sorry, I'm not up with executive speak. What framework?"

"Ha! Slip of the jargon tongue. Accountability frameworks were something Seb introduced, believe it or not. He heard about them at a CEO conference and it took his fancy. It means that you sort out with your boss exactly what your definition of success is for your role—sort of a big-picture look at how to judge if you're doing what you should be doing and getting the desired results. This includes your deliverables and what you will be judged on in, say, a year's time. You do this before you comb through the details of your position description, making sure you and the boss have a shared understanding of what it means.

Then you line this up with all the stuff that comes across your desk and prioritise it, so you're clear about what comes first and what's important, not just urgent." She finished the last of her drink in a long gulp.

"So when someone dumps 'policies and procedures' on your desk, you can calmly point out precisely which part of policies and procedures you're responsible for, rather than taking it all on. It helps you work out exactly which aspects of your job you can control and which you must influence and work with others to achieve. Finally, you sort out the resources you have, which aspects need strict compliance and which bits you can get done using your skills, experience, and judgment. This part is important because this is where you get to use your creativity and experience to do your job better, which makes for a more satisfying role, and a happier you!"

"Why haven't I heard about this before?" Pari's frowned as she finished her juice.

"You will. Although the concept is good, we had implementation issues. Seb seemed to see it as a way to keep his Executive Team in line and a tight rein on the budget. I don't think he was really interested in how satisfied with our roles we were. We liked it, though, because it gave us more role clarity and encouraged us to try new approaches to old problems. Even Anne and Elena saw the value of it once they got the hang of it. It seems that clinicians enjoy using their judgment to solve tricky problems, even when they're in management roles! It all fell over when the problems were uncovered in the medical unit, of course, which was a shame because we probably needed it more in that situation than ever! We've raised it with Carol and said we'd like to give it another shot. I think it will fit well with her focus on complexity, as complex organisations don't always work according to the rules. If we have time, we'll discuss it at the next exec planning workshop."

"Of course," Pari said, her voice regaining its usual confidence as the conversation moved into familiar territory. "Clinicians juggle policies and standards and guidelines with their own judgment every day because every patient is different, and clinical situations can change in a big hurry. Sometimes the rules don't apply. So you judge when to stick to the rules and when to deviate from them for the good of the patient." She paused to brush some crumbs off her shirt. "I see how that would help me. I'm swamped by requests and demands from all over the health service. To be honest, right now I feel like the KVHS spare pair of hands, rather than an executive!"

"It seems to be a problem with quality roles, doesn't it? From a People and Culture perspective, I'd say that's because there's no agreed role definition. We know what finance managers do. But quality manager jobs seem to be elastic and a bit all over the place." Kristen took a bite of her salad as Pari considered this point.

"Maybe that's because we're not clear on what the quality manager should achieve," Pari said. "And what the quality system should look like. And what it exists for beyond accreditation. And what we should measure. And what good looks like. And—"

"Got it!" laughed Kristen. "You're right. The more ambiguity about what something should achieve, the harder it is to decide how to get it done, and what's in and what's out. At least Carol understands this and is trying to sort it out." She scraped up the last of her salad dressing with a piece of pita bread. "You know, I think you could be great in this role. But it seems to me that you haven't been quite yourself the past few weeks. I've heard a few grumbles about you around the traps, and that's unusual."

Pari blushed at Kristen's directness. "Oh, I hate to hear that, Kristen. Working with people has always been my strong point! But … well, to be honest, I'm not surprised. I've turned into a bit of a quality dragon. I don't know why. Perhaps it's the pressure. There's so much to do and no time to do it."

"Anyone's first few months as an executive can be a bit weird. I was a bit weird when I started this job." Kristen smiled at the memory. "People see you differently; your words carry more weight, and there's more general authority associated with what you say. There's more pressure and new expectations for you to act like an executive. It's particularly difficult when you've been promoted within the same organisation. Not everyone is going to be happy for your success."

"Oh!" Pari stopped short as Kristen's words sunk in. "Ha. I think I just got it. I have been trying to 'act' like an executive, haven't I? And the 'ED of Strategy, Quality, and Governance Systems' at that. So—surprise!—people aren't responding to me like they used to." She leaned her elbows on the table and put her head in her hands. "No wonder people are running away from me in corridors. I've been using horrible quality jargon to try to impress on people that I know what I'm talking about. The other day I described a quality plan as 'a document that describes the standards, practices, resources, and processes pertinent to improving a specific product, service, or project.' The staff in the workshop looked at me as if I'd lost my mind. And I think I might have!" She looked up as Kristen chuckled. "Honestly, Kristen, I feel like I should have been able to figure this out by myself."

"Yes, you probably should! You know as well as I do, Pari, that the only person impressed by jargon is the one using it. But what are mentors and coaches for if not to help us see what's right in front of us?" Kristen replaced the lid on her salad container, then raised her eyes to meet Pari's.

"Here's some advice for you, to take or leave. Don't worry about 'acting'. Just work on being the best you that you can be. That will create more personal power than any job title or position description could ever give you. Grow your skills, do a great job and take on the added responsibility, but don't lose what makes you, *you* in the process. And don't lose what makes care, *care*. Carol's right: if all this improvement work doesn't improve what happens at point of care, what's the point?"

She started to gather her lunch things, then stopped. "Peter taught me that managers and staff aren't too interested in the committee structure or the reporting framework or the audit schedule. They may need to work with these systems, but that's not why they get out of bed every morning. Yet that's so often what we focus on as senior managers—and then we get disappointed because staff don't engage with us. In fact, they head for the hills! What they want is for us to provide systems that help them go home every day feeling that they've done the best they could for the people they've looked after. Make that the ultimate aim of your work and watch things improve. And something I've forgotten over the past year, but won't let myself forget again, is the importance of bringing something positive to every situation. Healthcare is hard enough without the relentless negativity so many staff project. A little positivity makes a big difference to the people around you. You need to exercise influence in your role. Influence requires respect and respect requires competence. But a little joy won't go astray either. KVHS needs it!" She glanced at her phone as it vibrated a meeting reminder. "Oops, look at the time. Gotta go."

Pari patted Kristen's arm. "Thank you, Kristen. You don't know how helpful this has been. I really appreciate it. I'm going to sort out my attitude and be a bit smarter about how I approach it all."

"No worries." Kristen stood up. "I'd like to say 'anytime.' But the truth is that sometimes I'll be able to help and sometimes I'll be up to my eyeballs in operational quicksand and won't be available. But when I can, I will. Don't ever be afraid to ask if you get stuck." She gave Pari a kind look as she threw her bag over her shoulder. "This team needs to start supporting each other a lot more than we have before. It's the only way we'll get through all this change and come out the other side relatively sane. By the way"—she nodded over Pari's shoulder—"if you want to work on your personal power muscles, there's a perfect opportunity sitting on the other side of the caf."

Pari turned and spotted Phil from the medical ward eating his lunch. He was alone. Pari had never had a one-on-one with him as there had always been other staff around. She felt a wave of annoyance as she remembered their conversation that morning.

"I don't think I can."

"I haven't spent thirty minutes of my life coaching you for you to say, 'I can't,'" Kristen admonished her. "You can and you must. We can talk about the theory of swimming all day, but if you want to be a champion, at some point you've got to get in the water. And there's a pool on the other side of the caf. Good luck!" With a thumbs-up, she was gone.

Pari sat for a minute, mulling over their conversation. Everything in her wanted to retreat to the safety of her office. But she took a deep breath and replayed Kristen's words in her head. *I do want to be great in this job and that means tackling the hard stuff. Positively!* She stood up, squared her shoulders, and strode across to Phil.

CHAPTER EIGHT

"Hi, Phil. Do you mind if I sit down for a minute?"

Phil looked up. If he was pleased to see Pari, he managed to hide it brilliantly. "Depends why," he responded. "If it's to whack me about the head with that pilot idea of yours again, well …"

"No, it isn't. I—I wanted to say sorry for bothering you this morning when I know things are very hard for you and your staff right now."

Phil's eyes widened, then narrowed. "Really? What's the catch?"

"No catch," Pari responded evenly. "I see now that in our meetings I was making it all about me and what I need to do, and not thinking about you and the team."

Then an unexpected thing happened. Phil smiled. Pari realised she hadn't seen him smile once since she met him. His face immediately dropped ten years of age and ten tons of attitude.

Encouraged, she continued. "I also wanted to ask you … apart from wanting more staff, what are the other things your staff would like to change if they could? Do you know their top three 'magic wand' wishes?"

Phil thought for a minute. "I was going to say, 'that's easy, here they are,' but then I realised that they're my three wishes. I'm not sure they'd be the same for the team. Why do you want to know?"

"Well," Pari began, a little uncertainly, "I'd like to help you find out. And then help grant one of those wishes, if I can."

"Now I know there must be a catch. Why on earth would you do that?" Phil frowned as he took a swig from his water bottle.

"I was a department manager for three years and a clinical team member for many years before that. I know that people can't concentrate properly on patient care if they hate too many things about their daily grind or if they feel unappreciated. The best thing I ever did for staff morale and engagement in my service was support my team to solve problems that were preventing them from providing the sort of care they really wanted to. I think we could both achieve something we want if we help your staff achieve something they want."

Phil checked his phone. "I've got five minutes before I'm due back on the ward. What did you have in mind?"

"Well, I haven't really thought it through," Pari began. (*Actually, I haven't thought about it at all, but here goes anyway.*) "But I realise I've broken the number one rule in the way I engaged with you and your team, which is Start Where They Are. I was starting where I was. I'd like to meet with your staff and have a conversation about what they think is stopping them from providing the kind of care they'd like to." She stopped for his reaction, but his face was blank. She forged on, feeling much less assured than she sounded. "It wouldn't take long. I have a brief exercise we could do to come up with the top three issues. Then we could look at which one best aligns with Great Care, and work on solving it together. I won't pretend I don't want to get something out of it, too. But we'll focus on the staff and their needs first."

"Fine," started Phil slowly, sounding less than not convinced, "but only if you come at afternoon handover on our 'quality' day. That's…"

"Tuesday," Pari finished. "Yes, I was listening this morning." Pari suppressed the urge to lecture Phil on the notion that quality was something ' done' once a week. She understood; it had been hard enough to stop her own staff using that language. It gave her a lot of insight into where they were quality-wise, however. If staff thought of quality predominantly as control—audits and compliance with standards and reporting, rather than as creation—defining and implementing the level of care they want to provide, she knew they would see it as a set of extra tasks. She also knew she could change that if she worked with them. "I'll be there. Thanks very much, Phil. I look forward to it."

"I don't know if I can say the same for us," Phil retorted as he got up to leave, his face regaining its familiar frown. "But we'll give it a go. See you then."

What a day—and a whole afternoon to go! But as she left the caf, Pari realised she was okay. Better than okay. She was grateful to Kristen for helping her see that she'd spent the first few weeks of her new job trying to be something she wasn't. She'd been completely preoccupied with meeting external expectations and progressing her agenda, and in the process had lost her empathy and ignored her own experience, intuition, and common sense. She knew she could be good at this job, but that it would take time to learn the ropes. She was going to make mistakes along the way, but to get the job done she would swallow her pride, admit the things she didn't know and not be afraid to ask for help. And she was going to be supportive, not demanding. *Time for the real Pari to make a comeback*, she decided as she headed to her next meeting.

*****

"Four months and counting." The stress showed on Kristen's face as she completed her progress presentation. The Executive Team had convened for their second planning workshop at the same venue as the first, and Kristen's presentation on the core operational problems had started the day.

The past few weeks had been a whirl of activity for everyone around the table. Anton, Elena, Kristen, and Jeff had been busy working on their issues list and supporting their senior leaders to engage with Great Care. Carol had run the Great Care workshop for the Board, the CPC, the senior managers' group, and two community and consumer groups, always with one of the other executives in attendance to show a united front, and for them to hear what people wanted from a KVHS experience. The Board had made "Great Care for Our Community" the focus of the new strategic plan. Once Pari was up to speed on the process, she had run more workshops for middle managers and frontline staff and developed and rolled out an online survey to allow consumers, community, and part-time, night, and weekend staff to have input into Great Care without attending a workshop. The initial Great Care framework had been fleshed out from this input, and an implementation plan was in the early stages of action. Driving progress with this was the focus of the second planning workshop.

Kristen's briefing on progress with the core operational problem list showed that progress was slow but steady and included a few wins, prompting an enthusiastic response from Anton.

"Yes, only four months, but look what we've achieved in the past two. And at least now we know where we're going—we just have to get there!" Anton spoke with more fire than usual, and Carol regarded him with interest. He tapped his foot and clicked his pen energetically. He and the other executives had been working together on a set of common goals since the first planning workshop, and Carol had commented a number of times on the valuable contribution Anton brought to the table. He'd been speaking up more about consumer-related issues, and his approach to thinking and planning added a new dimension to the clinicians' ways of doing things.

Kristen sat down and Carol nodded at her. "Thank you for that succinct overview of the operational issues, and congrats, everyone, on the progress. Let's keep at it. Kristen, do you mind keeping track of our decisions today? Pari and I are both taking notes, but I'd like you to develop some key messages from these couple of days for us to pass onto the divisional directors. We need to be consistent in the messaging about our plans and how that will affect staff." She looked around the group. "I recall that after our first planning workshop, the mixed messages we took back to staff created some confusion. We can't afford that; everyone has to be in the same boat, rowing in the same direction or we won't reach our Great Care destination as a whole health service."

"And whatever happens in four months," noted Elena dryly, "the world won't end, Kristen, even if our Department of Health rankings haven't improved. We'll still have a health service to run."

"True, you'll have a health service, but you might not have Nancy to chair it, or me to head it up, for that matter. And you're not the one who'll have to announce this to a national conference of over a thousand people."

There was an intake of breath as everyone looked at the CEO. *Whoops, that didn't come out quite as intended.* But some days she had less patience for Elena's attitude than others. The conference and the next performance meeting with the Department of Health were around the same time. If their results were bad, she was going to have to stand up and say so. She imagined someone in the audience— possibly from Mountain Health Care—holding up the *Kinsley Valley* Leader with STILL ROCK BOTTOM blaring from the front page. That would not be the uplifting end to the conference the organisers were looking for, quite apart from the humiliation she would suffer as a "failed" CEO and the disappointment of everyone associated with KVHS. She breathed through her annoyance.

"Elena's right, however," she continued. "You will all still have a job, I expect. Health services rarely close down because staff and patients are suffering. If they did, more health executives might pay extra attention to what's going on beyond their offices!"

"You—you could lose your job if our results don't change?" The realisation that there was more at stake than pride appeared to hit Anton like a blow, and both pen clicking and foot tapping ceased. He shook his head. "I hadn't thought about that. It didn't occur to me that you could be sacked, as long as the budget was under control, and they didn't catch you with your fingers in the till."

"Or in the drug cupboard," added Kristen. "But yes, Anton, the politics of healthcare are nearly as complex as healthcare itself. If our results don't improve, they might not sack Carol straight out, but they can make it mighty difficult for her to stay in the job."

"Okay, I didn't intend to go down this road *at all*." Carol held up her hands to indicate the end of this discussion. "Let's start over. Elena was right to say that the world won't end. I don't want anyone to panic. But I do want to keep the main thing, the main thing. Which is?"

Jeff responded without hesitation. "That's to get the whole organisation up to a consistently good level of care quality where we don't have unwarranted variation and patients don't need to depend so heavily on ending up in a 'good' part of the service to have a positive experience."

Carol inwardly breathed a sigh of relief. Back on track! "Precisely, Jeff. We can't achieve greatness in every area of the health service in a few months, but we can make a difference where it's most needed. Let's keep our eyes on that, and everything else will take care of itself." She went to the whiteboard and wrote:

1. Paint a Picture of the point of care quality we want to be known for.
2. Plot the components required to create the Picture into a framework, describing the Purpose (Goals), People (Roles), and Pillars (Governance).
3. Pilot the framework, practise implementation and learn how to make it work.
4. Plan to make the point-of-care Picture a reality across the whole organisation as simply as possible.
5. Put the Plan into Practice and Persist with implementation, even when challenging.
6. Promote and Promulgate Progress.

"Remember this roadmap from workshop one? We're here today to consolidate progress with actions one, two, and three, and to plan actions four and five. To make these steps effective, we must better engage with our consumers and community, and commit to stronger change and implementation actions. This will be the focus of the next couple of days. Action six is all about evaluation of the model: Is it working to create consistent greatness at point of care?" She paused to make sure that everyone was with her and was pleased to see their faces set in concentration. "If we get our measures right in actions two and three," she continued, "it will make answering this a lot easier. Now that we're crystal clear about what we're trying to achieve, matching the right measures to tell us if we're achieving it should be relatively straightforward. Collecting the data may be another story, though." Carol sat down. "Right, let's get on with it. Ready, Pari? You're up."

Carol noticed the stress in her shoulders and a familiar leaden feeling in the pit of her stomach. She hadn't planned to go in so hard today and realised she was feeling the pressure more than she'd admitted to anyone, including herself. Now that the discussion was back on track, it was time to get herself back on track. She sat very straight and took some deep breaths.

Pari's cheeks were flushed and her voice a little unsteady as she stood to make her first formal presentation to the Executive Team: the final KVHS Great Care framework. She started with the new KVHS strategic plan, noting that the Board had decided to make their strategic aim "Great Care for Our Community." She led the group through a quick refresher on the three key components of the GC framework: the purpose, which was the definition of "Great Care," translated into four concrete goals to guide everyday work; the people, which described the Great Care characteristics, roles, and responsibilities of people at every level of the organisation from Board to bedside (or chairside, in the case of community health, aged care, and outpatients); and the pillars of governance that provided the support and systems for managers and staff to pursue and provide Great Care every day, and to know how much progress they were making.

Jeff frowned. "That looks like what you came up with at the first exec planning session. I read the notes," he continued, in response to Elena's raised eyebrows. "Are you sure that defining Great Care isn't manipulated in some way so we get a consistent result?"

"Classic doctor!" Kristen laughed. "Come on, Jeff, you were at the medical staff forums. Didn't they come up with almost exactly this definition of high quality care?"

"Yes, I suppose so …" But Jeff's face was a study in scepticism. He took his glasses off and polished them, head tilted to one side.

Carol, feeling much better after her few moments of focused breathing, joined the discussion. "It's unsurprising, really, since we use the same scenario to elicit the feedback with each group. If anyone said anything radically different, it would be in there and we'd highlight it. The fact is, what most consumers, community, and staff want from a caring service is consistent across all sectors. It's not rocket science. There will always be individual needs for every patient. But that's what the goals are all about: care that is safe, effective, connected, and personal *for each person*. Some actions within those goals will be the same for everyone. And some will be different. But if we make those four goals the daily purpose of everyone who works at—or governs—KVHS, we'll be on the way to providing a platform for consistently good care that we can build on."

Pari moved to the next slide. "And as you can see, Jeff, the goals are really just four of the key 'dimensions of quality' the US Institute of Medicine[6] came up with many years ago, some of which have been reinforced by the Eight Picker Principles of patient-centred care.[7] She ran her pointer over the eight principles.

"I love that I get this now!" Anton said, clicking his pen rapidly. "We came up with the same things that researchers came up with because they're what all people want from care and services."

"Yes!" Pari said. "It's nice to have the research to back it up, but in the end, we know these are the things we want for the people we love, and for every KVHS patient. People want their care to be safe, to be right for them with the best possible outcome, and to hang together and make sense. And they want to be engaged as a respected partner." Pari moved to the next slide, showing a table of which Great Care dimensions they already systematically addressed. "Safe and Personal Care are largely covered by accreditation requirements, and access and timeliness are taken care of as performance measures for our funders. It's our job to make sure that the dimensions not addressed by external requirements don't slip through the cracks. Effective and Connected Care should receive just as much attention as the others. They are equally important to consumers, as we've seen through this exercise."

Elena twirled her necklace self-consciously. "It's true. After our first workshop, I ran the scenario with six of my senior nurses. Probably not very well. But even so, we got more or less the same result." She leaned over and removed the clickling pen from Anton's hand.

"Great!" Kristen said. "What did you do with the information?"

Elena put the pen down a safe distance away from Anton. "Not much. I'll admit it was a good exercise, and the nurses got quite excited. But I didn't follow up. Too busy."

"No wonder there was eye rolling when I ran it with the whole senior nurse group!" Pari exclaimed. "I guess they thought it was just another management fad, where there's a fuss about something and then nothing happens." She caught herself and stopped. That was the first time she had showed irritation in an Executive Team meeting. But in this case, she felt it was justified. Starting something and not following through was about the most destructive thing a senior manager could do for staff morale, culture, and belief. They'd be better off not doing anything in the first place.

Elena's mouth formed a thin straight line.

"Credit where it's due." Surprised faces turned to Carol. "It's not ideal not to follow through on something started, but I thank you for taking the initiative, Elena. Change isn't linear or straightforward, particularly in the complexity of healthcare. We take steps and some of them work better than others. I really believe in learning by doing when it comes to Great Care. It's every bit as useful as the systematic side of planning and implementing. I agree that we need to be consistent and continue the things we start, but life sometimes gets in the way of our good intentions. Let's move on. Have you got the stocktakes, Pari?"

Pari clicked to the next slide. She took a few seconds to look around at the faces turned expectantly towards her and noted the signs of tiredness and stress. She allowed a little more warmth into her voice as she began moving through two stocktakes: showing the KVHS strengths and gaps against the purpose, people, and pillars of the Great Care framework, and discussions she'd had with department heads and the Health Information Manager about their perceptions of Great Care strengths and gaps around the health service at point of care.

"Two things I found incredibly useful, and which surprised me"—Pari wrinkled her brow—"were the conversations with Carolyn, the Health Information Manager, and those I had with managers and staff about the informal processes that guide and shape how care is delivered and work gets done. I went into these discussions all prepared to find out which systems they would need tweaked to support Great Care, such as training, procedures, and position descriptions. Everyone agreed that these are important for change. But we ended up talking much more about corridor conversations, traditions, buddy systems and influencers. These have a big impact on how decisions really get made every day. I realised that both formal and informal systems are important, but that if we don't address the informal systems, we may not get Great Care embedded as business as usual."

"Of course!" Kristen tapped the table in vigorous agreement. "It's the sort of thing we don't pay enough attention to when we try to make change. We assume that work gets done through the formal processes we can see on paper. But what's agreed in a tearoom is probably more powerful than any new policy. We should add this to the change model so we don't forget."

Pari nodded and continued with her final couple of slides, which covered an overview of progress with the organisational governance and systems "engine room," including a care and governance risk heat map that Susie had expertly prepared. "Over to you for the details," she concluded, waving her hand around the group before the sat down and took a long drink of water.

"I have to ask—why did you ask the Health Info Manager about care quality?" Kristen looked bemused. "HIMs don't go near a patient!"

"That was my idea," responded Jeff, nodding at Pari. "HIMs work with patient records every day and read every one, to code them for funding and research purposes, including complications and readmissions. Carolyn probably knows more about what goes on with clinical care in this health service than we do! If you want to know which doctor to choose—or not choose—to look after you, or which part of the health service to be admitted to, ask a HIM!"

Carol was more than pleased to note that the other team members were no longer passive observers of quality, but active participants in drilling down on the governance systems required for Great Care. Kristen joined in with the discussion on staff recruitment, retention, skills, and characteristics required for Great Care, having worked with the People and Culture team to determine what would be required to equip managers and staff to provide it for every consumer. Jeff and Elena led the discussion on clinical competence, credentialing, scope of practice, standards and guidelines. Anton had some figures prepared on resource planning, and the changes required for IT, reporting, and information flow to support GC. Carol covered consumer partnerships and CPC support, and she and Kristen discussed the visible leadership, messaging, and culture gaps. Pari fleshed out the monitoring, improvement, risk, and measurement changes that would be required to drive and support Great Care.

"Great work, everyone!" Carol was genuinely impressed by the collaboration she'd witnessed, and she thanked her lucky stars, not for the first time, that Pari had taken the job.

"What are you going to do about Professor Yang and the surgical M&M meetings?" Elena asked pointedly, glancing sideways at Kristen with a knowing smile.

"What are we going to do, you mean," Carol snapped, annoyed that Elena had chosen to target a key medical gap that Jeff had identified.

"There are a few issues to work through there," Jeff answered, stroking his beard. "I admit that I thought we'd addressed them months ago, but it turns out we hadn't, not to senior medical staff satisfaction, anyway. I should have known better. Anyway, we're resolving sticking points relating to confidentiality and use of the information that comes out of the meetings, and we're quarantining some time for medical staff to meet as well as participating in the interdisciplinary meetings. It will take some organising, but I think the information we'll get out of it will be worth it. At least the interdisciplinary surgical M&M meetings are back on the table, and Pari and I have designed an email template that makes it easier to record and distribute the lessons learned from the meetings." He leaned back in his chair and looked at Carol. "Prof Yang wants to lead the changes—again. I don't know if that's a good or bad thing. But she has the credibility and relationships we need to get this done, so I guess we should give her a second chance."

"I also spoke to Professor Yang." Everyone looked at Pari. "I wondered if there was anything she could gain from helping us fix the M&M meetings. You know, Start Where They Are." She and Kristen exchanged smiles. "I found out from the surgical business manager that Prof Yang wants to present at the next World Surgical Conference but doesn't have a topic yet. I, well … I met with her and suggested she present on the implementation and outputs of surgical interdisciplinary M&M meetings. She seemed to like the idea, so I offered to help with compiling some information for her about the process and outcomes of the meetings."

"So it was you who waved the magic wand!" Jeff exclaimed. " I wondered what happened. One day the Prof was saying 'no way,' and the next it was, 'so when are you going to get those interdisciplinary meetings going, Jeff?' I seriously wondered if I needed to be worried about her! Thanks Pari—I owe you." He gave her the thumbs-up.

"We all do!" Carol said with a wide smile. "But keep a close eye on progress, Jeff, please. Why don't you offer to write a joint article with Prof Yang for a journal? I'm sure there'd be enough interest. I could help, and we'd all get a publication out of it."

"Doesn't that seem like a bit of a … bribe?" asked Anton.

"I guess you could see it that way." Jeff looked nonplussed as he considered this take on Pari's approach. "I prefer to think of it as positive collaboration and exchange. It's how healthcare works, for better or worse. And a conference paper and journal article on this topic would be excellent for KVHS, quite apart from the patient care improvement that would result from knowing more about our mortality and morbidity!"

"I'm a great believer in getting what we want by helping others get what they want," added Carol.

"This is all very well," interjected Elena, waving Anton's pen at Carol. "But can we move on? Now we know where we are in great detail. I'm sure that's important. But how do we make all this happen? Wasn't there supposed to be an implementation plan?"

"I know you'd rather be getting on with making things happen, Elena," Carol said, moving over to the window to close the curtains against the bright morning sun that had crested the nearby hills. "We do like to rush to action and solution in healthcare, and sometimes we need to. But doing that without being sure exactly where we want to go, and exactly where we're starting from, is a recipe for failure, particularly with an organisation-wide transformation like this. Now that we're clear about our origin and destination, we should be able to plan some highly effective and targeted implementation tomorrow that will help us get some quick runs on the board. We've got two guest speakers coming today, remember, and I think both those discussions will significantly influence our approach to making Great Care a reality across KVHS. Don't worry, we'll get there." She looked at her watch. "Andy will be here at eleven, so let's have our break now."

"Andy, the Consumer and Community Partnerships Committee Chair? Isn't it a bit unusual to have a Board member provide training?" queried Kristen. "I don't think we've ever done this before."

The vigorous nods of agreement around the table indicated they'd all been thinking the same thing.

"Not unusual when you have a positive Board–Executive Team relationship," responded Carol. "Which you may not have experienced here at KVHS for the past few years. And not when you have published experts on the Board like Andy. He specialises in the psychology of community collaboration and facilitating community and consumer engagement and works with some of the big retail companies as well as community and indigenous organisations. He's not here to tell us how to do things, but to give us some guidance about best practice in this area and some feedback from the CPC." She picked up her phone and stood up. "I don't know about you, but I could use a little help with this! Any objections?"

"Sounds good to me," said Kristen, picking up her bag. "Come on, Pari, you'll need some sustenance after that big effort. These workshops really take it out of you, you know. I hope they've got those fantastic cacao protein balls for morning tea that they had when we were here last time."

*****

Andy and Carol were waiting in the conference room when the others returned from their break. The room had been refreshed by the hotel staff; tall jugs of iced water and a bowl of fruit sat on the table. A gentle warm breeze wafted through the room from an open window, just enough to disturb any loose papers lying around. Carol waited until everyone was settled before she began.

"I've asked Andy to challenge us to think about Great Care through a different lens," Carol explained. "We're already working on a number of initiatives with consumers, such as building systems and skills for shared decision-making and more effective information exchange. The new national accreditation standards in this area have pushed us to progress our thinking and our latest consumer satisfaction measures show some improvement." Kristen and Pari exchanged a glance, acknowledging the hard work they'd done together to get these results. "But there's plenty of potential for us to grow in this space, and we have much to learn from the Consumer and Community Partnerships Committee, who've been thinking about Great Care from their perspective."

"Thanks, Carol," Andy began with a nod. "The CPC has been busy since Carol ran the Great Care workshop for us a few weeks back. Thanks, Pari," he turned to the screen as Pari brought his presentation up. "It was fantastic to see the committee, and fifty of our closest friends"—he clicked to a photo of the large group of workshop participants from the KVHS community—"have their lightbulb moment about what high quality care is, and how they want that to look in our health service, created by them and expressed in their own words. I'm not going to take up too much of your time today, but I do want to cover two important things. The first will be some key tenets of consumer focus from the CPC perspective. Second, I want to share with you the Great Care ideas we came up with at our workshop. Sound like a plan?"

Everyone nodded.

Andy clicked to his next slide. "Let's start with some defining questions." He grinned. "Here's something for you to ponder, for a start. Which do consumers value the most when in our care: a wash in the morning, or to be involved in their decision-making?"

Everyone had an opinion. Andy sat back with an amused look as the group went at it hammer and tongs. Finally, Kristen turned to him in desperation. "Put us out of our misery! Which is it?"

"Turns out, it depends." He laughed as everyone else groaned. "If you're an elderly person, it's the wash. If you're young, it's the decisions.[8] This is an important question, though, as it reminds us that the challenge of true consumer focus is only going to grow as we attempt to meet the needs of different generations. Healthcare has created the expectation that consumers will be partners in their care, so it's up to us to make it work for both consumers and staff. This extends to 'the dignity of risk,' something that aged care and mental health have been grappling with for many years and is now creeping into acute care."

"Don't we know it," said Elena. "If a patient refuses a drip because it's uncomfortable, where does that leave us? This sort of thing is happening more and more. The nurses are really stressed about it. Not only that, the younger chronic patients transferred back from the city hospitals all seem to want day passes so they can attend social events."

"Let's not get side-tracked into clinical pros and cons for now," laughed Andy. "But these are good examples, Elena. Consumers have the right to make informed choices about their care, but sometimes that's going to increase their risk. There's nothing easy about trying to balance choice and control on the one hand and keeping people safe and getting the best clinical outcome on the other. But this is what's coming down the pipeline as part of true consumer focus. It may be that we get better at explaining the benefits of uncomfortable interventions or find ways to make them more palatable as we encounter a generation who may not be quite as stoic as we're used to. So the CPC would like to get ahead of the game and find out what our consumers really do value, and how well we deliver it."

"Including holding social events in the hospital so they never have to leave," Anton deadpanned.

The next hour flew by as Andy pushed the group to think beyond their current norms of consumer focus and participation. He posed a set of four core consumer focus questions for them to discuss, including:

- How easy do consumers find KVHS to deal with?
- What are the top three pain points for consumers at KVHS that they would change if they could?
- How cared about do KVHS consumers feel?
- What one thing would most consumers like us to do differently?[9]

"Consumers aren't only invested in the Personal goal, of course," Andy said. "They want Effective, Connected, and Safe care as much as you want to provide it. These questions should be applied to each Great Care goal."

He clicked to the next slide, which showed a flow chart for a surgical patient pathway. "In the second half of the workshop after Carol had run the defining GC exercise, we worked on how we could use the Great Care goals to improve the KVHS consumer care experience. With a lot of help from Susie and her Lean method expertise, we constructed basic surgical and outpatient pathways. Then we applied the consumer focus questions to both pathways: Are we easy to deal with? What are the top three pain points in this pathway? Do consumers feel cared about in this pathway? What would they like done differently? We looked at last year's patient satisfaction and complaints data to see if we could answer these questions."

He paused to drink some water, and Pari refilled his glass. "Of course, we found that we know more about an inpatient journey than an outpatient. But some of these questions we can't answer for either. We need better data! But not data that takes twelve months to collect and analyse. That has its place, of course. Anyway, this is what we were able to do with the information we had."

He pressed the remote and a few red pain points appeared, scattered along the pathway. He moved to the next slide where the surgical pathway was laid out again. As he clicked the remote, the pathway appeared to contract instant measles. Multiple red dots signifying pain points and difficult dealings popped up all over the slide.

"This is drawn from the experiences of the people in the workshop," he explained. "We had no trouble answering the core consumer focus questions for this pathway using stories from the people in the room. As you can see, it isn't all good news, but at least we know more now than we did before the workshop. No one there could recall ever being asked if they felt cared for, whether we were easy to deal with, and what the pain points are. We've had the same feedback from subsequent community meetings about Great Care."

The group studied the screen in silence. Elena's eyebrows shot up, and Pari's shoulders slumped. Even though she knew this was coming, she took the problems the CPC had identified to heart.

"At our latest CPC meeting," Andy continued, "we reviewed the information from consumer and community meetings to see how we could answer the core consumer focus questions for the four Great Care goals. Here's what we came up with." Andy clicked to the next slide, which listed four questions:

- Do consumers feel that their care is delivered as a caring, responsive, and respectful partnership with them—and is it? (Personal goal)
- Do consumers feel safe with us—and are they? (Safe goal)
- Do consumers think their care is right for them and doing what it is supposed to—and is it? (Effective goal)
- Do consumers think that their care is well organised and seamless—and is it? (Connected goal)

Carol was familiar with the material, having been at the CPC meeting, and she watched closely as the other executives studied the questions and wrestled with four questions going into four goals.

"I see what you're trying to do." Jeff sat up and pointed to the slide. "They're the subjective and objective sides of the GC goals. You're suggesting we find out consumers' perceptions of how they experience the four goals and compare it with objective information we collect for each goal. Interesting."

"How do we find a way to get all this information in real time?" asked Anton, his brow furrowed. "We don't have anything set up to collect this sort of information right now."

"I think"—Kristen paused while she collected her thoughts—"that we could answer the subjective questions quite easily. The objective ones will be harder because we don't currently have the information to answer them fully. We have some, mostly in the Safe goal, as it's what's required for accreditation and funding purposes, but it would be harder to find or collect data within the other goals."

"Yep," agreed Jeff. "There'd be some effectiveness data in the outcomes information that the doctors review within their specialties and with their colleagues. More and better in some units than others, and its use for improvement would vary. I know, for example, that the gastrointestinal and colorectal surgeons have done some excellent process and outcome improvement work here—they're quite renowned for it, with many publications. I believe the oncology and O&G units have impressive clinical review and improvement programs as well, although I'm not across the detail yet. We did redesign work in the ED, of course, as part of the move into the new building. That will help with the Connected goal. And—"

"Don't forget allied health," Pari interrupted. "They're all looking at how to improve their treatment outcomes. Effectiveness is not all about the docs."

"Ha. True! And a lot of the work I'm talking about was interdisciplinary with nursing and allied health. It's just that I want to get medical effectiveness data used more consistently and usefully over time. We don't really use it on an organisational scale, but it's interesting to think about. What proportion of our patients overall achieve their planned health outcomes? You could also look at it from the negative perspective and review complications data to see how many encounter setbacks in achieving their planned outcomes due to ineffective care or clinical practice variation. Many doctors would really appreciate us supporting their research and improvement work more than it has been in the past. That would win you some fans, Carol!"

"Well," said Elena, "in my experience, the doctors won't share their data outside of their units." Jeff stroked his beard but said nothing. "Nurses know about outcomes as well, you know. They live with them every day. Good and bad." She looked around, and Carol wondered if Elena was about to scuttle the first positive discussion they'd had on clinical outcomes.

"We might be able to collect some real-time outcomes data on the ward," Elena continued. "I'd like to compare the nurses' perception of how well our care works with consumers' experiences and the doctors' perspectives. That would be rather fun."

A pin was heard dropping as the group absorbed Elena's idea of fun.

"Sounds fantastic, Elena." Carol said, scrambling to hide her surprise and relief.

"She has a point." Jeff nodded at Elena. "And we might be able to encourage more data transparency if we can show the benefits to patients and staff, beyond 'we need it for accreditation and the Department of Health.' "

"I think the Connected goal will be hardest," mused Pari, suppressing a smile at Elena's statement. "There's not much objective info around for that. We'll put our thinking caps on. When you look at the actions within that goal, a lot of it is about shared understanding and care panning out the way it's planned, so we could look at appointment cancellations and no-shows, for a start. Treatment gaps or overuse are harder."

"All good thoughts," Carol said, nodding. "But what about answering the subjective questions—Kristen?"

Kristen consulted her computer screen. "We have the state consumer experience survey, which gives us some of this. We also do our own exit survey for each patient and their family, if they want to participate, of course. It focuses on fairly traditional issues: Did you like the food? Was the room clean? Was it too noisy? Did we take care of your pain? etc. Maybe it's time for a makeover? We could craft some intelligent questions to find out from each consumer if we've achieved the GC goals, and in the process, we could tease out their pain points within each goal, and how we respond to those. This would help us understand how well cared for the consumers feel and how easy to deal with we are! It wouldn't be more work for the staff," she added hastily, glancing at Elena. "The volunteers ask the questions. But we've been asking the same things for so long and the results aren't really changing: communication is still in the top three problems, as it has been for years. We should use that process far better than we are and really unpack the issues. And we could modernise it by recording the answers on computer tablets rather than paper forms."

"Um," Anton mused. "I reckon one of my staff could whip up a nice spreadsheet for that fairly easily."

Elena twirled her necklace for a moment. "I wasn't going to complain about data collection. I was thinking that we could do some of this as part of discharge planning as well. We might be able to collect the nurses' perspectives on how safe, personal, effective, and connected the care was, which we could compare to objective information, and also what the patients think."

Pari looked up from her notes, eyebrows raised. She wasn't the only one.

"What?" Elena looked around. "Don't be so surprised. It's about time we were included."

"I agree, that would be really interesting and useful, Elena." Carol broke the silent response to Elena's new-found enthusiasm for the topic. "Do you think we could put that on a device as well, Anton, so we could use it across more than one service? I'd also like to get more real-time information like that in aged care and community health than we do currently."

Anton grinned. "We'll do our best, boss!"

"I'd like to survey GPs and community health providers to see how many 'surprises' they get after one of their clients has a hospital admission due to poor or no information." Jeff ran his hand over his crew cut distractedly as the ideas tumbled out of his mouth. "And if all this came to pass, we'd have real-time information about how well the GC goals were being achieved, which we can supplement with objective data as we collect and report it. We could look at using PROMs and PREMs, too. We've been thinking about it but haven't got any further than that."

"Great, Jeff." Andy turned to the whiteboard and wrote: Patient-Reported Outcome Measures = PROMs, Patient-Reported Experience Measures = PREMs. "There are some really good tools around now to help us get measurable consumer perspectives on their experience and outcomes. Go on, Jeff."

"The information could be fed back to department heads for them to discuss with their staff and reported to quality committees," Jeff continued. "It could also be channelled into the central data collection, so we can look at it across the organisation and use it to develop improvement strategies to better meet the GC goals." Jeff turned to Pari and Anton. "Let's set up a time to discuss data collection."

Andy looked pleased at the energy his input had generated. "The CPC will be happy to work with you by applying the information to different pathways—surgical, outpatient, community health, mental health and aged care—to really ramp up our consumer focus and generate a great consumer experience across the organisation," he said as he sat down.

"What about the communication issue?" Kristen asked. There was silence for a minute.

"Conversation stopper!" Kristen laughed. "Poor communication has been in our top three consumer complaints for as long as I can remember."

"You're right, it's a perennial problem," responded Andy, looking thoughtful. "But it doesn't need to be. Part of the issue is that we don't identify the specifics of what makes up the communication problem. So everyone shakes their head and pops it in the too hard basket."

"Yes, but the information you've shared with us should help to identify more bite sized chunks to address," said Carol. "Great Care will require that we improve communication, or we won't be able to deliver the GC goals. Communication is a means to that end, not an end in itself. And even with the best training in the world, not everyone is going to be a skilful communicator. It's not possible, so we can't rely solely on that. We'll have to use all the smarts and creativity we can gather to find ways of communicating that support personal, effective, connected and safe care. Some of this will require more formal and recognised partnership roles, for family members for example, around which we design information exchange. Some might be enabled through technology. We might develop master communicators to act as translators and intermediaries. Who knows? I'm sure the consumers and staff will have way better ideas than these! But one thing is non-negotiable: it's time to get more serious about this.

"We'll get started on using the information you've presented today right away." Pari suddenly looked and sounded like her old energetic self. "It's all gold, which will help decide our GC implementation priorities. Thanks, Andy!"

Over the next half hour, the group planned their renewed approach to the KVHS consumer focus. There was a buzz in the room that Carol had not experienced with this group before. She felt her spirits lift as she surveyed the scene and allowed her shoulders to relax. The lead in her stomach had disappeared without her noticing. *People support what they help to create,* she thought, as she had at the first exec workshop. And healthcare people really do want consumers to have positive experiences. Maybe sometimes they made it too bureaucratic and abstract, whereas this discussion had purpose: we want to know what consumers experience so we know if we're achieving the GC goals.

Eventually she took advantage of a pause in the conversation to point to her watch. "We're out of time," she noted with regret. "We must stop for lunch. Thank you so much, Andy. As you can see, you've sparked the imagination of the group! I have no doubt we'll make great progress from here. I'll thank the CPC members personally at the next meeting, but in the meantime, would you please pass on our thanks for their hard work and inspiration?"

"Of course." Andy picked up his papers. "One more quick thing. When you're implementing the Personal goal, don't force it. There's nothing worse than artificial inclusion." He looked around at the puzzled faces.

"I've got my psychologist hat on now. It's worth taking longer to implement, so you can take the time to help staff to see the value in partnering with consumers; for them and for patients and families. If staff go through the motions of engagement because they have to, we'll never reap the benefits. Consumers will hate it and so will staff. We need staff to partner because they want to. Because it speaks to what they come to work for—to meaningfully connect, to contribute and feel good about themselves and their work. Do the 'between the ears' work on engagement, as well as the policy work."

"Hear, hear! We'll try! And we'll see you at the next community meeting. Stay for lunch?" Kristen clapped appreciatively and everyone joined in.

Andy held his hands up in protest. "No need to thank me. We're all really pleased to contribute to work that is so critical to the KVHS' future. It will be great to take the notes from this session back to the CPC and discuss it with Carol at the next meeting. Anyway, must run; can't stay for lunch; have a diary full of clients this afternoon. Enjoy the session on change—I have a feeling you'll find it more than interesting. Bye, everyone!"

CHAPTER NINE

The whole team was back in the conference room on time after lunch—except Carol.

"She's gone to meet the speaker," Kristen responded to the enquiring looks as she turned on the air-conditioning.

"Who is it, do you know?" asked Anton. "I haven't had a minute to think about these couple of days and realise I had no idea we even had guest speakers on the agenda."

"Someone from the local uni," answered Jeff. "I haven't taken much notice either, to be honest. Too much else going on."

"The university! Please let it not be too academic," groaned Kristen. "We know Carol has a weakness for research into practice, but I can't make myself find it quite as fascinating as she does."

They were laughing as Carol walked in. "Everyone, it's my great pleasure to introduce Chen Lee, Professor of Organisational Change, Innovation, and Transformation at KV University."

Introductions were made as Chen set up his presentation. He noticed Kristen looking at him, head on one side.

"You look very familiar, but I don't know why," she said, peering at Chen.

"I think I can solve the mystery." Carol smiled. "Remember when we bumped into each other at the hockey game a couple of Friday nights ago? I was talking to Chen. When he's not being a professor, he's the Kinsley Valley Under 18s coach."

"Oh, yes!" Kristen tapped her forehead. "I remember! Good, now I won't be wondering about it in the middle of the night. But how do you know each other?"

Carol explained how she knew Chen and gave the group a brief summary of his CV. "Basically, Chen has dedicated his life to trying to find out how to engage staff in change that sticks," she concluded.

"And much more importantly, he is married to an amazing woman," announced Kristen, which made them all laugh. "I've been on a couple of fundraising committees with Angela and she's a gem. I didn't know we had a mutual acquaintance, Carol!" she said, sitting back and crossing her arms comfortably. "I admit I had my doubts about this session. After all, I'm supposed to know about this stuff, but as far as I'm concerned, you may proceed." She gestured to Chen with a flourish.

"I'll second that," agreed Anton. "As long as there are a few sports stories in there, I'm all yours."

"Thank you so much," Chen responded with a small bow and a big smile. "Let's start with some examples of where change has not stuck, with disastrous results."

The next thirty minutes were spent dissecting case studies from industries all over the world and close to home. Chen related his hockey team's unsuccessful finals campaigns, and everyone else in turn contributed a story about change they'd been responsible for that hadn't worked over the long term.

Anton was enjoying the discussion about failed change. "I saw so much bad change at the bank that I could talk about it for days!"

"Change is a challenge in most organisations for many reasons," Carol said. "People get into habits, they don't like to stop doing things they've gotten good at or that give them power, it's disruptive, it slows you down, it can create conflict. There's a wealth of literature about why change is hard." She couldn't resist contributing to the discussion, despite trying to stay in the background and letting Chen do his thing.

"Successful change requires a clear picture of three things," Chen continued. "Your destination, your origin—where you're really starting, not where you'd like to be starting—and your map for getting from one to the other, including topography. Only then can you chart your course to get to your destination in the best possible way."

"Topography?" queried Pari, eyes bright with interest.

"Basically, a mud map of the challenges you'll face along the way: the mountains, valleys, quicksand—and even road tolls," he finished with a broad smile.

"What do you mean by 'tolls'?" Kristen and Anton asked in unison.

"The price you pay to get from where you are to where you want to be. There's always something, and I like to identify it in advance, if possible, so I'm ready to pay, or to bargain. It could be a minor thing—for example, the staff might do the new thing if you help them with an old thing that's bugging them. Or take a redundant task away from them. Or it might be a major trade-off involving something like working conditions. You can't always predict it; but if you can, it really helps smooth the change."

Anton's face broke into a broad grin. "I've thought of an example of a project that was started at a false origin and so took a wrong route that would never have gotten them to their destination. Did you hear what happened with the new bridge they're building over the river?"

"What's the problem there?" asked Carol, remembering her conversation with Nancy about the build.

"Well, they mapped out the project plan and got started on the construction, and then they realised that the report on the riverbed soil that had informed their planning was full of incorrect information. When they dug the foundations, they found that the soil didn't look and act like the report said it would, and their planned foundations would not work. After a lot of mucking around, they realised that they had the soil information for a bridge of a very similar name in another state. The soil surveyor had surveyed for both bridges and sent them the wrong report. They had to start all over with the right information, and now they're six months behind the original schedule."

"So, they weren't starting where they really were," Chen said, and nodded. "That's a great—but disturbing!—example. Especially as those roadworks already feel like they've gone on forever. What about you, Elena? You haven't told us a story yet."

Elena had remained quiet throughout the discussion, but at Chen's prompting, she reluctantly described trying to implement a more rigorous assessment process for aged-care residents. "It was fine while I kept my eye on it," she concluded. "But then I went on leave, and when I came back it was as if it had never happened. I couldn't believe it. I thought I'd done all the right things, but obviously, I hadn't."

"What were those 'right things,' Elena?" asked Chen, moving to the whiteboard.

"Oh, well, you know, the same as everyone else has been saying. We held some meetings to discuss the change, revised the policy and procedure, ran some training, raised awareness with posters, and communicated with emails."

"Ah!" smiled Chen. The classic PACEM change model: policy and procedure, awareness raising, communication, education, and meetings. No one ever formally developed or introduced it, yet it's used in human services all over the world, usually to mediocre effect." He noted Elena's head toss and continued hastily. "I don't want to be negative; they're all important ingredients, but they're not very effective without using other, stronger change levers as well. By themselves, they're weak predictors of sustained change."

Kristen noticed Elena's reaction and spoke up. "But we all do it like that! Not only Elena."

"Of course!" said Chen. "I'm not making an example of you, Elena, far from it. As I said, it's by far the most common approach to change that I see. I used PACEM for many years myself until I learned there was a better way. It's important not to throw out babies with bathwater, either; as I said, each of the PACEM components has its place in change. But there's more to it than that. Does anyone have an idea of why I'd say that?"

Jeff raised his hand. "Anything that relies on people to 'try harder' or 'remember' or follow a procedure is a weak lever for change. Medium-strength levers actively steer staff to the right action, like a checklist. Strong actions make it hard for the staff to do anything but the right action, like new software or removing the old way.[10] I studied safety and human factors in my PhD," he added in response to Pari's admiring look.

"Honestly, I had no idea that change could be managed when I started out in healthcare." Pari shook her head. "I used to tell everyone what they had to do differently, change the protocol, run some education, raise awareness, and hope for the best. Then, when nothing happened, I'd blame the staff for not engaging with the change. Not very savvy of me."

"And sometimes removing the old way is nearly impossible," chuckled Kristen. "Has anyone else here tried to get rid of an old form? Those things have a life of their own!"

"There are a couple of key reasons why PACEM doesn't work very well in a health service," Chen said, nodding at Kristen with a smile. "First, human beings are not consistently logical or rational, nor do we always think things through before acting. It depends on the situation. When we're planning an important dinner party, for example, we use what some call 'reflective' thinking. We work out what we want to achieve and how to get it done. We might even get some training in a particular cooking style or learn a new recipe from our favourite chef. But when a situation requires us to act fast, a different part of our brain takes over and we use 'reactive' or 'automatic' thinking.[11] That's when we get home from work late and must whip dinner up in a hurry for our cranky kids, so we're likely to fall back on something tried and true." He looked around to make sure everyone was following and was pleased to see that all eyes were fixed on him. "PACEM primarily works on reflective thinking, which is fine for people who have thinking time, like managers. But for busy staff who spend their day using a lot of reactive thinking to respond to situations, PACEM is not going to equip them well to do something differently in those situations."

"Unless the training is reinforced and practised, and therefore becomes automatic," added Jeff, "like the training airline pilots do."

Chen nodded.

"But we seem to keep using PACEM, over and over, getting the same result," groaned Pari.

"We're creatures of habit!" agreed Chen. "Also, you're trying to make change happen in a complex environment, thus tripling the degree of difficulty compared to making change in a factory, for example. I presume Carol has talked to you about complex adaptive systems and resilience?"

"Only every second day," sighed Kristen, mopping her brow theatrically.

"Great!" laughed Chen. "I'll get to that a little later when we dive into the Will and Skill model of change. And add a little socialisation for good measure. But first, a parable."

"What?" chorused Anton, Kristen, Elena, and Jeff. Pari and Carol grinned, their interest piqued.

"I'm not sure I do parables," said Anton in his manliest voice, and Elena and Jeff nodded in vigorous agreement. "I thought we were going to talk about sports! And didn't you guarantee there'd be no funny business at these workshops, Carol?"

"I did, and I meant it," responded Carol, suppressing a laugh. "Give Chen a chance. I'm sure that if he wants to share a parable, it's for a good reason."

"Trust me—no funny business," Chen assured them as he sat down. "There's method in the madness." He sat up straight, placed both his hands on the table, and began, "It's called, 'The Trouble with Vegetables.' "

Elena, Jeff, and Anton exchanged doubtful glances as he began.

There was much happiness in the kingdom of Complia when the Prince announced his engagement to the Princess of Transformania, a kingdom across the sea.

Before he left for the wedding and royal honeymoon tour, the Prince called the Chief Farmer and Chief Quality Controller to his office. The Chief Farmer was a trusted employee and had overseen the thriving orchards of Complia for ten years—so well that the delicious fruit they produced fed the whole Kingdom.

"In six months, I will return to Complia with the Princess. One of the things she will miss most about her home in Transformania is her vegetable garden. She has tended it since she was a small girl and loves every plant. It is beautifully laid out and is a very pleasant place to spend a sunny afternoon. The Princess is also an amazing vegetarian cook and likes nothing better than to create delicious dishes full of fresh garden vegetables.

"I'd like you to prepare a vegetable garden for her here. When we return in six months, I want to see a beautiful garden filled with magnificent vegetables, ready for our first feast here as husband and wife. The garden must have peas, beans, tomatoes, and potatoes, because they are my favourites. I'm not sure which are the Princess's favourites; just make sure there is a comprehensive range of delicious vegetables for her to choose from. Oh—and this garden must be even more beautiful than hers. The aesthetics must be perfect."

The Chief Farmer shifted uncomfortably from foot to foot. "Pardon me, sir, but, as you know, we've just opened up a large number of new orchards for export. No one has any spare time. Are you going to supply new staff to work on the vegetable garden?"

"More staff! Are you kidding? The royal budget is stretched to the limit as it is, what with my brothers and sisters producing ever increasing numbers of children. And the development of the new orchards has been a very expensive exercise, as you know. This is a vegetable garden. How hard can it be?"

"Well, sir, to be honest, I've never put together a vegetable garden before. I'm an orchard specialist." The Chief Farmer looked uncharacteristically nervous.

"Really! Well, personally I can't see the difference. A plant is a plant. I don't want to hear

excuses. I'm sure you'll figure it out. Don't we have excellent, committed orchard staff who come to work every day to do a great job?"

"Er, yes, sir, but—"

"So, they should be able to produce a high quality vegetable garden, shouldn't they? If they put their mind to it and work a little harder? I'm sure you can organise and delegate the staff to get this done, can't you?" The Prince's voice rose. "Or do I need to replace you with a Chief Farmer who can deliver this for me?"

The Chief Farmer loved his job. "No, of course not. I'm right on it." He bowed and turned to go.

"Oh, and by the way," the Prince called after him, "tomorrow I'll send you the resources you'll need to create the garden. There will be mulch and fertiliser and timber and tools, and a fancy ladder and a robot hoe that I bought off late-night television. I'm sure they'll come in very handy. You can buy the seeds when you decide what to plant. And—there's one more thing. You must use the TQM method of growing: Total Quality Meatless. The Princess mentioned she heard about it at a conference and was keen to try it out. Imagine how impressed she'll be when she arrives here and finds we have used it to build a whole garden from scratch!"

"Ah, sir … I don't know what that is."

"Look it up on YouTube, then! Where's your initiative? Anyway, the Chief Quality Controller will have the job of monitoring your progress and reporting it to me while I'm away, so you can work on it together."

The Chief Farmer winced. "Of course, sir," he muttered with a sinking heart as he passed through the heavily guarded door.

The Chief Quality Controller watched him go. "Sir, I haven't had much experience with vegetable gardens, either …"

"Honestly!" The Prince banged his desk. "What do I pay you all for? If you don't know, find out. And when you bring me the progress reports, I only want to hear about the excellent progress being made. Unless there's a disaster—but obviously that won't happen. Are we clear?"

"Crystal, sir."

"Now, leave me. It's time for my wedding suit fitting."

Chen stopped, drank some water, and looked around at the group. "So, what's going on here?"

There was silence while those who hadn't been giving the story their full attention frantically scanned their short-term memory. Pari had plenty to say, but she decided to hold her fire. Carol had no intention of bailing her team out, so apart from a supportive nod in Chen's direction, she said nothing.

"Well," began Kristen, breaking the silence. "The Prince seems to be making a lot of assumptions about the capabilities of his staff to get this job done."

"Yes! And why is that, do you think?" Chen responded encouragingly.

Elena broke in. "Why shouldn't he? That's what he pays them for, isn't it? To know what he wants, and to be able to do it? It's not like they're new staff. They should know what he wants."

"I tend to agree," said Jeff with a nod. "These people are obviously good, trusted professionals. The Prince is letting them get on with it without micromanaging them."

Carol smiled inwardly. True to their roots. But she could see they were interested in spite of themselves.

"Anton?" continued Chen.

"I think Jeff and Elena are right. But Kristen has a point, too, I suppose. I'm not sure this Prince dude is going to get what he wants."

"Because?" Chen prompted.

"Because he hasn't been very clear about what he wants…yes, yes, a beautiful vegetable garden, we know that much," he added hastily as Jeff and Elena frowned, "but we know in accounting—and IT—that the devil is in the detail. And there's not much detail here."

"Thanks, Anton. Pari?"

Pari pushed a stray lock of dark hair behind her ear. "I think that if the Prince gets exactly what he wants, it will be by good luck, rather than good management. He's unclear about what he wants beyond a vague idea of 'beautiful,' 'high quality,' and 'perfect.' These things are difficult to interpret unless you agree on exactly what they mean. Then he's expecting busy people to fit it into their day, and he's providing them with resources that may or may not be useful because he hasn't involved them in this decision, and therefore hasn't asked them what they need to do the job. He's also asking them to use a particular model or method to get the job done that may not be fit for purpose and that the staff have never heard of." She looked around the table. "I took notes!" she finished, in response to the others' wide-eyed surprise.

"Okay, that woke me up." Jeff straightened his chair and leaned forward. "I do agree with Elena here. She and I see staff as highly trained and committed professionals who should know their job and do it. But I see that you're looking at it through a different lens. You're looking at them as real people who might get a job done better if they're clear about the outcomes and expectations." He sat back and polished his glasses, seemingly oblivious to the implications of his statement.

"Get *out*! Clinicians real people. Amazing!" laughed Kristen. "Well, Jeff, you may not know, but I ran the human resources' service—now People and Culture—for a few years. I spent a lot of time mediating and organising counselling for staff, including medical and nursing staff "—she nodded at Elena—"who'd been bullied because they hadn't delivered, or because they'd done something wrong, or didn't meet expectations. Sure, some were just lazy or incompetent. But most of them didn't have a clue what the expectations were, or how to meet them. As a non-clinical executive member, let me state for the record that clinicians are not always the best communicators."

"Thanks for the unsolicited critique, Kristen," drawled Elena, crossing her arms defensively. Jeff ran his hand over his crewcut.

Kristen continued with an amused grin. "Hold your horses, you two. I'm on your side! 'Real people' tend to do a better job when they are clear about their role and responsibilities and supported and encouraged to enact them. Even if they have a 'Dr' in front of their name." She glanced sideways at Jeff. "Even if they're on an executive team. I don't think we pay nearly enough attention to this in healthcare, as Pari and I have discussed. To me, giving staff active support and encouragement to get their job done is key to a high-performing organisation. Our staff need it from us in the same way that we need it from Carol."

THE POINT OF CARE

Chen broke the tension. "What is the impact of the Prince's approach to change on his staff?"

Anton leaned forward and pushed his glasses up his nose. "Let me have a go. They'll be stressed—obviously—which means they may not perform as well as they should to get the job done. They're not really sure what he expects, or if they've got the skills to make it happen. And they're stuck with this ridiculous-sounding TQM method that they're told to use so the Prince can impress the Princess. But it probably won't even help them."

"And they really don't want to make it happen, do they?" asked Pari, turning to Chen. "They can't see the sense in it and have no ownership over it."

"Exactly. You've all hit on at least one aspect of what these staff are up against. Let's continue. Yes, there's more," he smiled in response to Jeff's grunt and Elena's loud sigh. "Don't you want to know what happens?" He took a sip of water and went on:

Soon after, the Prince left for his wedding and royal honeymoon tour. The months passed. The Chief Quality Controller made many visits to the new vegetable garden and held many meetings with the Chief Farmer. She researched the TQM method and ran education for the orchard workers who had been selected by the Chief Farmer to fit the vegetable garden into their already full work schedule. She dutifully reported progress to the Prince every month via email, producing pages of colourful graphs and fascinating tables showing planting and growth trends, as well as tracking the rainfall and temperature. In time, there were photos of plump peas, long green beans, ripe red tomatoes, and large potatoes. She also included a first-hand story from one of the garden workers in every report, usually discussing how the latest plant disease or bug infestation had been overcome. The Prince was impressed.

"I'm sure the Princess will be so excited when she sees these vegetables that she will forget all about her home garden in Transformania," he emailed. "And these are beautiful reports. You are doing a fine job, Chief Quality Controller. You are in line for a promotion when I return! With your quality skills and our committed, hardworking garden staff, we have the perfect team."

The Prince and Princess returned to Complia six months to the day from the Prince's departure. There was much hustle and bustle to harvest vegetables for the welcome home feast.

Just before sunset, the Chief Farmer received word that the Prince and Princess were on their way to inspect the vegetable garden. The Prince arrived leading the Princess, who was blindfolded. He whipped the blindfold off with a flourish as he announced "Surprise!"

The Princess looked around and smiled at the Chief Farmer and Quality Controller. "Surprise what?" she asked.

"Oh, er, this is where I was told to come—perhaps I've got the wrong spot. Chief Farmer, where should we look to see the surprise?"

"You're looking at it, sir," muttered the Chief Farmer, who looked a lot older than he had six months ago. He exchanged a glance with the Chief Quality Officer.

Down the hill from the group was a large field, dug into rows. Some of the rows had been tended with care and were filled with flourishing plants. Some rows were almost empty, except for a lonely group of plants at one end.

Silence. Faces dropped. The Prince turned an unbecoming shade of purple. The Chief Quality Officer and Farmer edged away.

"This looks NOTHING like the Princess's vegetable garden in Transformania," the Prince spluttered. "It's in a FIELD. It's not beautiful, it's not planned, it's not orderly— and I'm guessing it's not producing very much—is it?"

More silence.

"Such beautiful reports full of good news! Month after month! The best garden staff with the best intentions, working hard every day, using the TQM method! Explain to me HOW it is that we do not have a magnificent vegetable garden?"

The Chief Quality Controller's mouth opened, but nothing came out.

Eventually the Chief Farmer forced himself to speak, finding courage in his desperation. He was going to lose his job anyway. "S-s-sir. If I may. I told you I was no kitchen garden expert. So I did what you said: I researched vegetable gardens based on the TQM method with the Chief Quality Officer. But I was also running the orchards and getting the new ones going you've put a deadline on those as well, as you know—so I had limited time to run a new project. In fact, I did most of it at night. I delegated different vegetables to different workers, but they also had to do it in their 'spare' time.

And some of them were more motivated than others …"

The Prince looked baffled. "But the reports! The photos! The stories! And I was told the TQM method was fool proof! What happened?"

Everyone looked at the Chief Quality Controller. She took a deep breath. "Sir, you asked for good news. So I gave it to you. I photographed the best-looking plants and interviewed only the workers who had triumphed over a problem like an infestation. And to be honest, the TQM method was very confusing. I spent hours trying to work it out and … you know, I don't think it's a good fit for our climate and soil. Once we were sure we'd have the vegetables you'd requested, fighting with the Chief Farmer and the garden staff for anything beyond that got too hard. I'm sorry. I gave up."

The Chief Farmer broke in. "And I also mostly concentrated on the peas, beans, tomatoes, and potatoes. Their quality was good, but I didn't know how much of each we were expected to produce. I was guessing. It looks like we'll have just enough of them for the first feast, though," he added brightly.

"What about the aesthetics of the garden?" enquired the Princess, as the Prince appeared incapable of speech.

"We didn't really know what you meant by 'aesthetics,' " the Chief Quality Controller muttered, cheeks blazing. "There are so many different ways you can lay out a vegetable garden … we just weren't sure where to start."

"Didn't I supply all the materials and resources you needed?" the Prince spluttered.

"Yes—well—you supplied some resources," said the Chief Farmer. "Some were useful and some not. That robot hoe couldn't dig a straight line if its life depended on it. We never got around to using the ladder. You see, we didn't really know what you wanted. I did what we thought was right, and what was easiest and quickest, which was finding a fallow field and allocating each worker a row for their vegetables."

"So, you didn't even try to design a beautiful garden with decorative motifs and raised beds and sharp edges and comfortable seats?" The Prince could barely get the words out. "No, don't answer that. And, I imagine we won't be seeing a comprehensive array of vegetables at the first feast, either. Do we have anything beyond peas, beans, tomatoes, and potatoes?"

The Chief Farmer stepped forward and picked up a basket. He removed the covering cloth, revealing a motley mix of vegetables. "Sir, many of the extra vegetables didn't grow. We didn't have the time to work them properly. But we do have some for the first feast. Here's the samphire, Brussels sprouts, and parsnips that didn't do too badly."

At this, the Prince put his head in his hands. "Brussels sprouts! Parsnips! I hate them! And what on earth is samphire?"

"Well, we heard it was hardy ..."

The Prince held up his hand with a sigh. There was another silence while everyone gazed from forlorn basket to forlorn field. The Princess asked sadly, "Spinach? Cauliflower? Carrots? No?" She turned to the Prince. "Remember I promised I'd make you my world-famous spinach, cauliflower, and carrot pie as soon as we settled in? Well, you can kiss that goodbye. You know, if you'd involved me, I could have helped! As nice as surprises are, something as important as growing quality vegetables requires more than guessing and hoping. And it works a lot better when you can draw on real experience and knowledge. I could have told you exactly what we needed and helped make it happen."

The Prince groaned and turned his gaze on the Chief Quality Controller. "You've always been so good with the quality of the orchards, researching the best methods and developing useful tools. What happened?"

"Sir, we—we ... didn't know enough. We didn't have a picture in our heads of what you wanted the finished garden to look like and produce. We didn't have a blueprint or a plan. With the orchards, we know exactly what the expectations are and what we're trying to achieve. Without all that, we had to guess, as the Princess said, and use the resources we had, which were a bit random and not really what we needed ... and this is what we got.

"The other problem was—I must be honest here—I don't have any line authority over the Chief Farmer. I'm not his manager. I could make suggestions, but he wasn't interested in my input. We ended up arguing about what was important and how to do things. It wasn't like the orchards, where we're both engaged in working together to make the orchards the best they can be—because they benefit everyone. This project was all about ... well, you, and no one else was excited about it. So we focused on the peas, beans, tomatoes, and potatoes, because they were mandatory. Anything else was an extra, including the aesthetics, and in the end, they didn't get done very well—or at all ..." Her voice trailed off.

The Prince took a deep breath, and the Chief Farmer and Quality Controller braced for impact. But the Princess spoke first. "So—we ended up with some of the things the Prince wanted, but not what we all needed."

The Chief Quality Controller decided to throw herself on the Princess's mercy. But as she was opening her mouth to plead for her job, a surprising thing happened. The Princess winked.

"It seems the Prince assumed that you both knew what was important and gave you instructions and tools that were less than helpful." She glanced at the glowering Prince. "Might as well be brutal here, my dear, or we won't learn anything. And you can be a bit vague with your instructions, and overly optimistic about how well people read your mind and have your best interests at heart. Everyone tried their best, but of course they focused on what was mandatory—and what else they could get done with the time, resources, and knowledge they had. And, my dear, may I say that designing and growing a successful and beautiful vegetable garden is—like most things—a lot harder than it looks, and takes constant oversight, which I've never felt you quite appreciated..." The Prince grimaced. "If you're going to run a successful kingdom, it will be helpful if you could be a bit more specific. Even great staff are not mind readers—or superhuman," she finished softly.

The Prince was silent for a long minute. Then—amazingly—he smiled at the Princess and turned to the Chief Farmer and Quality Controller.

"The Princess is right, as always. Well, here's my shot at honesty: I did not give this the time or attention it deserved. I didn't work with you to develop the vision or the concrete outcome I wanted, nor did I bother to find out what the Princess wanted. I didn't supply resources designed to achieve that outcome; in fact, I burdened you with tools and methods that looked good but didn't help because, well, I thought it would impress the Princess. I didn't make sure you had the skills and information you needed or ask enough serious questions about progress. I didn't want the brutal facts about where things weren't going well, or where the gaps were. Basically—I set you up to fail. I'm sorry."

The Quality Controller and Chief Farmer leaned on each other, weak with relief—and admiration for their fabulous new Princess.

"Okay," said the Prince, taking the Princess by the hand. "Let's start again. This time, the Princess will lead the project, as I can tell she's itching to get her hands on it." He turned to go, then stopped.

"And in six months, we'll hold a second 'first feast,' celebrating the Complia vegetable garden version 2.0. First, we'll get clear about the food we want to serve and what we can produce in this climate. Then we'll develop a shared vision, find the production model that best fits our situation, develop the plan for making it happen, and supply the right tools, skills, and people for the job. We might even instigate a vegetable sharing scheme with those who work on the garden, for a little added motivation. I can't promise you'll get all the resources you'll need at once, but you'll get what you need to start off properly and I'll commit to resourcing it as you progress.

"Speaking of progress," he glanced at the Chief Quality Controller, who gulped, "this time I want the real story, so we will work together on how best to present it. Fewer selective photos and more facts, perhaps? Stories that cover both the successes and failures, so the Princess and I can do what it takes to guide the garden to success?

"And Chief Farmer? Here's my first clear instruction for version 2.0: no parsnips or Brussels sprouts. I'll reserve my decision about the samphire until I've tried it."

And with a regal wave, he was gone.

Chen took a drink and looked around at the group. "Why do you think I'm putting you through this exercise?"

"As you're here to discuss change," Jeff said, "I'm guessing this is to show us how badly we do it in healthcare. We can't expect people to read our minds and perform miracles just because we want them to. If we want a change to work, there's a bit more to it than that." Jeff sat back, looking more engaged now that the parable was complete.

"Yes, Jeff, spot on," agreed Chen. "Elena?"

Elena thought for a minute. "As a matter of fact, the way the Prince reacted when he didn't get the garden he wanted reminded me of when I was a student nurse on my first hospital rotation. Yes, I still remember, before you say anything, Kristen."

"Who, me?" exclaimed Kristen, looking innocent.

"Anyway," Elena continued, "when I started out in nursing I used to get into trouble—a lot. My first ever charge nurse reminds me of the Prince. I always tried my best, but sometimes I needed a little more explanation and help to understand than the other students. I'd had a few weeks off with a broken leg just after we started our hospital rotations, and I got behind the rest of the group. No one ever helped me catch up, and when the charge nurse did occasionally speak to me, she made things so complicated and used so much jargon that I had no clue what she was on about. I was thinking of dropping out, but in my second rotation the new charge nurse noticed straightaway that I was struggling and gave me some extra help. She was so patient with me and explained everything three times if I needed it and made sure I knew what the expectations were and how to do things properly. I was much happier, and so were my patients because I was better at my job. So, yes. I see your point."

"Thanks, Elena. That really brings it home. I've been thinking. We don't only make these mistakes individually. We make them collectively, as an Executive Team. So does the Board."

"What do you mean?" asked Pari, struggling to see the connection.

"In healthcare generally, and at KVHS specifically, the Board and Executive Team want and expect staff to deliver high quality care. We act like the Prince and expect to get the garden we want. And when we don't, we blame staff and wonder why. Over and over."

"It's true," agreed Kristen, nodding. "Now at least we have a definition of high quality care. But for many years, we didn't. And we didn't spend any time helping staff to understand exactly what we expected. We probably gave them the wrong resources and expected them to fit it into their busy day. Or we didn't help them to better organise their work so they *could* fit it in."

"And we were happy to take the positive quality reports without too much questioning." Elena leaned forward and took up the story. "Seb didn't like bad news. And he transmitted that reluctance to the Board. We were all so preoccupied with the new building and the budget problems and everything else that we didn't take much notice of the reporting. Everything looked good and we took it at face value."

"In the end, our organisation didn't end up as a beautiful patient care 'garden,'" Kristen added. "No matter how beautiful it was on the outside, on the inside, we got a straggly field." The emotion in her voice showed how personally she took the failures.

"KVHS is not the first health service to do that and it won't be the last," Carol said sympathetically. "Chen is reinforcing what we already know we should do. Clear, agreed goals that are aspirational *and* achievable. Specific roles for achieving the goals, supported by great management, tools and resources. And reporting and feedback to inform and drive progress. A pragmatic plan for change that considers the complexity of the environment and doesn't try to dump solutions from other organisations without adapting them." She exchanged glances with Chen, not quite sure how this concept had landed around the table.

"Aspirational goals, pragmatically achieved," Pari said. "I like that. As long as the aspiration bit doesn't include too many 'shiny things.' Honestly, there are faddy quality methods and tools everywhere you look. Many of them do the same thing in different packaging. I thought I knew most of them, but since I've been in this job, they keep coming out of the woodwork! Every department in this place seems to be using at least one tool or technique they've learned at a conference or in a course. Some of them are great—really fit for purpose and helping the service to change and improve. But some are just sucking time and resources and not helping the staff to do anything better; in fact, they're a burden. But because it's the department head who loves the tool, no one's game to complain."

"Exactly," Jeff said, nodding. "The quality improvement industry is expert at rediscovering fire! I think it's more about egos than tools." He chuckled. "Medicine has been dealing with this for years. And I admit to indulging in shiny things myself at times. Everyone wants to be the first or the best at the new, usually 'internationally acclaimed' technique or tool, even if it doesn't improve on how things are already done. Just as well we have an approval process for all that now. I'm afraid in the past some patients were subject to quite a lot of 'shiny thing practise' without their knowledge or consent."

"Tools and methods are only as good as how well they help you do what you need to do," added Anton. "You soon learn that in IT where just about everything is a fad. You can get so distracted by the technology that you end up not really achieving what you're trying to get done. Sometimes the shiny tech even makes the work more complicated—but at least it looks more attractive while you're working harder," he laughed.

"At least now we'll be able to evaluate the tools, because we know what we're trying to achieve," Carol said. "If something doesn't help us make KVHS Great Care happen for every patient, and we don't need it for funding or accreditation, we ditch it. We'll judge improvement tools and methods on the basis of their helpfulness in identifying, planning, implementing and evaluating the changes we need to make. Just like the diagnosis and treatment cycle, Jeff: you wouldn't be bothered with anything that didn't help you to accurately identify your ED patients' conditions, treat them appropriately, and evaluate the outcomes, would you?"—Jeff shook his head—"So why would we put up with unhelpful tools when we're trying to do the same thing for our organisation?

"Time for a break. Let's make it brief. Is fifteen minutes enough? There are a few more important issues to work through before we finish today, including understanding why it's diabolically hard to do things consistently well at KVHS and what we can do about it. Come on, Chen, I'll buy you a free coffee." Carol stood, and she and Chen walked out together.

CHAPTER TEN

Kristen shut the blinds against the hot afternoon sun as Chen picked up his whiteboard marker and wrote "Great Care = doing the right things consistently well."

"Equals hard, let's face it," groaned Pari. "Or we'd be doing it already."

Chen grinned. "Hard, yes. But not impossible. Let's get right into some of the nuts and bolts about making things happen consistently well, which requires the right change that sticks. Carol, you mentioned complexity before our afternoon break, and that's exactly what I want to talk about now. I'm sure Carol has likened KVHS to the road system?" Chen enquired of the rest of the group.

Heads nodded vigorously.

"Once or twice … or ten times," chuckled Anton.

"Great. Let me give you an example of why doing things consistently well is challenging in a complex system, and where resilience fits. A few weeks ago, some uni colleagues and I drove to the city for a conference. On the way there, the weather was good, and we had a good trip and made good time. But, a few days later, when I was driving, the return trip was completely different, for reasons we couldn't control. Not only did they have new detours in place due to the bridge works, but those big storms—remember?—hit us right on dusk. The poorly maintained roads that hadn't bothered us when the weather was dry were suddenly a mess of mud, water, and potholes. Tree branches were all over the place. There were massive farm trucks coming the other way, on their night runs to the city markets, and we could only hope those drivers didn't make our situation worse. As it got darker, I decided to pull over at a rest stop and hand over the driving to one of my colleagues. Why do you think I did that?"

"Because you were scared?" suggested Kristen. "I would be. I hate that road at the best of times."

"Not scared, exactly. I do a lot of driving for work, like all of us living in a country town. We've all been up and down that route to the city a million times. But I could see the situation was deteriorating, and that my perfectly fine driving on the way to the city was not now as effective in this new situation. I also knew that my colleague was better equipped than me to handle the conditions, so I decided to respond by handing over the driving, so we would have more chance of achieving the outcome we wanted: getting home safely."

"What was so special about him?" Jeff asked.

"Her," corrected Chen. "Monday to Friday, Lana is a mild-mannered academic. On weekends, she likes to indulge her passion for rally driving."

There was a collective "Oh!" as the group saw the sense in Chen's decision.

"I can't put my hand on my heart and promise that Lana drove in an orthodox manner or obeyed every road rule. The main thing is, we got home in one piece. Can you see the relevance to complexity and resilience at KVHS?"

Everyone was quiet while they pondered the analogy.

"I think I can," began Jeff slowly. "Situations in healthcare can change and deteriorate rapidly, often due to things you can't control. Patients can go downhill, or something can go wrong with equipment, or a system fails or someone makes a mistake and it can all go to hell. Something you think will be quite routine suddenly turns into a nightmare. It happens all the time in emergency medicine, of course. And the 'rules' don't always help you in that situation. The policy or guideline that works perfectly well at 0900 on a Tuesday can be a waste of space at 2300 on a Friday when something is going wrong." Nods of recognition spread around the table. "In that situation, you use the best skills, expertise, and judgment you've got at your disposal to decide the right course of action."

"Thanks, Jeff, I can't improve on that explanation." Chen grinned.

"But what's this got to do with change?" asked Kristen. "Sorry, I'm a bit lost."

"Good question," said Chen. "When I teach change in complex systems, I combine it with resilience, because people in complex systems work exactly the way Jeff just described. There's no point making change all about getting people to slavishly follow new rules if sometimes we need people not to follow the rules to keep patients safe and things working. Complex systems differ from complicated in many ways; but for today's conversation, suffice to say that they're unpredictable and have many interdependent moving parts, some of which you can't control. They're also relatively heavily people-dependent, compared to a factory production line. You can't have a rule for every situation because of the unpredictability, so you also need well-trained and experienced people ready to respond, and *permitted and supported* to play to their strengths, and respond, within clear parameters, when situations change, and without dropping their bundle."

Elena cocked her head to one side, eyes narrowed with concentration. "Isn't that how clinicians already work? My nurses certainly do, the good ones anyway. They know that their job is to do what it takes to keep patients safe. So why are we making such a big thing of it?"

"The good ones, yes," Jeff responded evenly. "However, I'd be surprised if that sort of mature approach to care was consistent across KVHS. You insist that your nurses provide excellent care, Elena. And I don't dispute that is the case sometimes. Maybe even most of the time. But I doubt if it's all of the time, and the data appear to back that up. That's not a slight on them; it's the reality of life in the complexity of a human service organisation." He ran his hand over his crew cut. "It's the same right across KVHS. We know it's really difficult to do anything consistently well in any human service environment. Partly that's because of the constantly changing conditions and challenges we face every day. Partly it's because we work within myriad systems. And partly because we're only human."

"And partly it's because we're only now beginning to take a specific, strategic, and systematic approach to providing excellent care," Carol said, looking up from her note taking. "Unless we've made the pursuit of excellence explicit and provided specific permission and support for staff to develop proactive and resilient approaches to pursuing it, it really comes down to individuals' motivation. Especially the managers' motivation. Are they just trying to get their service through the day? Or supporting their staff to create a really good service? I'm sure, Elena, that you and I could list which manager is which at KVHS. And there would be some who won't have even thought about it. We want staff to think and act resiliently in their everyday work. And we also must develop specific team resilience for responding to common risk scenarios."

Elena nodded slowly. "True. But we can't have everyone doing what they feel like. We must have some rules!"

"Take Chen's driving example," Anton reflected, clicking a new pen. "They encountered an unexpected and deteriorating situation and got home safely because they followed the rules *and* responded with their skill and judgment. We can all respond more or less resiliently to sudden changes in driving conditions through our experience. But drivers who have done focused training, like 'defensive driving' courses or rally driving, are experts in the basic rules and skills. They have strengths in that area that we don't have. They also know how to work outside the rules when required to get the best possible outcome. You have to know the rules before you can break the rules. We need to think about supporting our expert staff to work resiliently, because a mix of standardisation and responsiveness is our best chance of providing consistently Great Care in a complex environment. And it allows people to develop and play to their strengths, which gives them more job satisfaction."

"I agree," Jeff said. "Elena has a point, though. Most clinical protocols are there for a reason: they're evidence-based and therefore non-negotiable. We don't want people running around implementing their own ideas about surgery or infection control, for example, just because they think their ideas are better than the evidence. We're trying to reduce harm due to unwarranted variation and overuse of tests and treatment, remember? That's why we use statistical process control charts for our key risk monitoring, so we can identify and respond when our systems are not controlling our risks and our results are moving outside of expected boundaries. Resilience is more about supporting staff to respond appropriately, working to their strengths, when the unexpected happens—and the unexpected happens a lot more frequently in a complex system than on a factory production line. We want people to think about their response and provide Great Care, not blindly follow rules and routines that are not helping the patient. It takes a bit of juggling to get the balance right, though."

"That's like saying that it takes 'a bit of juggling' to get to the moon." Kristen rolled her eyes expressively. "I'd say it takes massive amounts of juggling. There's nothing easy about this."

Carol gazed at the ceiling. "No," she said, suppressing a sigh. "There's nothing easy about making consistently good care business as usual. I wish! It's not set and forget. There's no point changing a few protocols, running some education, and giving people a Great Care checklist. We need to work with the way things really get done by real people, and not pretend KVHS is a factory populated by robots programmed to strictly follow every step of every protocol. Life in healthcare doesn't work that way."

Chen nodded. "You'll need to work with clinical leaders, managers, staff and consumers to implement change in an environment where sometimes the rules get followed, sometimes they don't, and every day is slightly different. Consumers and staff can help you develop useful protocols and systems based on how work really gets done. And we also want to develop staff thinking and provide permission and support, so they know when to, and how to, deviate from the rule book when required, to achieve Great Care."

"This sounds like our accountability framework!" exclaimed Kristen. "You remember, Carol, we've discussed it with you. It was one of the more progressive things that Seb introduced, even if his motivation was about us all hitting our budget and targets, rather than achieving something like Great Care. But the framework was helpful: Be really clear about what you must achieve and deliver, your boundaries, and the rules. But within that, you have permission to use your skills, experience, and creativity to make it happen better than it can with rules alone." She got up to open the blinds as the sun disappeared behind dark clouds and the room dimmed. "And to make it more fun!" she threw over her shoulder.

Anton tapped rapidly on the table with his pen. "And just as our accountability framework did, I'm guessing we need to develop resilience in our non-clinical staff as well?"

"Yes, of course," responded Pari. "Non-clinical staff, particularly those who interact with consumers, must also be able to respond to new and changing situations. For example, the receptionists are always dealing with tricky requests and questions, as well as managing long waiting times. We need them to follow the booking procedure, but to use their judgment when the system throws up an 0800 appointment for a patient who has to travel two hours by bus to KVHS from an outlying farm, or to spot an elderly person who clearly shouldn't wait two hours for anything. We want our staff to think first, and then act to get the best outcome for consumers. We're a ways from this happening for every consumer"—she shook her head in frustration—"but I think we can do it. If people understand the intent of Great Care, and want to make it happen, and have permission to use their skills and judgment and strengths to make it happen, they'll be able to make things go well whatever the situation is, because, well, because …" Pari paused, searching for the right words. "Because they'll really get it."

Kristen laughed. "Yes, 'getting it' is of paramount importance! Wow, Chen, this is great stuff, but I think my head is about to implode with all this thinking."

"We're on the home stretch, Kristen," Chen said with a grin. "But you're right: it's time for a quick brain break."

*****

Yellow light from the late-afternoon sun reflected off the walls of the conference room, creating a cosy atmosphere. It also reminded them of the long day they'd had and there were a few yawns around the table as they took their seats. Chen noted the fatigue and wasted no time in getting on with the last lesson of the day: the 'Will and Skill' model of change.

"'Will' is the 'I want to' component and 'Skill' is the 'I am able to' component of change," he explained. "Of course, they're interdependent. It's like a reinforcing loop. Sometimes you must build the will before people will engage in building the required skills for the change. In other situations, helping people acquire a skill makes them more willing to engage in the change. But we must address both." He looked up to see Kristen nodding in agreement. "We'll mostly focus on the 'Will' in the time we have left today, as this is usually where the challenges to change lie." He expertly laid out the essential Heart, Head, and How[12] actions to fostering the will for change, explaining that most Will work in healthcare targeted the Head and often forgot the Heart and How actions, paving the way for weak or failed change.

"Information supports understanding, but feelings drive action," he reminded them. "Why else does so much TV advertising try to make us feel positive about a product?" He described the Heart actions as:

- Finding meaning in the change with those affected by it.
- Using visual representations and stories from the staff and consumer perspective that show the desired change destination, benefits of the change, and/or the problems with the current situation.
- Helping staff to feel involved and look good.
- Peers and managers providing support for each other throughout the change.
- Starting where they are (SWTA), not where you are.
- Not starting from scratch but building on what already works.
- Acknowledging wins.

- Socialising the change by making it part of everyday conversations, behaviours, and decisions; something that old hands want to teach newbies; something that defines a ward or service that they're proud to be associated with.

The Head actions he listed as:

- A clearly described, reachable destination, preferably one decided with those who will make the change happen.
- Facts and data about why we need to go to that destination.
- Credible leadership and peers involved in helping to get to the destination.
- Clear, doable steps on how to get there.
- Regular data, feedback, and discussion along the way to show how the journey is progressing.
- To build on what already works well.
- Simple rules that act as reminders and prompts for what we are trying to achieve.

He finished by noting that the How must:

- Create a path that's the easiest way to get to the destination—downhill if possible!
- Start the path to change with how work is really done, not how it's meant to be done in the policy and procedure.
- Remove the old way, or some of the old way.
- Clarify individual and team roles and expectations for reaching the destination.
- Identify and acknowledge the likely boulders and barriers on the path and how to overcome them with the people who will be navigating them.
- Organise the physical environment and organisational systems to support the new way of doing things.
- Show that the new path is workable by engaging with some early adopters and getting them started on doing things differently.

There was a silence whilst people absorbed this. Jeff sat up, looking the most energised. "I love simple rules," he said with enthusiasm. "We used them in the city ED I worked in, along with our human factors work. I'd like to do more of both here at KVHS. We used human factors in the ED redesign, but I haven't had any luck introducing simple rules yet."

"Simple rules?" queried Anton, shifting restlessly in his chair.

"Simple statements that guide behaviour to get to a desired result. They cut through the complexity by clearly stating what's required to happen, rather than a long list of steps for how to make it happen. Sometimes they trigger action, and sometimes they stop it." Jeff stood up and went to the whiteboard. "I'm sure you all know a simple rule, you just don't think about it that way. For example, patients are triaged in ED according to simple rules. Let's see what we come up with."

"How about 'Do unto others as you would have them do unto you'?" Carol said. "That's a simple rule that replaces a long list of 'dos' and 'don'ts' to live a good life."

"Great example," Chen said, as Jeff wrote. "And many people use simple rules to guide their eating. For example, I have three: 'No second helpings,' 'Fish twice a week,' and 'More than half the plate is plant food.' And here's one from my hockey team: 'No arguments on the field.' No matter how annoyed we are with each other or the other team during a game, or how wrong a referee's call is, we save it for the locker room. On the field, we present a united and calm front, even if we're not feeling that way."

"My dad had a simple rule for his construction company," said Anton. "I hadn't thought about it that way before. He always said: 'Only deal with suppliers who've been in business more than five years.' He might have paid a bit more for his supplies because of this rule, but it meant he was dealing with companies who had track records for quality and reliability that he could count on."

"You can see that simple rules help with both the Will and Skill aspects of change." Chen looked around to make sure everyone was on the same page. "They are very useful in making it easy to understand the change and remember how to make it happen."

"I like Will and Skill!" Pari said with feeling. "It reminds us to equip people to own the change as well as implement it. Without both, you end up like the Prince's staff: zero enthusiasm or understanding for the task, and not really equipped to make it happen, which usually ends up in half-baked change that doesn't get you what you need."

"And the socialisation aspect of change is what we were talking about yesterday— except that we called it the 'informal' aspect of change." Kristen turned to Chen with a thoughtful look, brow creased. "I knew instinctively that this was important, but I'd never named it. What we really want is to hear one staff member say to another: 'This is how you provide Connected care,' or 'That wasn't very Personal care.' Then we'll know it's in the bones of the way they work and how they interact, which creates the consumer experience. Got it! Now we just have to make it happen!"

The group continued their discussion, considering how best to work on the Will side of the Great Care changes by developing and communicating stories about real Great Care experience for consumers and staff. Chen reminded them of the old, time-tested AIDA[13] formula for getting a message across and making it stick:

ATTENTION: Why it's useful for the recipient to know this.

INTEREST: Relevance to the recipient and others that are involved.

DESIRE: Head and Heart information that stirs a need in the recipient to act in response.

ACTION: Clear and easy next steps to take.

Chen turned to the CEO. "Carol, did you remember to bring an example?"

"I did," responded Carol, pushing her hand into her briefcase and pulling out a piece of paper. "Here's something that was on the cafeteria noticeboard when I first started. As the date had passed, I took it as a souvenir, thinking it might come in handy—and I was right." She handed a copy to each of them. It read:

You are invited to a meeting to discuss how to reduce pressure injury rates in rehabilitation. With accreditation only two months away, this is an issue that affects everyone: doctors, nurses, and allied health. Meeting Room 3, Tuesday 5th at 1200.

"Sounds good to me," said Jeff, grinning. "Short and to the point." Anton nodded. Elena said nothing but looked up expectantly as if she knew what was coming next.

"And how did that meeting go?" asked Chen.

Pari shifted uncomfortably in her seat. "It didn't," she said curtly. "Only the rehab OT who drew up the notice, the nursing pressure injury prevention coordinator, and one other nurse bothered to come. We couldn't believe how slack everyone else was. We had to reschedule and spent hours chasing people to make sure they'd turn up."

"We're not having a go at the OTs, Pari," Carol said gently. "We're all guilty of sending messages like this. Sometimes we put them on a wall, sometimes in an email. We're not marketers and have limited skills in effectively getting messages across. We're using this to learn how to do it better."

"That's right." Chen smiled. "And that's exactly what I want you to do now. Split into pairs and I'll give you five minutes to develop a more powerful message about that meeting, based on what we've discussed so far about change."

The group went to work and the room was filled with talk and laughter as the pairs re-worked the information. After five minutes, each read their messages out. Elena and Anton led with some alarming statistics about pressure injury prevalence. Pari and Jeff emphasised the important role every clinician had to play in preventing pressure injuries. Carol and Kristen told a heartrending story about a fictional aged-care resident and the effect of a stage-three pressure injury on her quality of life and the staff caring for her.

Chen made notes on the whiteboard and nodded appreciatively as each pair shared their new message. "You've each got at least one element of success, so you're more likely to attract people to the meeting than the original message. Now—here's one I prepared a little earlier." He read:

> Doctors, Nurses, and Allied Health Staff: Do you feel like you're working harder? You are! We've been collecting data and found that if you work on the rehab ward, you're spending an average of thirty minutes more per day on pressure injuries than six months ago, due to the rise in stage two and three PIs. If the PI rate keeps rising, it will be an hour more per day by Christmas. Who has an extra hour per day? Attendance at our "longer and stronger" resident exercise class has halved in the same time period, due to the increase in residents with pressure injuries, and we're concerned this will soon result in more falls. Our residents are suffering unnecessarily! Not from the pain of pressure injuries, but the way it's affecting their lives. Take Margaret, for example, who cries now when the exercise class is on because she used to look forward to it every day—and was making progress with significant strength increase—but now her pressure injury stops her from participating.
>
> It's time to do something about it. We've done our homework and found three evidence-based techniques for preventing and treating pressure injuries that we could implement, building on what we currently do. We'd like to discuss these with you and get your advice and input on

implementation. The next time you're on the rehab ward, please see Alice (day) or John (evening) at the nurses' station. Don't be surprised if they remind you! Or—write your name on the bottom of this notice and we'll give you a call or email. We'd like to start implementing by the end of June, and we need your thoughts by the 15th of June so we can get our planning organised.

Thanks for your help—let's work together to fix this.

Everyone laughed. "It's too long," complained Elena, leaning over to remove Anton's clicking pen from his hand. "But, I have to admit, it's interesting."

"Can you see the AIDA in the message?"

"Yes, it's all there," Kristen replied. "I tried to identify each one as you read it. Am I right in saying that it also has a good dose of the 'building Will with Heart, Head and How' actions we discussed earlier? I can hear SWTA, stories, data, and a doable path." Her eyes creased with amusement as Anton glared indignantly at Elena and his stolen pen. "But you went even further and made it easy for people to show their interest. They didn't need to put themselves out to attend a meeting."

"Yes, but as I said, it's too long," Elena repeated. "Who has time to read that?"

"Well, this is a long version, I'll admit," chuckled Chen. "As you become more confident with different ways of messaging, you'll learn to craft it into different lengths without losing the impact. However"—he looked around the table—"you'd be surprised how many people will read something this length when they find it of interest and relevance to them. Some marketing people think messages should be even longer than this one. Of course, you can explore different media. You could get the same message across with a thirty-second video shot on someone's phone. And for the skimmers, make the key points bold so they stand out."

They stopped for a quick stretch break, and Kristen moved around the table, refilling coffee cups for those who wanted it. Anton took a long gulp from his sports drink and Pari made herself a cup of herbal tea.

"Last couple of points before we finish," Chen reassured them as they took their seats. "You all understand how important it is to equip people with the skills and practicalities they need to be able to make a change and do things differently, so I won't go on about it. I really want to make the point that the Skills part of the change model is not only about effective training. If we help people develop new skills and knowledge to participate in a change, they must be able to dock this with a receptive environment in their workplace, where they are supported to practise and apply those skills."

Jeff put down his coffee cup and sat back. "Not sure I get that. Why would we train people and then not let them use the skills?"

"Ha! I'm not sure why we'd do that, Jeff—but we do it all the time!" Kristen said with an expressive shrug. "Don't start me. I couldn't count how many staff I've watched attend training to gain a new skill only to return to their workplace and have their peers or manager actively discourage them from using it—or never encourage them to use it. What a waste of time and money. That's certainly not socialising a change! And don't even mention conferences. Yes, it's nice to go away and meet up with colleagues and hear what others are doing and present a paper. But if I asked you to calculate the return on that investment, Anton, you'd cry."

"So what should we do about it, Chen? Let's have a quick brainstorm. I'm happy to scribe," Carol said, getting up and moving to the whiteboard.

"Sure," Chen said. "Let's combine knowledge and skills with a broader view of implementation that includes staff empowerment—and socialisation. If staff aren't empowered to use new skills to make a change, and it's not 'acceptable' for them to apply those skills, you might as well forget it. So, what do staff need to feel the permission and ownership to exercise new skills and do things a different way?"

After ten minutes, the whiteboard was full of suggestions. Chen quickly transposed and rearranged them onto a large piece of flip chart paper. "Great work. I think you've identified just about everything in the last model I'm going to teach you today: the DKRS Empowerment Model."

The group studied Chen's list:

DIRECTION

- The why: What's the destination, purpose, advantage, and meaning?
- The roadmap: Where are we starting? And how will we get to the destination?
- Leadership: someone showing the way.
- Goals: clear and concrete.
- Beliefs: from old to new.
- Quick wins in short cycle pilots.
- Clear roles, decision-making boundaries and defined authority and autonomy to make the change.
- How we'll get there.

KNOWLEDGE

- Value and use of local knowledge, creativity, and intuition to make the change.
- Working to strengths.
- Technical, interpersonal, data and decision-making skills put into practice.
- Organisational information required to understand, implement, and track the change.
- Learning from mistakes.

RESOURCES

- Tools and materials.
- Right physical environment.
- Streamlined and relevant systems and processes.
- Guidelines and standardisation.
- Equipment.
- Time (e.g., remove redundant tasks when introducing new tasks).
- Funding.
- People.
- Technical input to make the change.

SUPPORT

- Change embedded in social structures such as peer-to-peer teaching and feedback.
- Manager behaviour modelling and decision-making.
- Relationship development between individuals and teams.
- Coaching and feedback.
- Resilience.
- Regular reminders and discussion using current and new communication channels.
- Acknowledgment of, learning from, and celebration of progress and successes.

"This kind of sums up Will and Skill," observed Jeff.

Kristen sat up. "And MMAAP as well!" she exclaimed. "It was a previous CEO's 'map' to staff satisfaction. Remember Peter and his map Elena? He used to say that as long as he had his 'map' with him when dealing with staff issues, things always worked out. That's Meaning, Mastery, Authority, Acknowledgment, Purpose,"[14] she added in response to Chen's enquiring look.

"He was right!" Chen said. "There's plenty of research to back that up. If you can build those characteristics into job roles, there's a fair chance that people will be happier and more satisfied with their work. Will and Skill and MMAAP are different slices of the same thing: engaging staff and empowering them to lead change. Rules alone won't do it, although healthcare appears seriously wedded to rules as the key drivers of care—and change."

Kristen rolled her eyes. "It's rooted in our history," she sighed. "Health service organisations have traditionally been constructed on military model hierarchies and principles of 'Do what you're told and follow the rules'. Too often we treat people like robots and then expect them to act like caring, thinking, human beings. It's proving a hard habit to break. The concept of people wanting meaning in their work and helping them to thrive so their care does as well is a very slow burn. And MMAAP? Obviously good stuff, but each of those characteristics is a potential threat to authority and the way hierarchical human service organisations run. Many managers don't think that their staff should have a say and are afraid of the consequences of giving people autonomy. We're trying to break this down, but it's like swimming in treacle."

"I'm guessing that achieving the organisation's potential through helping staff to achieve their potential isn't high on the agenda either?" Chen grinned. "Or crafting staff engagement in improvement so it increases their job satisfaction? Without that, trying to get people to take initiative is always going to be an uphill battle. Making sure that the human need for meaning, mastery and connection are part of supporting and developing staff is the basis for getting the best out of people. It helps to operationalise change as well as motivating people to be involved in the first place." He smiled around the group. "As an outside observer I don't think command and control is serving you well. It creates a whole lot of unmotivated staff and learned helplessness, blocking the initiative and proactivity required to create great care every day. It's a particular challenge in human services."

"It is! Breaking down the hierarchies and providing some hope that things are getting better—and engaging staff in that—are our key weapons against helplessness. But you don't change these long established patterns overnight." Carol glanced at her watch. "I've lost track of the time thanks to this fascinating discussion! We'd better wrap it up. We've packed a lot in for one afternoon and you've given us plenty to chew on." She looked around the table. "Let's do a quick re-cap so we capture the key points for our discussions tomorrow. What do you know about change now that you didn't at lunchtime?"

Chen turned to the whiteboard and wrote as the group made one last effort. After two minutes, the list read:

- Change in complex systems requires staff to want to make the change and be able to make the change.

- Staff must internalise the need for change using both emotions and facts.

- Develop both the Will and Skill for change, with the first focus on Will (Heart, Head, and How).

- Use SWTA and AIDA to work on fostering the Will, and DKRS to reinforce Will and anchor the Skill.

- Try to make the new way increase job satisfaction and help staff to flourish by building in as much MMAAP as possible to the new way of doing things.

- Implement change using 'freedom within a framework' to support staff to make the new way of doing things work in both the predictability and unpredictability of business as usual.

"Phew," sighed Anton.

"Looks like a great afternoon's work," countered Carol cheerfully. "Yes, when you look at it like this, in a list and after a long discussion, it does seem overwhelming. But we'll develop it into our own KVHS model so it's easy to remember and work with. We want to get Great Care into the heads, hearts, and systems of KVHS without too many false starts. We already do many of these things, but now it's about doing them systematically, every time we want staff to take something and run with it. From now on, we're going to dig the foundations for change before we build the house, so the house doesn't fall down as often." She looked at each of her team in turn. "I'm hoping this will save us time in the long run, because there won't be so much rework for failed changes or so many arguments with staff because we won't be using ineffective PACEM change techniques." She turned to Chen. "Thank you so much, Professor! You've wrapped a semester's worth of lectures into one afternoon for us. We really appreciate it, and we'll use it—I promise."

"And we're still standing," chuckled Kristen, "even though we're sitting down."

"Thanks, everyone," Carol continued, putting her computer in her briefcase. "We've got a two-hour break until dinner. I suggest we all take advantage of this beautiful evening and get some fresh air before it gets too dark. Please don't sit in your room and do emails, as tempting as that might be. I'll see you in the restaurant at seven. Come on, Chen, I'll walk you out."

Much to her surprise, as she and Chen turned to go, a ripple of applause broke out around the table.

"We appreciate great material when we see it," Jeff said with a smile. "Our brains might be full right now, but there are some valuable processes and tips in there that I can see will go down really well with the doctors. Thanks."

Carol and Chen smiled back at the team and turned to go.

"And thank you from me again," said Carol sincerely as they descended the stairs. "As much as the change knowledge is valuable, the mindset shift I think we made today is more important. I couldn't have done it without you. Say hi to Angela for me and let's catch up soon."

"Sure, and when we do, the word 'change' is banned from the conversation!" laughed

Chen as he crossed the threshold into the warm evening.

The team did make the most of the break. Carol went for a swim in the hotel pool, Kristen and Anton did battle on the tennis court, Jeff hit the gym, Elena went for a walk and Pari used one of the vineyard bikes to take a ride around the property. A couple of them squeezed in a quick power nap. And they all still found time to dig into their emails before dinner.

Gathering dark clouds and a freshening breeze made them rethink their plans to eat outside as they met on the balcony for a pre-dinner drink, so they took a table inside. The restaurant was nearly full, as a bus of tourists was visiting the winery and staying overnight, so the group was pleased to find a booth in a corner of the restaurant where they could have a conversation without shouting above the hubbub. The evening passed pleasantly as they discussed a wide range of topics, excluding work, which Carol banned from the dinner table. The mood seemed convivial, and Carol allowed herself another moment of hope. Maybe they could pull a rabbit out of the leadership hat after all.

After their intense workshop day, they all welcomed an early night. "Be ready at 0800 hours sharp tomorrow for the next exciting episode!" Kristen reminded them as they scattered to their rooms.

Little did they know that the excitement awaiting them would not be the enjoyable kind.

CHAPTER ELEVEN

Carol was waiting in the conference room the next morning when the rest of the team arrived, chatting cheerfully. The banter died on their lips, though, as Carol did not return their greetings.

"What's up, Carol?" enquired Pari as they took their seats.

Carol held up a copy of the *Kinsley Valley Leader*. "Has anyone seen this?"

"That's today's edition? I had a quick glance online at breakfast to make sure we weren't on the front page—and we weren't—so I didn't look any further," replied Jeff. "What's wrong?"

"Yes, it's today's edition. They were delivering it to reception as I got back from my walk this morning, so I picked it up. I was happy to see we weren't on the front page as well. Until I saw this." She opened the paper and turned it to face them. "We're not on page one, thanks to our local politician's corruption scandal. But we did make page three."

" 'GREAT CARE CAN'T MASK BIG PROBLEMS,' " read Anton. "Bloody hell. How do they know about Great Care? What does it say?"

"It says"—Jeff had opened his computer and was reading from the screen—"that 'the CEO of KVHS has introduced a new fad, called Great Care, promising to provide Great Care for every patient. Staff have been told that they must now use this term, although there is no guidance on how to make it happen in practice. Sources close to the health service say it's just another attempt by the new CEO to inflict something new on staff to paper over poor management and bad care.' It goes on … but you get the gist," Jeff said, looking up with a frown.

The mood around the table plummeted as everyone digested the latest blow from the *Leader*.

Pari's face creased with indignation. She glanced around the table. Kristen looked too surprised for words. Anton was slumped in his chair reading the article on his tablet, while Jeff sat bolt upright, ready for action. Elena was grim faced, giving nothing away. Carol's face was flat and expressionless. She put the paper down and clasped her hands in front of her, knuckles white.

"How dare they portray Carol as a bad manager trying to cover up problems with a fad when in fact she's doing the exact opposite!" Pari exclaimed, crossing her arms defiantly.

Kristen recovered her powers of speech. "*Who* is giving them the information? It's time to get it stopped, once and for all. Not only is it untrue, but if it continues, it's going to kill any hope of embedding GC. I know some people who are already using the bad press as an excuse not to participate, and this is a boost to their cause. And we'll never win back the community ... oh, no!" She slapped her forehead dramatically. "Our next Great Care community workshop is next week. It won't be a happy crowd!"

"It'll be alright," Jeff reassured her. "It gives us an opportunity to counter the *Leader*'s rubbish, at least. As for who is doing the leaking, they may have slipped up by providing so much detail."

"What do you mean?" Pari uncrossed her arms and leaned forward, intrigued.

"Well, by my reckoning, it's got to be someone who's actually attended a GC workshop," replied Jeff. "There are details about Great Care in that article that could only have been gleaned from being there in person."

"That's around a hundred and fifty people across ten workshops now," said Pari, quietly.

"That's not too many." Jeff shuffled impatiently in his chair. "Pari, can you get us the workshops lists? There can't be too many people there who are disaffected enough to take this risk. We should be able to narrow it down without too much trouble." Pari nodded. "I know your strategy has been to address this quietly and not give it much oxygen, Carol," he continued, glancing at his silent CEO. "And at first, I agreed with you. But it hasn't worked. Someone is playing with us, and it's time to confront it head-on."

"And we have social media!" Anton announced, fingers flying over his tablet. "Don't worry, just the usual haters who are happy that today's Leader has given them something else to attack. Nothing worth our attention."

Carol grimaced. *When did "the usual haters" become an acceptable term?*

"You haven't said much, Elena," continued Jeff, who was on a roll, responding to the crisis with typical ED-physician vigour. "There must be some dissatisfied nurses. There usually are."

"Well, seeing as they make up the biggest slice of the staff, you should expect that there will be more unhappy nurses than other staff," responded Elena testily, lips pursed. "And what about allied health and non-clinical staff?"

Pari gazed at her thoughtfully. She wasn't sure that Elena's heart was really in what she was saying, whereas the other team members were stirred up and ready for action. "I know, I've got my antennae up. But I haven't seen or heard anything unusual from the allied health-ers," Pari said.

"Elena has a point. We shouldn't focus only on clinical people," continued Jeff. "Kristen and Anton, we'll need you to have a look at the workshop lists as well."

"You bet. Bring it on." Kristen and Anton chorused their assent.

"Hold it!" Carol held up her hand and everyone stopped, surprised. "Look at us. We're giving whoever it is exactly what they want. This has completely distracted us from what we're here to do, which is to get Great Care embedded at KVHS."

"But we can't just roll over, Carol," said Anton. Everyone nodded their agreement.

"'Roll over'? Believe me, I have no intention of rolling over." Carol sat up very straight and looked each of them in the eye. "If you think that, you don't know me very well. Jeff's right, I did want to keep this problem quiet and try to fix it behind the scenes. I didn't want to make a big show of it, because people who indulge in this sort of ridiculous behaviour are usually attention seekers, and I had no intention of giving them what they wanted. But that doesn't mean I've been sitting on my hands."

"I know you haven't," asserted Kristen. "How many meetings have you had with the editor of the Leader since you started here—three? And the Board members are using their community networks to scan for clues."

"One of my staff has been monitoring social media, as we agreed a couple of months ago," added Anton. "But no luck, yet, unfortunately."

"Don't mistake a low-key approach for not caring," Carol continued. "I'm absolutely determined not to let this sway us from our path. We're doing something great here at Kinsley Valley, something that's going to make a difference to thousands of lives: consumers and staff. We're going to lead the way in providing consistently high quality rural healthcare. I believe that together, we can do this. Unless the government gets rid of me, nothing is going to stop me from making that happen." She brushed a strand of hair behind her ear and took a breath, weighing her words. "The future is in our hands today, and this morning's planning session is critical to our progress. Having said that, I agree with you all: it's time for more direct action to tackle this. I propose we complete our morning as planned and spend lunch on a new *Leader* response strategy. All in favour?"

"I'm with you!" Anton saluted.

"Let's go!" urged Kristen.

Jeff and Elena nodded their assent. Pari threw a relieved smile Carol's way.

Maybe the Leader has done us a strange sort of favour, mused Carol, noting their determined faces. The familiar leaden feeling in the pit of her stomach reminded her that the newspaper had delivered her a body blow, but the positive energy in the room was definitely helping. And she meant every word of her speech. She had no intention of letting bad press get in the way of getting this health service back to where it needed to be for the KVHS community.

"Great," Carol said. "Ready, Pari? Let's talk 'where to from here.' Has everyone got their copy of the framework that Pari presented yesterday?"

Pari handed out a high-level plan for the Executive Team's role in embedding Great Care, as everyone turned or swiped to the framework in their papers or on their computers. They studied the plan as Pari talked them through it.

"This is an extrapolation of Carol's great care roadmap, to give us more guidance on our role," Pari explained. "I've taken the six key roadmap actions and developed sub actions within each that the exec really has to get done to progress things." The list read:

One: Paint a Picture of the point-of-care quality we want to be known for.

1.1. Define the components of KVHS Great Care with a broad range of staff and consumers, and the organisational systems and roles required to provide it for every consumer, every time. Make it real for staff using plain language and reflecting what they come to work to do each day. Link with staff and consumer experiences of good and poor care at KVHS.

Two: Plot the components required to achieve Great Care into a framework: Purpose, People, Pillars.

2.1. Define and align the roles of the Board, Executive Team and relevant committees in leading the establishment of KVHS Great Care across all KVHS services as a key driver of the KVHS strategic plan. Organise key safety and quality committee agendas using the Great Care goals and governance system components, and organise reporting and discussion using these headings. Ensure all Board committees are aligned with the KVHS Great Care goals.

2.2. Perform an organisational assessment of GC strengths and gaps—for the "front of house" point-of-care GC goals and actions, and the "back of house" governance systems—to identify areas requiring further development to support the achievement of KVHS Great Care.

Three: Pilot, practise and learn.

3.1. Share the KVHS Great Care goals and actions with managers and staff and work with willing volunteers to identify key organisation-wide and local strategies for achieving them in a limited number of services. Use the lessons learned to develop the organisational implementation plan.

Four: Plan to make the Point-of-care Picture a reality across the whole organisation.

4.1. Select priorities based on the stocktake gaps and identify the organisation-wide strategies required to close them, for both the point-of-care goals and the governance systems. Develop an annual operational point-of-care KVHS Great Care Implementation Plan with organisation-wide priorities, strategies and measures to be achieved in care delivery in the next twelve months for each goal and governance system. Incorporate current improvement initiatives and external compliance requirements.

4.2. Develop the "back of house" governance and support systems plan, integrating compliance requirements. Make required role, agenda and reporting changes to quality and safety committees.

4.3. Identify the measures and information required to monitor the achievement of each KVHS Great Care goal and develop new data collection where required. Incorporate external reporting requirements into goal monitoring and reporting.

Five: Put it into practice and persist to make it business as usual.

5.1. Discuss the implementation plan with consumers, managers, and staff. Work with department heads and service managers to develop their local annual plans for making the four Great Care goals a reality for their consumers every day. Incorporate consumer and staff ideas and relevant lessons from the implementation pilot/s. Clarify roles and responsibilities for achieving the goals and embed in staff management and support systems. Promote the GC goals as everyone's priorities, every day.

5.2. Put the plans into action. Implement the operational GC and local GC plans, as well as the GC goal monitoring and reporting system for committees and line managers.

5.3. Monitor, provide feedback and discuss progress in committees and through line management. Adjust organisation-wide strategies as required to achieve the goals.

5.4. Identify, learn from, and spread success.

Six: Promote and Promulgate Progress.

6.1. Annually, the Executive Team presents an evaluation of the Great Care strategy to the Board, using objective and subjective data to show progress with the Great Care goal consistency, lessons learned, and successes and changes in consumer and staff perception and experience. Engage consumers and staff in painting the picture of Great Care: where it is and where it needs to go."

Pari put her papers down and sat back.

"Thanks, Pari," Carol said. "How is everyone digesting that?"

"Makes sense." Anton was studying his computer screen with interest. "But we're not following the steps in order, are we? We're a bit all over the place."

"Exactly what I was thinking." Elena nodded her agreement.

"Yes, well spotted," said Carol. "We're not exactly progressing this in a linear fashion.

Clearly, we have several actions happening at once. That's life in the messiness of complexity. It's important to have a map, and to know where we are and where we're going, but it's never a straight line to get from A to B. Today, we're going to consolidate the actions we've begun and plan some that we haven't. Let's start with a check on action two, because if we don't get that right, GC really will be just a fad."

Over the next hour, the team worked in small groups to discuss leadership and committee roles for the next phase of Great Care development. Elena was unexpectedly the strongest of them all on clarifying their roles. She volunteered to take notes on the whiteboard as they divided up the leadership of implementation actions, goals, and governance pillars, according to their operational responsibilities.

"Don't look so surprised, Carol," Elena said as she recorded the last of their conversation and sat down. "I know that 'everyone's responsible' sounds good but doesn't work very well in practice. Nurses understand this. We each have to know exactly what our deliverables are. I've been working with my nurses on role clarity over the past few months. I can't very well expect them to commit to it if we do something different, can I?"

"Good job, Elena! I think we've got that sorted," Kristen declared. "If we're not all walking and talking the same Great Care language, we might as well not bother." She picked up the pot and poured some coffee. "And that includes Board and operational committees. I've already heard five different versions of what GC means from committee meetings I've been to in the past week. We've got to get those agendas aligned with the GC goals and governance pillars. Everything has to be about supporting managers and staff to make those four goals a reality for every consumer. My division will work with managers to embed GC into people's roles— position descriptions, induction, training, performance review, and professional development—so that it all supports people to fulfil their role in achieving GC."

"That reminds me," said Pari, reaching across the table to pick up a handful of almonds. "We've got the Comms Team and the Great Care Ambassadors working on creative ways to present GC visually, showing the goals and roles and governance supports in a way that everyone will understand."

"That's right – I've got their posters with me to show everyone. We've been careful to make sure the messages pass the 'take-home' test," said Kristen. "Seb liked lots of jargon," she added in response to Carol's enquiring look. "He thought it made us look like we knew what we were talking about. But it confused everyone, including us. It got so bad that I started a secret rule with my divisional heads: nothing went out to middle managers and staff—no email, memo, directive or poster—unless our families understood it. Honestly, some of the reactions I got from my mum about Seb's memos!" She shook her head at the memory. "Hilarious. 'Is this the United Nations or my local hospital?' she'd ask in disgust. My staff got pretty good at translating the bureaucratic gobbledygook into plain language."

She held up three posters.

"I've seen them around. They look great. And restructuring the quality committees and agendas around the GC goals should reinforce the messages," said Anton, leaning forward and pushing his glasses up his nose.

Carol's shoulders relaxed. The conversation about accountability in no way resembled the one they'd had at workshop one—fortunately! "Thanks, everyone. We're now miles ahead of many health service executive teams I've known who didn't engage with their care quality role." She smiled around the table. "Right, time for a break. Remember, it's small group work after morning tea, so go straight to the breakout spaces, and I'll see you back here in about an hour."

*****

After a quick break, the team broke into three groups to prioritise the point of care and governance gaps identified in yesterday's discussion, in preparation for developing the annual GC operational plan. Andy and Chen's content from the previous day was discussed and integrated into their plans. When they reconvened in the conference room, Elena and Jeff kicked off the report back from the group work.

"We think things are progressing, even if slowly," Jeff began. "Elena and I will continue working with the clinical leaders to improve results in the key Department of Health indicators. We've found that a lot of the related problems are due to erosion of compliance with policy and procedure over the years due to lack of focus. It's not that we don't know what to do, we're just not doing it consistently. So some of that, at least, should be relatively straightforward to resolve."

"We also found some policies that weren't being followed because they're … ridiculous," continued Elena. "Old policies that haven't been reviewed by the people who have to use them. The world has moved on, but the policy hasn't. We've also finally realised that it's a good thing to take tasks away from staff if they're not adding value. Change shouldn't always be more things to do. If we introduce a new way, we should remove the old way—or streamline parts of the old way that we have to keep. Otherwise, Great Care will be seen as adding to their work burden, not relieving it."

Jeff nodded as he consulted his notes. "There are a few things we've prioritised as not yet consistently addressed across the organisation, such as the use of evidence-based practice for some high-acuity and high-volume conditions under the Effective goal, and exchange of patient information for inter-ward transfers, under the Connected goal."

"We also want to work on nursing outcomes for the Effective goal," continued Elena. "And there's too much variation around the use of interpreters for care planning within the Personal goal. Some non-English-speaking patients are engaged well, but some have no idea about their care plan. Jeff and I were also thinking about a way to acknowledge individual staff or teams that succeed in delivering a GC goal as well, so we can capture and recognise good work. We want something that's meaningful and not frivolous. No ridiculous competitions."

"Hmmm." Carol cocked her head to one side. "That reminds me. Nancy mentioned something the other day about applying for an annual grant from the estate of one of her mayor predecessors—I can't remember her name …"

"Oh, that would be the Kath Phelan Fund!" exclaimed Kristen. "I heard they were setting it up. What a good idea! She was a great supporter of the hospital as well and headed up the volunteers for years after she retired from the mayor job. Perhaps the team or individual demonstrating 'the greatest' Great Care could receive some funds to spend in their service?"

"Sounds like a plan," agreed Jeff.

Anton and Carol held a quick whispered consultation before Anton leaned forward and pushed his glasses up his nose. "Carol and I will work on some of the gaps in the Leadership and Culture governance and systems. We'll first focus on budget priorities and developing a GC culture survey with Kristen's People and Culture team. We've already discussed committees and our leadership role today, and consumer partnerships yesterday." He glanced at Carol, who nodded at him to continue. "The other thing that's happening in that space is a more streamlined pathway for getting consumer and staff perspectives onto the Executive Team agenda and how to better keep everyone in the loop. As Carol says, if we stop listening, we're doomed. We're also working with the Health Information and IT managers to integrate the GC goals into the upcoming electronic health record."

"And," Kristen continued, "I've assigned my marketing and fundraising team to work with Pari to craft the information generated by the Great Care workshops and online survey into messages about creating Great Care every day, using the AIDA model. We've started trialling those messages at new staff induction, with Carol taking the lead on why KVHS is a Great Care organisation and asking the new staff what they bring to KVHS that will uniquely contribute. The Comms Team has done a great job with the visuals for this as well. " She held up a second set of posters as Jeff checked his vibrating phone.

"New staff also have a much better first week than they used to," Kristen went on as Jeff left the room to answer the call. "Now they have a buddy who welcomes them, keeps an eye on them and inculcates them into the ways of Great Care. They also have a meeting with a consumer or family member to be reminded first-hand about what's important, and a lunch with their new colleagues. What else? Oh, yes, the training and development team is organising the annual training calendar around the four goals, so that all training equips participants to make Great Care happen for every consumer. What's up next is a new Great Care supervision and mentoring system in the pipeline, and staff professional development plans to build strengths in the four goals. We also have a major proposal we want to discuss with you all, but we'll hold our fire on that until later."

"Pari?" enquired Carol, turning to her.

"My team needs to improve the improvement system, which sounds strange, I know." Pari paused for a minute to consider this before continuing. "Risk management was completely revised before the last accreditation assessment, so our focus now is on improvement science, change, and transformation. We need to work with Anton's team to broaden our measurement and reporting to include information on each GC goal, get it flowing in and out of committees and to divisional and department heads, and find ways to present the data so it makes more sense and is more user friendly. And the improvement team will develop its own skills, so we can support others better. They really need to be master Will and Skill change agents, and they aren't. But they will be," she concluded in a decisive tone.

"We'll need to integrate the CPC's ideas about measurement into that information flow," noted Carol.

"And all the current compliance measures and activities," Jeff said, catching Carol's comment as he returned to his chair. "We can't have Great Care in one place and compliance as a separate thing in another. Our compliance requirements and standards must be integrated into the framework, so they help us create Great Care." He ran his hand over his crew cut and took off his glasses. "Phew. That's a lot of water coming down the river. We don't want to ride staff too hard or we'll get a big push back. Remember, people, not robots. Standardisation with flexibility. Evidence with resilience. Freedom within a framework."

"Yes, Jeff!" Carol said. "Today's planning will be prioritised and implemented over the next twelve to twenty-four months. We'll stay aware of pacing, so people aren't too overwhelmed. There will be periods of overwhelm, of course; that's life in healthcare. But we'll try to keep it manageable." She noted that Elena's lip curled at this statement. "I know it's hard. So we have to work together. I rely on each of you to lead it and to keep in touch with your staff and 'take the temperature' regularly to see how they're coping with it all. Having said that, I'd like to remind you of a certain list that you didn't show much interest in last time I raised it." She handed around pocket-sized cards.

"What's this?" Anton asked, frowning over his card. It read:

Leading Great Care:[A4]

1. Start Where You Really Are.
2. Then Start Where They Are.
3. Develop a set of shared, non-negotiable goals for greatness.
4. Embrace the hard yards together.
5. Make it as easy as possible to win.
6. Model the behaviour you want to see in the team.

"Does *anyone* remember?" enquired Carol with mock despair. Apart from the sound of five brains furiously attempting to retrieve a memory, the room was quiet.

Elena broke the tension. "Oh, I know!" she exclaimed, looking pleased with herself.

"It's on your office noticeboard, isn't it, Carol?"

"Yes, that's right. I did try to raise it with you all a couple of months back, but the sound of your indifference was deafening," Carol joked. "So here it is again, on individual cards for your convenience." She chuckled. "I am serious about us all employing these tips when we're guiding managers and staff through the change process to achieve Great Care. A mentor gave them to me many years ago and I've found them invaluable. As you see, the tips incorporate a lot of what we discussed with Chen, so they're going to be helpful when you're working with your staff to make the changes required for Great Care." She glanced at her watch. "And something else that will help?—is lunch. I know you won't mind using the time to discuss a couple of things: the key messages for our staff from this couple of days and developing our KVHS *Leader* strategy." Carol sat back and sipped her water.

"Our KVHS 'leaker' strategy, you mean," muttered Kristen darkly.

"And after lunch?" asked Elena, gathering her things. "I don't remember seeing anything on the agenda. I fear you may have some horrible team bonding exercise ready for us."

Carol laughed. "Ha! No, that's not me. I believe the best bonding exercise we can undertake is what we've been doing here these past two days: working together to create Great Care. We don't need to climb trees or shoot rapids together to be a team. What we're trying to do is way more challenging than any team-building exercise." Carol was pleased to see Elena nod without hesitation. She continued. "This afternoon is blank, because once we're finished what we need to do, we're all going home. Everyone in this room has worked their backsides off over the past few months. I can't give you anything much in return except some time now and again. We're making good progress today and probably only have an hour or so of discussion left after a quick lunch. We're going to catch up on the incredible Great Care work that's being done around the organisation and discuss some big plans for embedding quality that have nothing to do with the quality team." She looked around at their surprised faces. "I know you don't have any meetings back at work as you expected to be here until four. I can't stop you from working at home—that's your choice—but please try to relax this weekend. Now, I'm starving. Let's eat!"

CHAPTER TWELVE

When the lunch strategy discussion wrapped up, Pari grabbed a coffee and made her way onto the balcony for some fresh air. The weather had changed; the air was chillier and dark clouds loomed overhead. She gazed across the vines to the sheets of rain obscuring the nearby hills, lost in her thoughts.

"That's good work you're doing with the medical ward," said a voice behind her. Pari jumped and turned. "Oh, Carol, you gave me a fright! I was miles away."

"Sorry to interrupt your reverie!" Carol leaned on the balcony railing next to her. "It's probably good for your brain to do a little day dreaming after this intense couple of days. I wanted to say thank you for your perseverance with all this. It will get better, you know. We'll plough through this stage of sorting out how to make it all happen; then we'll we put it in a plan and just do it!"

"Thanks, Carol, I appreciate it," said Pari, and smiled. "You know, the medical ward wasn't so bad once I got over myself and realised that they don't come to work to help me progress my agenda!"

"I know it's tough, Pari. Believe me, I've been there." Carol's brow furrowed at the memory. "I made plenty of mistakes and wouldn't have survived if it wasn't for the fabulous mentors and coaches I had." She turned to Pari. "So, I've been thinking. You seemed to enjoy Chen's session yesterday."

"Very much," responded Pari, grinning. "I still need to process it, but it really clicked with me: that we must work with our organisation as it really behaves, rather than as we'd like it to behave. That means that change won't often be cut and dried, more like messy and iterative. But it should stick!"

"Not to mention being reminded that our staff are actually real people, no matter how much of a shock that was to Jeff and Elena," chuckled Carol.

They looked out across the vineyard for a moment. Carol broke the silence. "I haven't forgotten I promised you a coach, Pari. How would you like it to be Chen?"

"Wow. That would be amazing," Pari answered with a wide smile.

"Think it over and let me know. If you decide you'd rather have someone else, no problem." She looked up at the dark sky. "Whoops, there's a drop of rain. Let's go back in."

*****

Carol led the group in a few deep-breathing exercises after lunch to get some oxygen flowing. "This will be a full session," she warned them. "But after that, the hard planning work will be done. Hang in there!" She sat down, picked up her tea and took a sip. "Kristen—your turn."

"All this talk over the past day and a bit won't get us anywhere unless we address the most important people in the whole change rollout," Kristen began, moving to the whiteboard and picking up a marker. "Anyone willing to guess who they might be?"

"Apart from us?" grinned Anton, clicking his pen. "Consumers?" asked Jeff.

"They are obviously critically important in helping us get this right, as we discussed yesterday with Andy. But I'm talking staff now. Anyone?"

"Oh! Of course. It's the middle managers," Elena stated matter-of-factly, arms crossed.

"Correct!" responded Kristen with fake shock.

"Don't look at me like that! I do know some things about running a health service," Elena observed curtly.

"Well, you are a surprise package." Kristen grinned.

"That's because health services pretty much run on their middle managers, especially their nursing middle managers," Elena shot back. "They can make things happen—and they can make things not happen, if they choose. Don't I know it," she finished quietly, shaking her head.

Kristen threw her a sympathetic glance and wrote "KVHS middle managers" on the whiteboard. "If we can equip and support the middle managers to lead Great Care in their services, we'll be nine-tenths of the way to making it business as usual. In fact, I think that a lot of our care quality problems would disappear. We've got to get away from 'doing quality on Tuesdays' as a set of compliance tasks that don't help staff create Great Care. We want 'quality' to represent the standard of what happens at point of care every day, and to do this, creating GC must become central to all managers' roles. Something they create." She made some notes on the whiteboard as she spoke, radiating like spokes around a middle manager hub.

"Line management isn't only about keeping services ticking over, meeting targets, and getting through the day. It's about them leading and managing their services to work well: to provide high quality care and experiences. As Chen said, they, along with the staff themselves, create the way work is socialised in their services. Staff take notice of what a manager appears to treat as important." She drew a loop with the words "competence" at one end and "confidence" at the other. "So, I'm proposing we introduce an intensive development program. Not only to help them implement GC, but to support them to be better managers more generally, so they feel more confident with things like getting the best out of their staff and creating a positive culture in their service that supports Great Care."

"More work for my already overworked managers?" drawled Elena, scanning the whiteboard. "And what's this competence/confidence business?"

"We actually want to help make clinical manager roles a bit easier." Kristen glanced at Elena but refused to take her bait. "They haven't had much attention over the past few years, have they? But we'll be careful about it. We'll ask them what they need to help them do their jobs better and how we can streamline their work where possible. We think that's the best way to build clinical leadership: building their strengths to help them feel more competent and confident, so they'll want to lead GC, every day and be able to do it. Happy managers, happy staff, happy consumers! We'll build in the MMAAP characteristics of roles that give the greatest job satisfaction: mastery, meaning, acknowledgment, autonomy, purpose; remember mentioning that yesterday? Resilience and working to strengths. Understanding what can be controlled and what must be influenced and how to do this."

She pointed at the whiteboard. "Competence breeds confidence, as Carol has reminded us, so our aim is to make them not only better managers, but happier and more satisfied in their role. That includes the doctors with management roles as well, Jeff."

Now it was Jeff's turn to look concerned. "Whoa!" he exclaimed, running his hand over his crew cut.

"What management training have your senior doctors had?" asked Carol, turning to him. "Not much, I bet. We seem to like to dump our clinicians in management roles and see if they sink or swim. If they sink, we blame them. But they can't magically acquire the skills they need overnight. Unless they choose to do a related qualification or training, in my experience, they spend their days struggling to manage their staff, meet targets, and make change happen, all the while trying heroically not to show how hard it is. Then we wonder why they get burned out and cranky."

"Don't worry," Kristen said, "the training will be well designed by my professional development team, using adult learning principles. Short, sharp, face-to-face sessions with supplementary online material. All evidence-based and no time wasting, with built-in MMAAP. We want to help managers thrive, not just survive." She sat down and handed the whiteboard marker to Pari. The room went quiet while Elena and Jeff digested the idea.

"Alright." Elena uncrossed her arms and sat up a little straighter. "If it's going to help the nurse managers, I'll support it—as long as I have input into the content."

"Input! We want you to teach some of it!" answered Kristen, looking relieved.

"But don't waste your time teaching them improvement tools," Elena continued. "All the nurse unit managers have done their Lean Six Sigma training. Seb was very big on the Lean method."

"Obviously worked a treat in the medical ward," Jeff said.

"Couldn't help yourself, could you, Jeff?" Elena shot back, sitting up. "Which is very game of you seeing as doctors created the medical service problems."

Jeff opened his mouth to respond and thought better of it. He busied himself polishing his glasses.

Carol jumped in. "Okay, that's enough. He's baiting you, Elena, ignore him."

"That's great that they have those skills." Pari took a breath and dived in. "Lean is really useful for improving flow, adding value, and reducing waste, and will be particularly pertinent for the Connected and Personal goals, I think. But it's only one tool in the toolbox." She turned to Elena. "We need to sort out exactly what we're trying to do and choose the right tools for the job. As the old saying goes: if the only tool you have is a hammer, you treat everything like it's a nail. My team is developing a practical improvement toolbox to support better data collection and analysis, problem definition, solution generation, change, and implementation. We'll work with Kristen's professional development training team to do a needs analysis, to ascertain what the managers feel they need to know and do to make GC happen in their service. Then we'll develop the curriculum from there, so it's absolutely focused and useful."

"Don't forget to include the defining consumer questions and Will and Skill," Carol reminded them. "And while we're discussing training, why don't you explain how you're developing the GC Ambassadors, Pari?"

Pari quickly ran through the "train the trainer" program to skill up staff across the organisation who'd indicated at the workshops that they'd like to have a role in making Great Care a reality. "I know they're already out and about, as we've seen from their work on the posters, because we can't curb their enthusiasm!" she laughed.

Kristen joined in. "And the good news is, I've already had two of my staff tell me how much they enjoyed the workshops and how excited they are to be GC Ambassadors. Great start, Pari."

Pari grinned and continued. "The GC Ambassadors will help make the point-of-care changes across the organisation. The idea is to have a large team of skilled people to guide our services to implement GC so we share the load and no one has to do too much. They'll learn from my team as we develop the GC pilots. We already have eight up and running."

"Eight!" exclaimed Elena. "How on earth did you persuade eight services to pilot Great Care?"

"Yes, what is this quality witchcraft you practise, Pari?" laughed Kristen.

"Isn't that too many?" enquired Jeff. "I'm a bit rusty on my project management, but I know to do these things properly takes time and effort."

"We didn't intend to run so many pilots," agreed Carol with a shrug. "We'd thought three—four at most. But we had lots of volunteers from the workshops and we didn't want to dampen their enthusiasm. It means that Pari and her team are super busy helping them all get set up and going, but it's a great way to build momentum and goodwill for GC, so we decided it was worth it."

"And each of them is based on data indicating a specific issue for improvement," Pari added, "either objectively or from consumer input and feedback. They didn't pluck them out of thin air. A couple are ideas the team has been wanting to try for months or even years, so are excited and motivated to pilot. And everyone is integrating relevant quality standards, so it combines compliance with improvement and, in a couple of places, transformation."

"I know of a couple of the nursing-led pilots, but what are the rest doing?" asked Elena. She put her phone down and leaned forward with interest.

"Oh, there's some amazing ideas for creating Great Care," Pari continued happily, relieved that she wasn't going to be told to reduce the number of pilots. "The projects are so creative. For example, rehab is working on 'G'Day.' When we explored their Great Care gaps, they said they were concerned that many patients were sitting around between exercise sessions with nothing to do. Some of them get quite down, and this appears to affect their attitude to their rehabilitation. The staff identified that this wasn't very Personal care and was impacting on Effective care. The rehab consumers suggested that being asked if anything could be done to improve their day would make them feel more cared about, so together they came up with the idea that everyone working in rehab—doctors, nurses, and allied health—will ask 'What can I do for you to help you have a good day?' "

"Doctors!" exclaimed Elena with a sniff.

"Yes! You know what a tight-knit team they are down there. Their nurse manager doesn't take no for an answer. Once the team identified this as the GC component they wanted to work on, she made it an expectation of everyone who works in that service. And it has to be sincere; no lip service, or she's onto them."

"I don't suppose you've made any progress with the medical ward?" enquired Jeff. "Well—" Pari began, but Kristen cut her off.

"Let me tell it! You'll be far too modest, Pari." Kristen gave Pari an encouraging look. "The medical ward is piloting a GC initiative. Hooray! Somehow Pari managed to turn them from reluctant to revitalised!"

"Thanks, Kristen," said Pari, feeling herself go red. "But they've been fantastic. Once I stopped haranguing them to meet my needs, and we discussed what would improve their lives by improving their patients' lives, the ideas started to flow."

Speaking rapidly, she outlined their idea and how the whole ward was contributing to it. "They're going to make videos explaining the three most common conditions on the medical ward. They have a lot of patients transferred back from city hospitals, where they've been diagnosed with and treated for chronic conditions. Many of the older patients who don't travel often to the city, even when they're well, are so stressed by the whole experience that they remember nothing that they're told. So the staff here spend hours explaining things like diabetes and cancer and heart conditions." She stopped to take a sip of her tea.

"They're not always very good explanations, either," Anton declared with feeling. "My dad was admitted here when he came home from a city hospital last year, after finding out he had a bad heart problem. He was back in here three times before someone explained properly to him and the family how to manage it."

"Exactly, and they've finally realised this," Pari said. "It's not good for the patients to be unclear about their conditions, and it's not good for the staff to see their 'instructions' misinterpreted. It often results in unexpected readmissions, which is bad for everyone." She looked sympathetically at Anton. "So, they've formed teams for each of the three conditions with the most frequently asked questions, including consumers, allied health, nurses, and doctors, to contribute to content and share stories. Each team is making a short video, using their phones, explaining how to look after things post discharge. They've invited the consumers and staff who love to talk and teach, of course, to star in the videos, and everyone else is having fun developing the content, using their experience as well as evidence." She reached into her bag and pulled out her phone, rapidly swiping the screen as she spoke. "I think it's made both staff and consumers feel more valued, because they know this stuff so well and have such great tips to contribute. They figure this will improve aspects of the Effective and Safe GC goals, and save staff a ton of time as well. I've got their first video here if anyone would like to see it."

Elena reached out for the phone and Pari passed it to her. "That's really impressive, Pari," Carol said, as Elena and Jeff watched the video, smiling and pointing at the screen as they recognised their colleagues. "And I hear that community health is looking at the Connected goal. Apparently, there's a chasm somewhere between acute and community mental health care where some consumers disappear without a trace from our services. Clients don't turn up for their appointments, or if they do, community health often doesn't have the information they need to treat them properly or has to ask them to tell their story all over again, which the consumers hate. They're going to work with the inpatient mental health team and consumer group to see if they can bridge it."

"I think they're calling that one 'Let's Stick Together.' " Pari smiled. "Then there's OT—of course!" she laughed. "There was no way they weren't going to be part of it. They're measuring the effectiveness of a new postoperative exercise method for elbow fractures with one of the orthopaedic surgeons and the physio team. It's quite a new treatment, so it's a good opportunity for them to see what's really going on from both the consumer and clinician perspectives and work on their Personal and Effective goals at the same time. They're measuring using PROMs."

"PROMs?" chorused Kristen and Anton, looking at each other.

"Remember, Andy and Jeff talked about them yesterday?" Carol reminded them.

"Oh, yes, but the memory chip in my brain is full!" Anton said. "Yesterday was so long ago. I don't think that item got saved." He rubbed his forehead vigorously.

"Patient Reported Outcome Measures," Jeff said as he handed the phone back to Pari. "Great video."

"Impressive work!" Elena added with a rare broad smile.

Carol took up the pilot story. "The other four pilots are probably closer to what we want Great Care ultimately to be about. Improvement projects are really important to improve certain aspects of care, as we discussed with Chen. They'll be stepping stones to Great Care. But to achieve Great Care every day for every consumer, we'll also need a broader, more holistic approach. We want people to *think* Great Care." She looked down the pilot list Pari had prepared for her. "The four remaining services are looking at how they can make one whole goal—including its component actions— happen for every patient. For example, Day Procedure Unit has chosen the Personal goal. With so many patients coming and going through the unit, care was becoming transactional and they weren't really seeing the person. They're working with a group of consumers on which actions in the Personal goal are not happening consistently, and what needs to change for everyone to experience the complete 'Personal Care' package."

"Then there's aged care and admissions," continued Pari, fiddling with the whiteboard marker in front of her.

"Aged care is working on 'Good Health, Good Life', reviewing all their Safe and Effective care goal actions, as the number of residents and home care clients with increased acuity and multiple chronic conditions continues to grow. They're sharpening their clinical protocols and refreshing all the care plans, to improve quality of life through better quality of health. It will also help them achieve the new aged care standards. And the admissions crew is collaborating with the bed and theatre managers and the surgical ward on the Connected care goal to see what it would take for all actions in that goal to be met for emergency surgical patients. They're working with Susie, using Lean method to redesign the flow from door to bed. Even the local ambulance service is getting involved. They've discussed it with Prof Yang and apparently, she's quite supportive. I imagine it won't be too long before they're knocking on your door for some IT support, Anton."

Anton clicked his pen with one hand and gave her a thumbs up with the other.

"And the last pilot must be the cancer service," said Elena, throwing Anton a look that silenced his pen. She ignored his indignant glare and turned to Pari. "I think they've developed a tool to spot when Great Care is not happening in real time so they can fix it and also measure it. Is that right?"

"Yes!" Pari nodded enthusiastically. "This one is a joint project between the cancer consumer collaborative and the cancer service clinical leaders. After meeting with the collaborative, the clinical leaders in the service decided to tackle all four goals with 'Project Lookout.' Staff will constantly scan for clues as they go about their work that tell them if patients are receiving Great Care. They're also trying to make it easy for consumers to raise or lower the Great Care flag, depending on what they're experiencing. The night staff have a big role to play in this one as risk doesn't disappear just because patients are meant to be asleep! It's a form of active GC management and real-time measurement. I think I've got a slide on it here somewhere." She clicked through her slide deck. "Ah, here it is. They've developed some simple criteria based on the core actions in each goal. No doubt they'll evolve it over time, but this is a good start that we can spread to other areas after the pilot. They've started to discuss the criteria at every handover." The slide read:

Personal

P1:   A patient and/or family asks for information we thought we'd given them.

P2:   A patient and/or family queries a care decision.

P3:   A patient does not feel clean and comfortable.

Connected

C1:   A treatment or service did not go as planned.

C2:   Something happened in the care pathway the patient/family didn't expect.

C3:   There have been conflicting messages given to the patient and family about the care plan.

Effective

E1:   The treatment is not achieving the desired results.

E2:   The treatment in place varies from relevant guidelines.

E3:   The staff skill mix is not a good match for the patient's condition.

Safe

S1:   The patient is in pain.

S2:   The patient is distressed.

S3:   The patient has experienced an adverse event and/or near miss.

The group sat back and regarded the criteria admiringly.

"You know, there's something interesting about these pilots," mused Jeff. "They're all interdisciplinary. We don't have doctor GC pilots, or nurse and allied health GC pilots and non-clinical GC pilots. They're goal-based. Maybe we can break down some of our silos after all." He studied the screen intently as he spoke.

"Of course," Kristen said with a shrug. "Consumers want connected care. They don't want silos any more than we do."

"I want to check something, Pari," Jeff continued, turning to her. "Are you also sourcing ideas from the literature and other health services who've done similar work? Where you can find it, at least? That's really important. Let's try to implement things with a track record where we can, even if we have to adapt them for our environment. We don't want to waste time reinventing wheels."

"We are." Pari nodded. "We're trying to marry the good ideas with what's worked in other places and preferably been well evaluated. It won't always work like that, but we're trying to give ourselves the best chance of success. And if that means borrowing ideas from other organisations, I'm all for it. We're also building on what's working in the pilots to spread across the rest of the organisation. I think I've got the planning questions we're using with service managers on a slide, if you'd like to see them?"

Heads nodded all around. Pari clicked to the slide, which read:

What are we already doing well to achieve this goal?

Where do compliance and standards fit?

What would need to change from the way things are done now? —in terms of:

- Care planning and practice?
- Policy and procedure?
- Skills and tools?
- Meeting agendas structured around the four GC goals?
- Reminders and triggers?
- Systems and roles?

How could we work together with consumers to help us make these goals a more consistent reality?

What creative and fun things could we do to make more of the goal actions happen for every person?

What support would we need from our organisation?

What can we learn about how to make this happen from the literature, other KVHS services or other organisations?

"It results in a really useful discussion," Pari continued. "We always make clear that the actions within each goal are all things that staff are already doing, or at least identify that they should be doing as part of their everyday work. And incorporate the standards which they have to meet anyway. Great Care is about making these actions happen consistently well." She paused as a strong gust of wind rattled an open window and Anton got up to close it. "We set up the pre and post data collection, develop the change plan, and away we go! We'll change the questions for the non-clinical departments, of course. Instead of asking about achieving the goals, we'll discuss who they support to achieve the goal—that is, which direct care staff do they help to do their job and how could they better support them."

"Thanks, Pari," Carol said as Pari sat down. "Looks really good. Could you all please let your pilot services know how much we appreciate what they're doing and make sure your divisional heads are providing visible support?" She looked at her watch. "I think that's plenty for now. Good work, everyone, thank you." Sudden rain pounding on the roof almost drowned out her words as she brought the session to a close.

"How do we keep track of it all?" asked Anton loudly, over the din. "That's a lot of activity."

"You're not kidding," Kristen responded with a loud sigh. "All good things, of course," she added, responding to Carol's look.

Carol laughed. "You're right, there's no kidding about the amount of 'stuff' going on, that's for sure. That's why we have goals, a model, a framework, and a plan. These help us keep track of what we're trying to achieve, how we'll get there and how everything fits together. We have a big advantage insofar as we know what the 'cake' looks like: that's the four GC goals. The framework gives us the ingredients, and the short-and long-term plans, which will be fleshed out from our discussions over the past two days, help us mix it all together."

"Is that what went wrong at KVHS over the past year? We didn't have a framework for great care?" asked Anton. "What?" he responded wide-eyed to Elena's narrowed eyes.

Carol ignored their byplay. "Many services have a project-based plan to improve the quality of their care. They'll pick certain issues to work on because they are compliance requirements, or their data identify things that are not working well, or they've had a catastrophe. As you say, that's very much as KVHS operated over the past few years.

"The difference is, organisations without a clear idea of the care 'cake' they're trying to make can't create consistent quality care. Their consumers get some good care and some not so good, but there's nothing driving a whole of organisation approach to fixing it, so the overall care and experience bar doesn't get raised. They can't answer questions about how good their care is, because they don't define how good they want it to be. They don't know how good it will be in one year's time, because they've got nothing concrete to aim towards and therefore can't plan to get there. Some parts of their organisation will improve. But not everyone changes the way they think about care delivery every day."

"Ah! No clear origin or destination." Anton nodded. "I might just be starting to get a handle on all this."

"That Quality System Kit course you made me—er, asked that I do," Pari hastily corrected herself, "described it really well. They said that trying to create consistently high quality care through improvement projects alone takes patients on a series of 'day trips' to nice locations, so they get good care in some parts of the organisation, but it doesn't move the whole organisation to live in a better place."

"When you know what you're trying to achieve and where you're starting, the rest is just the how," added Kristen. "Aspirational goals and pragmatic action to achieve them. I've heard you say that so many times, Carol! But now I really understand it."

"Yes, and then we keep moving towards the goals," Carol continued. "We won't always progress as far and as fast as we want to, and sometimes our excellent ideas won't work in practice, but we keep going, monitoring our progress and making adjustments to our strategies to get us where we want to go."

"The course also said, 'Quality is often planned on the high ground but implemented in the swampy lowlands,' "[15] mused Pari. "It doesn't always work out the way you think it will. But at least we have a map for where we want to go, and we always know where we are, even when we're stuck."

"We'll be fine as long as we focus on three things: the point-of-care experience, the people who make it happen, and the systems and governance that support it." Carol began gathering her papers together. "And when external compliance requirements land on our desks, we slot them into our framework. We use them as well as we can to help us achieve what we're trying to do, rather than letting them blow us off course. They're going to fit somewhere within our Purpose, People and Pillars of governance." She looked around. "We're done."

Everyone finished packing their things and stood up, anxious to be gone. "Thank you, everyone. It's been a big couple of days, but everything we've covered will stand us in good stead for the months—and years—ahead. Go home, and don't think about health services, change, complexity, or, dare I say it, Great Care for a couple of days. And drive carefully in this weather!"

CHAPTER THIRTEEN

The weeks flew by. Many meetings were held and much work completed. The Operational and Board Quality and Clinical Governance Committees modified their agendas and reporting to align with Great Care, and gradually information about progress with achieving the GC goals and the status of the governance pillars started to flow. The month-long GC pilots were evaluated and the lessons fed into the GC organisational rollout plan. The Executive Team members discussed Great Care with their directors and managers and got it on the formal and informal agendas of their divisions. The Consumer and Community Partnerships Committee advised on the GC gaps from their pathway work and ongoing community consultation. Colourful GC posters sprang up everywhere, showing how KVHS consumers and staff were working together to make GC a reality for every person. The GC Ambassadors completed their training and were assisting department heads with GC implementation. The middle manager intensives had begun, and the GC Awards were coming together.

"It's all going pretty well, I think," observed Kristen one evening as she popped her head around Carol's door to say goodnight. The building was quiet as most staff had left. Kristen blinked as the bright red of an ambulance light flashed past outside in the gathering dusk.

Carol jumped.

"Sorry Kristen—deep in thought."

Kristen peered at Carol. "You don't look nearly happy enough for a CEO who is kicking serious goals."

Carol forced a tight smile. "I am happy with progress, Kristen. It's just that I've been reading the healthcare funding promises for the upcoming election. It's not exactly uplifting. No one is predicting anything but slash and burn, once you get past the pretty wrapping." She closed her laptop with a sigh.

"It's getting us all down." Kristen moved inside the door. "But what can you do? There is hope, though. Some of our improvement efforts should show real savings next year, and that will help. Anton is working on it. We think that the improved effectiveness and connectedness in our top three volume diagnoses alone will save hundreds of thousands of dollars. But I predict that we'll see savings in every GC goal across the health service. And don't forget—we have had a win this month! The strategy to supply the newspaper with copious good news stories seems to be working. That was a stroke of genius from Rosie, reminding us that everyone in town likes to see their name in the paper—in a good way, of course. I don't know why I didn't think of it myself. My family goes nuts if one of us gets a mention on the bottom of page twelve. *The Leader* editor knows that, so he can't help but publish them. Did you see that they gave us half a page in today's edition on the aged care GC pilot? That's half a page of good news!"

"All true," sighed Carol. "But there's an equal amount of bad press, and it's eating us from the inside as well as the outside."

"I know." Kristen nodded. "A particular cohort of staff are using the negative Leader stories as an excuse not to get involved in Great Care. There's nothing we can do but find the leak and fix it—and we're pulling out all the stops to do that. But everyone swears black and blue that they're not giving information to the press." She put down her bag. "On the bright side, I wanted to say that your presentation at the staff forum today was spectacular. I loved the stories about how the GC pilots are changing things for consumers and staff. The video of the man talking about his wife in residential aged care, suffering from diabetes, was magic. Who would have thought that an overhaul of her medication would make such a difference to them as a couple?"

Carol nodded. "I know! She now feels well enough to go with him to the theatre again, after years of not wanting to go out. It's the very best of Great Care when consumers and staff work together to transform quality of care and quality of life. So powerful. Plenty of good things are happening, and people do seem happier in general, I think." She got up and pulled down the window blind against the darkness outside.

"It really helps that we get the new staff off to a flying start as well," Kristen said. "They all have a fabulous first day now, and the highlight is you and Andy introducing the 'I Am Responsible for Great Care' challenge."

"I enjoy it. Rosie grumbles about 'new staff' day because no previous CEO has spent so much time on it. But to me there's nothing more important to spend time on! You're right, though, there is a significant group of staff who are holding out against engaging in GC and all that comes with it. The senior doctors continued their argument with me today about increased scrutiny of their outcomes. And it's not only them. Plenty of work to do yet."

"You know, I understand that much more since Jeff joined the Executive Team. He's good at explaining how hard it is for the docs to balance the public's expectations with being a fallible human. It's not as if they're not interested in their outcomes—they are. But the data sharing and comparing bit is still new to some of them." Kristen bent over to smell the wildflowers on the table.

"True," Carol said. "And it doesn't help that the 'sharing and comparing' is often introduced as something that they have to do for accreditation and performance, rather than as something they'll be supported to do to improve their practice and outcomes." She moved over to her small meeting table. "I didn't much like it when I was running the physio department either, to be honest. I didn't think my outcomes were anyone's business but mine. Transparency of results has been a challenge for most clinicians at some time in their careers, I'd say, even when we know it's the right thing. But we have to keep working on it."

Kristen shrugged. "I guess we're learning how to do all this better as time goes on, but it's a slow process, all right, particularly when we're not all on the same page about it." She picked up her bag. "Now—go home!"

"Not just yet—and that's why," Carol smiled as Pari appeared behind Kristen. "We're having so much trouble finding time to catch up that we've resorted to after hours' meetings."

"Have you told Carol about Turbo Change?" enquired Kristen as Pari squeezed past her into Carol's office.

"Haven't had a chance," responded Pari. "It's on my list for this meeting."

"Turbo Change? Have we diversified into the engine business?" asked Carol with mock surprise.

"Don't laugh. Anything could happen around here the way things are going," warned Kristen, wagging her finger. "After the last exec planning workshop, Jeff, Pari, and I got together to work on our change model. We wanted something that captured all the good things that Chen had covered at the workshop without being too complicated. We came up with the Turbo Change Cycle."[A6]

"Go on." Carol folded her arms and sat back.

Kristen put down her bag again. "We think that seven change 'ingredients' are enough to turbo-charge any change, if they're the right ones. Busy staff don't have the time or headspace for much more than that. So we build a change 'engine' with staff when they're about to implement something new or modify what's already being done to 'turbo-charge' the change. We start with a clear goal and definition of success, that's number one. That's followed by the SWTA 'pre' data collection component, using subjective and objective data to measure where they're starting from and to set measures for the change destination. At this point we also identify the boulders on the change road, as there will always be people who only see the negatives in change. We figure we might as well use their dire predictions as intelligence and encourage them to help with strategies for shifting them! Then we get into making the case for change with heads and hearts: the 'Will' part of the change model."

Pari took up the story. "We paint a picture with them of what they want their everyday work to look like in 12 months' time as a result of the change. They plan backwards from that to identify the three big changes they'd have to make to get there and plot the steps they'll take to make each big change. Creative and social actions are essential steps for each big change, of course. We want people to discuss the change in the tea room as well as in the meeting room." She sat down at the meeting table.

Carol nodded approvingly.

"The 'Skill' part of the change model comes next: identifying the skills and knowledge they'll need to take those change steps," Kristen continued. "This includes learning from others by investigating if someone else has done something similar–internally or externally–or if there's something relevant in the literature. We also look for where we can use accreditation standards to support the change, of course. Then they test the changes, using DKRS as our pilot framework and building in MMAAP to make sure we're engaging and supporting staff and consumers, to give the changes a really good going over."

Pari grinned. "They do give their big changes a good going over! During and after piloting the changes they collect the subjective and objective inter and post change data. If the results don't show goal achievement, they don't implement. They go back to the goal and discuss if it's the right one for what they're trying to achieve; or course correct the big changes if the goal is right but the steps they took didn't get the job done, and pilot again. If the goal is achieved, they embed and spread the changes, which means they weave it into formal and informal daily processes and embed it in governance and practice. Then we move to spreading it beyond the pilot scope."

"And we're making sure the staff, and consumers where they're partnering in a change, have fun as well, Kristen said. "There are some incredibly creative and savvy people out there and it's nice to see them given the opportunity to use their ideas and their networks to create really useful change. It's freedom within a framework! We haven't got it right yet, but we'll refine it as we go. We base Turbo Change on a simple rule: 'Change is planned and implemented with those who have to make it and those affected by it: consumers and staff.'" She picked up her bag to leave. "Of course, it's technically the direct opposite of turbo-charging. Doing it this way takes longer than the usual PACEM change, because of the front end planning that goes into it. A minor detail." She waved her hands about airily. "But it sticks way better than on-the-run half-baked changes that don't last." She glanced up at the clock. "Look at the time! Gotta go! Not too long, you two." Kristen waved as she departed, shutting the door behind her.

Carol poured Pari and herself glasses of iced water, and they began comparing notes on Great Care progress and strategizing on the barriers they'd encountered. Pari showed Carol the work she and Jeff had done to integrate Chen and Andy's lessons from the planning workshop into their approach to Great Care with middle managers. "Apart from the eight formal pilots, we've developed three simple GC implementation packages for other services to work with. The first is the 'basics' package and is non-negotiable. This is where managers and staff use the accreditation standards and other compliance requirements to drive goal achievement in their services. That sets the foundation and makes sure we integrate compliance requirements with Great Care.

"On top of the 'basics' package we've developed two other implementation pathways for the managers who are keen and want to try out and evaluate GC beyond the basics, before we formally spread it across the organisation. These come with specific support from the Quality Team and follow the Turbo Change cycle.

One package focuses on just one goal. That's the 'deep dive' package, where a service specialises in getting one goal, including all relevant actions, implemented for every consumer. The other is a focus on one action in each of the four goals that's not covered by standards or compliance requirements but is particularly relevant to their consumers. That's the 'balanced' package. Over time we'll be working on every consumer receiving every component of each goal, every time, of course. But we reckon that achieving that could be a good two years away. We want everyone to have the opportunity to do some experimenting first, to figure out what works, to have some fun in the process and to see the potential of GC in their services. And for those who don't want to take on a 'deep dive' or 'balanced' package at this point, we also have Great Care 'freestyle.' "

"Freestyle?" Carol's eyebrows shot up.

"Yes! We wanted a way to spread Great Care to the services not formally involved in a GC 'package' to keep it on the radar, in some form, for everyone. Something they could do with GC that taps into their enthusiasm without burdening them. In the end, Elena and Susie came up with 'freestyle' when they discovered that there were staff all over the place who had started doing things every day to create GC, without any of us saying or doing anything. For example, Jeff is using 'freestyle' as an opportunity to trial some GC simple rules in ED; you know what a fan of them he is. The ED staff have instigated 'Ask Me About Your Loved One' with Mike, the chaplain. Who, by the way, is Rosie's cousin. They're like peas in a pod!"

Carol eyebrows shot up. "I should have noticed the similarities but hadn't made the connection. What's Mike doing in ED?"

"He's there for the three busiest shifts of the week, wearing a lime green top hat they bought at last year's KVHS fete. The hat says: 'Ask me where your loved one is.' He's so good with people and is very calming. He doesn't give families clinical information but finds out for them where their loved one is on the 'yellow brick road.' "

"The yellow brick road? Honestly, Pari, sometimes I think you're talking about a different organisation, one I know nothing about. What on earth is that?" Carol cocked her head to one side. "Unless it's better that I don't know about it?"

"It's perfectly safe and respectable," laughed Pari. "It's ED shorthand for the patient pathway. Consumer feedback in the ED is very clear that a lot of family anxiety comes from not understanding what's happening and why things take so long. So Jeff worked with a group of younger ED doctors and nurses to develop a simple rule about keeping families informed: 'All ED patients' families know where their loved one is on the patient pathway.' " She sipped her water. "They plotted an ED 'yellow brick road'—the key steps in the ED process, such as triage, examination, tests, diagnosis, decision-making, and treatment—and Mike provides the interface. He finds out where patients are on the 'road' and keeps families informed. The complete road, or patient pathway, is on a poster on the wall, looking like a yellow brick road—to Great Care, of course! And there are also A4 copies that people can take away. It's been so successful that they're thinking about developing an 'ED yellow brick road' app with the university. Such great work and helping to create more Personal and Connected care, in particular."

"Brilliant!" agreed Carol.

"That one's a biggie, but there are lots of others." Pari began counting them off on her fingers as she spoke. "The catering staff have decided to focus on Personal Care. They'll check with the patients whether they're eating and enjoying the food, and if they're not, they have a chat with them and record it on their tablet to let the chefs know. They're also using a simple rule: 'We always know why a meal is uneaten.' The Home Care Team is trialling different ways to make it easy for a new client to get to know their KVHS service provider and are also working with Pharmacy to integrate an easier way to explain medications. So they're looking at Personal and Safe Care. Medical Imaging is doing a gap analysis to see which aspects of Effective Care the accreditation standards do not cover in their service, specific to their consumers. And the Nursing Admin Team has put a couple of those fabulous Great Care posters around their office to refer to when they're working through consumer complaints to identify the issues, to provide more Personal care. My consumer experience manager is also using the GC goals to discuss complaints with department managers. He says it's good to have a framework of what good care looks like so they can agree where it did and didn't happen." Pari paused as an ambulance flew past, siren blaring.

"I'm sure there are more freestyle things happening that I don't know about. We're trying to capture them on the Great Care intranet page as we hear about them so we can learn and share. But none of them will formally be evaluated, of course," she finished in a disappointed tone as she rustled in her bag for a pen.

"Not everything that is valuable is evaluated," Carol said. "Remember, this is Great Care in action. We want people coming to work thinking 'How can I create GC today?' and to be encouraged in this by their managers, even if we're not measuring their every move. I heard a doctor in a meeting this morning say that he's using the Great Care goals to remind the youngsters, as he called them—I presume the junior doctors—to consider the patient as a whole person, not only a diagnosis. I wanted to do a happy dance, which may have disrupted the meeting somewhat!" She gave Pari a quick example of a seated happy dance as she spoke.

"That's Great Care making a difference to how people think and act, which is what we're trying to do: create a thinking, caring organisation. Not all ideas will work, not all pilot packages will be brilliant successes and not everyone will come on board right away. We need to keep learning, nudging progress and evolving our thinking. If consumers and staff are better off because people are trying new things, we're winning, and hopefully we'll see the results in our care measures and in consumer and staff feedback. How do you think the governance engine room work is going?"

"It's finally got off the ground after a few false starts. Making the systems helpful to managers to support the GC goals was a different way of thinking and took a while to get our heads around. We didn't quite know where to start! But once the GC committee completed their gap analysis against the governance accreditation standards, and we combined that with our straw poll on what managers told us they need from governance systems to help them, we had a plan. Even that new reporting policy requirement that arrived from the Department of Health has already been slotted into the GC governance engine room."

"Fantastic." Carol looked a little relieved. "I was wondering how that would land: as part of Great Care? Or as some separate thing that would distract us? Well done!"

Pari shook her head. "Nothing to do with me. Elena and Jeff spotted how it could help us report on GC, so thank them! The four GC goal committees are also set up now so they'll incorporate those new reporting requirements into their agendas. I think Kristen's middle manager course is starting to have an effect as well. I've noticed that some managers and staff around the place seem more, well, energetic than usual. And the CPC's ideas for improving painful consumer touch points have been so useful when planning our organisational GC improvement priorities. Now that we're more tuned into where KVHS consumers find us difficult to deal with, I can see we've made so many wrong assumptions in the past about how things really work on the ground."

"Ain't that the truth. We see our organisation through a completely different lens!" Carol put down her pen and stretched. "I think we've covered enough for tonight. But before we finish, I wanted to ask how you're doing in all this organised chaos?"

Pari hesitated for a moment. "I'm okay, I guess." She shrugged her shoulders. "Sorry, that's not a very illuminating answer! It's just that things go up and down. Some days people run away from me in corridors and no one wants to talk to me and I feel I'll never get done all the things I need to do. And some days are amazing because I get to work with incredible people who are improving the lives of consumers—and staff—because they're making really innovative changes to achieve Great Care. That makes it all worthwhile."

Carol nodded. "I know the feeling all too well, Pari. And apart from the new role, it's always a big step up to the Executive Team, not to mention that we dropped you in the middle of Great Care and said 'Swim!' You're doing incredibly well."

Pari's embarrassment showed as she shifted in her seat. "Thanks, Carol," she said, face flushing. "I appreciate it. Chen has been a big help as well. Last time we met, we talked about earning respect and developing influence. I already had respect in the OT world, but I realised I had to start all over again in the quality and executive world. We've worked on some tips. Want to hear them?"

"Sure do," said Carol, sitting back.

"I bet it won't be anything new for you. We tried to relate the material specifically to a senior quality role." Pari pulled a notepad out of her bag and flicked through the pages. "Here we are. Six Tips for Building Influence:

"Number one: Don't rely on passion alone. Most people who work in healthcare are passionate about providing good care and services. So that alone is never going to be enough to earn respect, even though a lot of people in quality roles over-rely on it. But you've got to know your stuff as well. Always enact your passion through competence and knowledge."

"That's a good one that we don't hear discussed enough," Carol agreed, nodding. "Over the years, I've been surprised by self-described 'passionate' quality managers who don't know some of the basic literature on quality and safety, or how to change, measure, and improve, or even key quality results in their own organisation. Whereas truly passionate people can't help but learn as much as they can about their topic."

"Yes," agreed Pari. "I must admit that there have been a few passionate quality managers I've known over the years who have put me off, because by telling me how passionate they were about good care, they implied that I wasn't! But they didn't always have the skills and knowledge to turn their passion into results. It fits beautifully with the next tip which is, 'Be useful.' Within the framework of a job description and the boss's expectations," she smiled at Carol, "and my own goals, aim to be really useful. Understand the customers of your service and make it easy for them to work with the quality system to achieve what they want in their role and for their consumers. Say what you mean and deliver what you say.

"Number three is 'Balance the bad with the good.' Focusing only on all the stuff that goes wrong or isn't right won't win you friends nor help you to influence people, as we found out with the medical ward. Get into the habit of acknowledging and spreading things that go well. You'll not only make people feel prouder of their success, but we know that in the complexity of human services, learning from the good things is a powerful tool for improvement."

"Hear, hear." Carol tapped the table for emphasis. "And I'm already seeing this working at KVHS."

"The next is 'Get results.' Results shout louder than any talking, particularly in healthcare. Help people make a real difference for consumers and staff and help them to measure the change. That alone will foster respect.

"Number five is 'Be easy to deal with.' Everyone who works in human services is trying to improve lives in their own way. Be the positive person people want to know. Clinicians don't come to work to help you achieve your objectives. They're busy with their own! A little empathy for their challenges goes a long way. I learned that with the medical ward, too. Building relationships will get more done than ordering people about. Work on helping each other do what you both need to do. Help others get what they want and you'll get more of what you want."

"There's definitely not enough of that in healthcare," Carol observed.

"I know! It seems to be at the root of so many of our problems," Pari sighed before continuing. "The last one we decided on was 'Have more fun.' Quality roles can be really challenging, but it's not going to be any easier if you're grumpy and miserable. Yes, it's serious work, but 'you don't have to be sombre to be serious,' as John Cleese said. We know that the interesting, quirky and creative captures attention—and brings a little more joy—way more than the dull and bureaucratic."

"True, true, true!" Carol applauded. "That's a great set of actions for building influence,

Pari. I hope you've shared it with your team." She crossed her arms. "I wish I'd had it when I was younger. I did my best, but if I had my time over, I'd do a lot of things differently. The quality role in any human service is hard, partly because 'quality' has been implemented as compliance and extra work rather than something we create with our consumers."

Pari nodded her agreement.

"You know that Juran taught quality management as a three-legged stool: control, improvement, and planning,"[16] Carol continued. "The planning bit I call 'strategic creation.' Unfortunately, we seem to have completely forgotten about the planning aspect in most human services, and we've focused control and improvement largely on compliance. We focus on tactics and forget the strategy. The 'planning' component relates to what we're trying to do here with Great Care. I think that's why health and human services haven't got the results they should have considering all the work and resources applied over many years."

"Is that why?" asked Pari. "I've often wondered why progress has been so slow."

Carol paused, head on one side. "There are probably a zillion reasons. There's the complexity of our services, which we've discussed, and the tendency for us to treat our organisations like production lines, when they're not. It doesn't help that whatever we do to our consumers, they keep coming through the door because we're an essential service. Also, we don't have the commercial and external pressures that make a 'quality product' imperative as strong as it is in other industries because consumers don't have the same options they would if choosing a hotel." She drained her water.

"Along with all this, the public believes us to be perfect because they trust us with their lives-until they find out we're not of course. Add to that our 'craft production' origins, where everyone is an artisan and expert in their own work,[17] and thinks they do a pretty good job. These add up to a unique set of circumstances that make it hard to find impetus to strive to be great. That being said, I'm constantly grateful that we do have so many high-performing, committed people in health and human services that work towards better care every day."

"Yes, and I'm beginning to see that without the line managers taking responsibility for creating GC, it can only ever happen in patches. It's traditionally been a bit of a 'hero and the help' process, hasn't it?"

"Is this another pilot?" laughed Carol.

"Nooo…." Pari took a moment to consider her answer. "I'm starting to wake up and really think about all this, and this is how I'm seeing it now: the heroes are the senior clinicians and managers here and there in health services who get involved and lead improvement, and the help are the quality managers and teams who slog it out every day, trying to get the rest of the organisation involved. While it's nice to have the heroes doing what they do, it's not a very effective approach when you step back and look at it. Seems to me it's a workaround of the real problem, which is that some senior managers can't or won't insist that their line managers and staff enact their everyday responsibility for creating and providing a high quality service. No wonder human services haven't made the progress they should have by now."

"It's a good summary," Carol said, smiling. "And that responsibility starts with the Executive Team. As I'm sure you can now see, we're doing our best at KVHS to shake up the 'hero and the help' model. I know it's frustrating. But don't forget, on the down days, that we're striving to do something great here. I'm really happy you're part of it."

Pari beamed as she picked up her pad and pen. "Me too."

*****

On a rainy Saturday, two weeks before the rural health conference and the release of the next set of quality data from the Department of Health, Carol and Angela took their mothers out to a local winery for Carol's mother's birthday. Carol relaxed as they sat down at a table overlooking the vineyard. She hadn't had too many non-work social occasions since she started at KVHS, mainly because there were so many work-related functions she was expected to attend. Seb, her predecessor, had enjoyed the status that went with the job and had attended every function he was invited to. It seemed that not even an envelope could be opened in Kinsley Valley without the KVHS CEO in attendance. Carol's quarantined down times were her exercise, Friday nights with Chen and Angela, and spending as much time as she could with her mother, who was hugely enjoying being Carol's "plus one" at some of the weekend functions.

She knew she couldn't keep "living to work," as she currently was, nor did she intend to. Now that she was established in the town, she would relinquish some out-of- hours functions to the rest of the Executive Team. She had already made plans to train with the seniors' hockey team next season, to see if she was good enough to get a game, and also to join the Kinsley Valley Big Ideas group, which combined local wine, food, guest speakers and creative planning for the town. She had even got back on her bike again. Finally, after months of feeling like a fish out of water, and deeply missing her city life and friends, Carol could feel herself putting down tiny roots in Kinsley Valley. She was looking forward to working at a less frantic pace once they got Great Care embedded and their core problems fixed. But for now, being out with her good friend and their mothers was a welcome respite, despite her heavy weariness.

She was especially glad to be diverted from some unwelcome news she'd had from Nancy the night before. "I think we may have found our culprit," Nancy had announced when Carol answered the phone.

"What? Who?" Carol felt an internal tug-of-war between wanting to know and being afraid to know. She braced for the pain of disappointment she was going to feel.

"Jodie Jones called me today with a piece of information that may have cracked the case. Guess who's the aunt of the *Leader*'s editor? Wait for it: Anne Bixton's partner, Hillary."

Carol gasped, mentally wrestling with this unexpected twist. "But how … why …"

"Don't know," responded Nancy curtly. "It means that we still have someone at KVHS spilling the beans to Anne. But at least we know how it's getting to the *Leader*, and that it's got to be someone Anne knows reasonably well, or she wouldn't trust the information. It also explains why no one at KVHS has owned up to passing information along to the press, as technically they're not. They're just making sure Anne knows, and she and Hillary do the rest."

"But … why would Anne do this? Does she hate me that much?" Carol didn't remember sitting down, but she found herself seated at her kitchen table.

"I doubt it. Anne is too pragmatic to hate. I suspect, having known her for a long time, that she's having some fun at your expense, and making herself feel better for retiring just a little earlier than she had intended to, in the process. She probably has no idea of the real impact it's having on your plans."

Carol had been in a whirl of narrowing down the "friends of Anne" line up ever since. Just as they finished dessert, Carol heard her mother say, "Isn't that Dr Bixton over there? Is that her partner with her?"

Carol looked up with a start. Indeed, Anne was sitting with a glass of wine in a booth on the opposite side of the crowded restaurant. But it wasn't Hillary with her. It was Elena.

Carol suppressed a gasp as a jolt of electricity flew through her. The pair was engaged in deep and animated conversation—about what, Carol could only guess. Elena!

"Let's go," she urged, grabbing her bag.

"But we haven't had coffee!" Angela complained with a surprised look.

"I've heard the coffee here isn't great," replied Carol, standing up. "Let's get some at that new café back at Kinsley Valley. Theirs is meant to be the best in the region. I'll pay if you'll help Mum into the car." She raised her eyebrows in an "I'll explain later" expression.

Angela looked baffled at this sudden change of plans, but she knew her friend well enough to realise that something was up. They were out of there as quickly as she could decently move Carol's mother down the steps and into the car park.

Carol wrestled with her next steps for the rest of the weekend. How to manage it? Confront Anne directly? Ask Nancy for advice? Let it go for now, but keep a close watch on Elena? By Sunday night, she'd made up her mind. *First thing tomorrow*, she thought as she drifted into a restless sleep, in which she chased a line of flying white coats down the Kinsley Valley main street until morning.

At 0800 Carol made her way to Elena's office and poked her head around the door. "Good morning. Do you have a minute?"

Elena glanced up, looking less than happy to see her. "I have five minutes. I'm off to the regional Chief Nursing and Midwifery Forum today, and I'm chairing, so I can't be late. I'm only here because I forgot to print off some handouts on Friday." Carol heard the printer grinding away in the adjoining office.

Carol sat down. "Elena, I have something difficult to broach with you. We have reason to believe that Anne Bixton may be providing the leaked information to the Leader."

Elena's eyebrows shot up, but she said nothing.

"And so, of course, that narrows down our internal search considerably, as whoever is providing the information to Anne has to be someone she knows—and trusts."

"Your point?" said Elena icily. Carol cursed her internally for making this as hard as she could.

"Well, Elena, I need to ask you, as I will all Anne's close colleagues from her time here, if, if … you are supplying her with information to take to the newspaper."

There, she'd said it. There was a long silence. Carol noticed that the printer had stopped.

Elena turned an unbecoming shade of deep red. She stood and looked down at Carol. "I've never been so insulted. How dare you accuse me," she said in a low tone.

"I'm not accusing anyone. I'm asking you a question. I must be completely transparent, Elena. I saw you with Anne on Saturday."

"What? Are you following me around now?" Elena's ice turned to anger.

Carol stood and looked Elena in the eye. "No, of course not. It was a coincidence."

"I have to go." Elena pushed past Carol and stalked out. Carol heard a few minutes of energetic stapling, followed by silence.

That went well, she muttered to herself as she looked around Elena's office. In pride of place on the wall was an award for Nursing Leadership Excellence, from the College of Nursing and Midwifery, presented five years ago. Could this be the person who was undermining Carol and the whole of KVHS in the process? Elena had certainly seemed upset at the very notion, but then, she hadn't answered the question, either. Carol sighed. Time to get to the 0830 huddle. She squared her shoulders, slipped on a positive CEO expression, and walked out the door.

*****

The weekly Executive Team meeting was the last item on Carol's agenda that day and she was ready to lay her cards on the table. She had decided that if she wanted them to be a team, they had to face this situation together.

"You don't look so good," Kristen observed as she sat down.

"Not feeling that great, either, and you'll know why in a minute."

"Where's Elena?" asked Pari.

"At the regional CNMO meeting, so she'll miss Exec today," responded Kristen, regarding Carol curiously.

Once they were all seated, Carol took a breath and opened her mouth to begin. To her surprise, Jeff beat her to it.

"I've got some news," he began, looking serious. "Me, too," Carol said with a frown.

"I think you're going to want to hear mine first, if you can hold that thought, Carol." He cleared his throat. "On Friday night, I went to Dr Walters's retirement dinner, put on by his former Department of Health colleagues. He used to be the mental health regional director, you know."

"Retirement? I didn't think he was retiring for a couple of years," said Pari.

"Yes, when he gave me six months, I thought he fully intended to outlast me," added Carol.

They paused as the door opened and Rosie glided in with the coffee order.

"He wasn't supposed to retire yet," Jeff continued. "But his wife's been unwell, and they've recently decided it's time to work less and live more. He's still got a month or so to go here, and I suspect he'll fit in as many farewells as he can between now and then—and after. Anyway, I sat next to him, and it was obvious he was very much enjoying the excellent shiraz. Over-enjoying it, in fact."

"I heard he was as full as the last bus," observed Rosie, handing out the cups. "Rosie!" Carol admonished her.

"Just saying," Rosie threw over her shoulder with a grin as she closed the door behind her.

"She might not be far off," Jeff sighed. "Martin was very talkative and loud. After an hour I was desperate to change seats and excused myself. But he insisted I stay to hear something hilarious he had to share with me."

"We're all ears," said Kristen, leaning forward.

"Well … he told me, with great pride, that he'd been hugely enjoying himself these past few months, *spreading the word about the incompetent new KVHS CEO.*"

Jeff sat back, having thrown his bomb. The stunned silence was eventually broken by Kristen. "Good lord! Dr *Walters*! Why on *earth* would he do that?"

The executives stared at each other, minds racing.

"Is it … is it because Carol's a female CEO, do you think?" asked Anton, daring to go where the others wouldn't.

"I doubt it." Jeff shook his head. "It mightn't help, but Dr Walters has no time for any CEO, female or male, good or bad. Calls them bureaucratic wastes of space. I didn't know Seb, but it sounds like he didn't have much to do with the doctors, apart from on the golf course and at the football club"—Kristen nodded confirmation—"but Carol has asked for more accountability from all the medical unit heads, which hasn't gone down well with some of the older group. And Dr Walters in particular."

"Even after what happened in the medical ward?" said Pari, recovering her powers of speech. "Can't they see that stronger accountability for patient care was needed?"

The conversation buzzed around Carol, but she barely heard it. Dr Walters! Of course! Everything was immediately clear. Why hadn't she seen it before? She had suspected Professor Yang, but of course, it was Dr Walters who'd given her six months to survive in the job. He was obviously giving her a helping hand out of the organisation. And to top it off, he and Anne Bixton had probably bonded over their shared contempt for CEOs, particularly those who interfered in "doctors' business." Carol didn't know whether to be sad or glad. She felt a rush of relief as she hugged the thought that it wasn't Elena, followed by a painful pang of anxiety.

"But he didn't feed the information directly to the *Leader* himself," continued Jeff as the others stared at him. "He did it through—"

"Anne," finished Carol. "I know the rest of the story, Jeff. Nancy figured out that side of it and told me on Friday night." She allowed this to sink in for a minute before fixing her gaze on Jeff. "Why on earth didn't you call me over the weekend?"

Jeff shifted uneasily. "Well … I called Elena first. We thought we might be able to work it out together and make the whole thing go away. To be honest, I didn't want to throw the old guy to the wolves when he was leaving anyway. And I thought there was a chance he may just have been taking credit for someone else's dirty work, so I wanted to speak to a couple of his close colleagues today to check out the story. I've done that and it's him, all right." He ran his hand over his hair and looked around the table. "The other confounding factor is that Elena and Anne are friends. So we both wanted to at least try to fix it quietly. Elena has been wondering for a while if Anne had something to do with it and intended to ask her about it. We agreed we'd wait to contact you until after Elena had met with Anne to ask her to stop the undermining."

Carol's low tone revealed the depth of her frustration. "Oh, Jeff, I wish you'd spoken to me. I understand that you want to protect your colleagues, but it's gone way too far for that. And, unfortunately, I saw Elena with Anne on Saturday. I asked her about it this morning." "Oh, no," said Kristen slowly, her face dropping as realisation dawned. "You thought it was Elena passing on information to Anne? What did she say?"

"Not much. She didn't confirm or deny. She seemed pretty upset and had to leave, unfortunately, to go to the CNMO meeting, so we didn't get a chance to discuss it. Bugger." Carol could have kicked herself for her own assumptions. But she was still mystified by Elena's reaction. *Why didn't she just tell me it was all a mistake*?

Kristen read her face and her mind. "Elena's very proud, Carol. She wouldn't have taken kindly to you thinking that she'd undermine KVHS. She may not be your biggest fan, but she does appreciate what you're trying to do for the patients and staff."

"It gets worse," sighed Jeff. "She didn't have any luck persuading Anne. They had a huge argument, apparently. Elena was very upset about it as they've been friends for years. She put that friendship on the line for KVHS, Carol."

Carol sighed, her stomach full of lead. But now was not the time to fall in a heap. There was much to do, and the sooner it was done, the better. She sat up. "Okay. I hear you. It's a mess, but we can fix it if we work together. I'll call Elena as soon as we're finished here. But first, we need a strategy for Dr Walters ASAP." She picked up her phone and turned to Kristen. "Could you find your People and Culture manager and ask her to come in, please? In the meantime, I'd better let our Board Chair know what we're about to do."

CHAPTER FOURTEEN

Carol stood in the wings of the stage, listening to her introduction by the national rural health conference Chairperson. There had been some difficult days in the time since that Executive Team meeting, but she felt a sense of freedom as she stood there, waiting to go on. The undermining roots at KVHS had been weeded out and the air cleared. She and Elena had had dinner together and built a bridge to what she hoped would be a fruitful partnership—not a friendship exactly, but something that would benefit them both. She had called Anne and had a terse discussion about the issue. As expected, Anne had been unrepentant. But she had agreed to talk to Elena, at least. Dr Walters had been eased out three weeks early and denied his big hospital farewell— another hard decision, but the right one. She smiled in the darkness. It was all behind her. No more dreams of marching doctors—she hoped! And now, something good to boost KVHS into the future.

At her cue, she strode to the lectern and heard a small cheer from some of the KVHS staff in the audience.

"It's my privilege this evening to share with you the KVHS story of the past year. It hasn't always been pretty, and it's never been easy. I've always liked the idea of 'honouring the struggle,'[18] but there have been times this past few months when I wished the struggle would disappear to kingdom come." She paused while the audience chuckled.

"A year ago, we were at the bottom of our state league ladders for both consumer and staff satisfaction. We'd had a review into poor and unsafe care and an unsuccessful accreditation assessment. While our beautiful new building was going up, our organisation was falling down. I was extremely fortunate that, when all these problems came to light, the KVHS Board and Executive Team made a brave decision not to be that health service anymore, but to strive for more. And not to be content with reaching the middle of the pack, but to provide every one of our consumers and their families with consistently Great Care." Carol paused. In the quiet of the auditorium, she thought the audience would hear her heart thumping in her chest. It was no easy thing to lay bare the struggles of the past few months. The bright stage lights shone in her eyes, but as she looked down, she could see the first few rows of audience members watching her closely.

She sipped some water before going on to describe their pathway to Great Care: the ups and downs, successes and failures, and the lessons learned. "I want to thank my staff, Board and Executive most sincerely for their hard work and commitment to KVHS Great Care over the past months. I'm incredibly proud of each and every one of them. And a special thank you to the KVHS consumers and community who got behind us and contributed their wisdom and skills, making it possible for us to take a new direction. What a team." Loud applause broke out from the KVHS audience members.

"I'll finish by sharing my top ten hard-earned lessons learned. Basically, these are my 'Quality Rules.'"

She clicked the remote and a blank slide came up on the screen. As she clicked, the leadership rules appeared and she spoke to them in turn:

"One. Get the point. Make the pursuit of greatness a shared purpose across your organisation. The point of any human service organisation is point of care. You can't be a great organisation unless you're achieving greatness where staff and consumers interact. It's not enough to say we provide 'excellent,' or 'amazing,' or 'best in the world,' or 'best in the known universe' care. To claim it requires you to prove it. And to prove it, you must first define exactly what high quality care looks like at the interface between caregiver and consumer. The point of quality is point of care! It's deceptively easy to forget this and to lose line of sight between Board and bedside.[19]

"Consumers are not mysterious avatars. What they want is what you want. To be treated with dignity, respect, and compassion. To know what's going on in a way that supports informed decisions. To be as physically and psychologically comfortable as possible. To participate in real choices that take their lives and families into account. To receive the right treatment and care that gets the best possible outcome. Consistent, accurate messages about care plans and progress. Not to be harmed. To deal with an organisation that wants the best for them." She paused as she clicked to the next slide.

"Developing organisational alignment around point of care takes determination, intelligent planning, and relentless action. Hoping that care is great is not a strategy. Trusting that everyone out there is doing a great job is not purposeful action. The pursuit of greatness must be meaningful to what staff do every day or it will remain a boardroom dream. Staff must see—and believe—that this is where you want them to focus their precious time and attention." She paused to scan the audience, trying to get a feel for how her messages were being received.

"Crucially, your messages about high quality care must pass the 'take-home' test. In other words, when you test it on your family, they shouldn't run screaming from the room, afraid they will die a slow death from boredom, confusion, or the pain of extreme jargon. And if your staff say, 'Yep, that makes sense, get on and do it,' you're on a winner. If they also say, 'Looks great—let me at it!' you've hit the jackpot. Patent it immediately and get on the international speaking circuit."

A ripple of laughter ran through the audience.

"Two. Pursue greatness with 'aspirational pragmatism.' Overconfidence about the quality of care experienced by your consumers is the biggest of the big red flags when it comes to effective quality governance. Studies show that we are naturally positively biased towards the things we're involved in constructing.[20] This can lull us into complacency about how things really are. Set aspirational goals to achieve Great Care for every person, every time, and pursue them with gusto. But develop a realistic mindset about what it takes to get there. Doing anything consistently well in the complex system that is a health service is hard work because of the sheer number of factors involved and the way they interact with each other. It requires dynamic and practical pursuit, not a passive set-and-forget routine."

She clicked to a photo of a famous sporting team. "Think about a professional sports team that achieves success over a period of years. Achieving a good day for them takes more than good players trying hard during games. More than committees, reporting, and rules behind the scenes. It requires great players, surrounded by great systems, actively supported every day by great leaders. These super fit people require a super fit organisation behind them to realise their objectives. Organisational fitness requires planning and work to achieve and maintain, just as physical fitness does." Carol paused to glance at her notes, feeling the auditorium's stillness.

"But most of all, it requires working with things as they are, not as we would like them to be. The players aren't perfect, nor are they robots. They're human beings that have good and bad days and make mistakes. Every game is different and unpredictable. Success is achieved by working with that, not pretending that everyone is going to play their best game every time and that everything will go according to plan. Look at how much data coaches collect during games these days. Do you think they would do that if they didn't intend to learn and adapt as the game progressed?" She placed her hands on either side of the lectern and leaned forward, pleased to see some decisive head shaking in answer to her question.

"So it is in healthcare organisations. Great Care is created by great people at point of care, supported by great systems and governance. Get out of the ivory tower and down into the messiness of the everyday and start the journey from there. To embed Great Care as business as usual, it must reside in the bones of the organisation. That means using formal systems such as plans and policies and position descriptions and training. Focus these quality governance systems on supporting point of care to be great, starting with an honest assessment of how well they work now.

"Equally, if not more importantly, it also requires working with the informal systems that determine how work gets done every day. Influencing corridor conversations and tearoom agendas, and how decisions get made and priorities decided in real time. Shaping what managers treat as important and what influential staff members support. Helping people to thrive, not just survive.

"Three. Always be insanely curious - and honest - about what goes on for the people under your roof and in your care. Remember that these are human being with real feelings, in some sort of physical and/or psychological distress, on the receiving end of your organisation; which translates for consumers as whoever is looking after them and dealing directly with them. If I came into your service as an undercover consumer, what would I find? Would it depend where I was in the service? What shift I presented to? Who was on? Do your consumers feel cared for? Do they think your organisation is easy to deal with? Do you know their key pain points? Remember, one day it will be you, or a member of your family. Work hard on getting really good information on what's happening at point of care from both subjective and objective perspectives. Then act on it to get closer to where you want it to be."

Many audience heads nodded.

"Four. Stop 'doing quality.' Why? First and foremost, it makes no sense. When staff say they 'do' quality on Tuesdays, this is not a good sign. Usually it means they see 'quality' as a series of compliance tasks they would really rather not be 'doing.' Using this term cements a negative mindset about the whole process of improvement. Make great care a positive and active pursuit. There are only two verbs associated with quality: you're either *creating* great quality care directly with consumers, or you're *supporting* someone else to create it through effective systems and robust governance. And all embedded in a shared mindset that near enough is not good enough for our consumers and organisation."

Carol heard murmurs of agreement and noticed that an increasing number of phones were being raised to record her Quality Rules. She experienced a hit of adrenaline as she allowed herself to feel the audience engagement.

"Five. Understand that 'everyone is responsible for quality' probably means that no one really is. If 'everyone' is responsible, it's easy to interpret that as 'plenty of other people to take care of it.' Unless individuals understand their specific role in creating Great Care, and receive specific support for that role, they are unlikely to enact it. Here's a challenge: aim to get a critical mass of staff in your organisation answering the question 'Who is responsible for the quality of care in your organisation?' with: 'I am! And let me tell you exactly how.' Embedding that change alone will transform the quality of your care and consumer experience. Staff can't be held accountable unless they first have crystal clarity about their individual and team responsibilities and the support to enact those responsibilities.

"Six. Apply the blowtorch to jargon and fads. Einstein said something like: 'If you can't explain it simply, you don't understand it well enough,' and I'm a big fan of this principle. Conceptually, the pursuit of quality care should be simple, but it's often overcomplicated. Care quality is created together by the people who provide care and those who experience it. Tools, methods, systems, and governance are only effective if they help people create Great Care. Confusing and annoying people by waving shiny things with unintelligible names about or giving them extra tasks and calling it 'quality' are not useful strategies. Staff will judge you on your ability to make the process for creating, monitoring, and embedding Great Care simple, relevant, and helpful, not on your command of quality-ese. As with any tool, 'new' is not always 'improved.' And yet, sometimes it is. We have to assess each new approach on how well it can help us to achieve our quality goals—not on whether or not it's the latest 'thing.'" She paused to see if this home truth had hit the mark with the audience and noted with satisfaction a number of people making comments to their neighbours and pointing at the screen.

"The really skilled people are the ones who sort this out and ask: 'will this new tool or approach help us get where we want to go?' Under the layers of jargon and fancy wrapping, most quality tools and methods exist to help you plan, detect, understand, change, streamline, or measure. Choose the tools—old and new—that help you do this in the easiest, most effective way, explain them in plain language, and your staff and consumers will thank you.

"Seven. Remember that people support what they help create. The days are gone when we can dump a quality plan on managers out of the blue and expect them to be excited about it. Designing new plans, policy, processes, rules and training without the people who are charged with their implementation, and expecting positive engagement and sustained change, is a path to despair.

"This quality rule also reminds me to seek the people who are creating Great Care and acknowledge them. Good care is more than the absence of bad. Focusing only on the things that go wrong doesn't always inspire people to do them right. Seek and learn from the good stuff; it's every bit as important as seeking and fixing the bad stuff. Find the amazing things people are creating in your service; and adapt and spread like mad. Build on the strengths of your people: help them to flourish, and your organisation will flourish. That also means that we need to think before we dump extra tasks on people in the name of 'quality'. Don't limit your conversations to improvement about what more can be done. Also ask staff what they can stop doing—without compromising care or neglecting compliance requirements. Staff will support a 'stop doing' list that they create and will appreciate the gesture.

"Eight. Live the truism: 'Information drives understanding, but feelings drive action.' To engage people in creating Great Care, hit them with the facts, and then get out of your head and paint the human picture that shows the need for change. Health and human services love their rules and data, and of course they're important. But relying only on these may not get you caring and responsive services. There's a reason that advertisers spend their precious and expensive media minutes more on eliciting feelings than on presenting data. Changes must be introduced to go beyond an 'Oh, that's interesting,' response to the facts, to get a 'Wow, we should do something about that!' response from the heart. If you can achieve this, you'll spend less time pushing and more time leading. I know which I'd rather do!"

More heads nodding.

"Nine. Put your meetings to work. Use meetings as a progress reality check and driver. So many graphs, so much paper. But is all this helping us to get on top of our hotspots and risks and moving us closer to achieving our objectives? Or are your meetings a procession of process and a cavalcade of compliance, with the impact on point of care concealed in the mists of mediocrity? Okay, enough with the alliteration." She smiled into the audience.

"Ten. Last but not least. Lead with Quality Intelligence. We're not born with the smarts required to lead the creation of Great Care. Improving safety and quality is a technical specialty, requiring what I call 'Quality Intelligence': a specific set of knowledge and skills that must be developed. We all fall into the trap of thinking that the bureaucracy of quality is the quality system. Human services leaders work hard to implement governance systems, care processes, committees, compliance, improvement activities, measures and reporting, hoping to get good care as a result. But these are only supporting structures. The quality of the consumer experience hinges on people: the motivation and ability of managers and staff at point of care to create consistent greatness with consumers from the chaos of complexity. " She heard a murmur of assent.

"Good managers are critical to this because they can point everyone in the same direction and build teams that work to their strengths to create Great Care. These managers - and the and quality teams that support them - must be equipped with the skills they need to play their role in providing great care. At the very least they should have a working knowledge of complexity, change, resilience and measurement. They should know how to get the best out of people in a challenging environment and understand how to work with consumers to create positive experiences and outcomes. People aren't born with this knowledge, nor do they necessarily acquire it on their rise through the ranks. Basically, if we want great care, we have to develop great managers."

Carol paused as she clicked to her final slide, emblazoned with the KVHS Great Care logo, and many photos of KVHS consumers, staff and committee members.

"And where has all this left us? Just before this session I received a text containing our state DHHS results." A hush descended over the audience. All that work and commitment. Did it make a difference?

"I can announce … that out of thirty-five health services, we came in *eighth* on consumer satisfaction, and *third* on staff satisfaction!" she declared with relish.

The audience clapped enthusiastically, and Carol heard cheering from KVHS staff in the middle of the auditorium. She peered past the spotlight into the audience. Rosie was hugging Kristen. Pari sat next to them, beaming and dabbing her cheeks with a tissue. Jeff was grinning broadly, and Anton gave her a thumbs up, which Carol enthusiastically returned. She sought Elena and found her sitting farther back, being congratulated by a group of nursing colleagues. Their eyes locked. Elena nodded, almost imperceptibly.

Carol soaked up the scene. *Doesn't happen very often, might as well enjoy it.* Apart from the Mountain Health crew, who looked less than impressed, Carol could see that the audience was happy for the KVHS' success. She allowed herself a huge smile of relief and joy. Wild waving in the front row caught her eye and she saw Nancy jumping out of her seat to get Carol's attention, whilst simultaneously pumping the hand of the Minister for Health sitting next to her. "Thank you," Nancy mouthed. "Thank *you*," Carol mouthed back.

She took a breath. "To conclude"—she clicked to the next slide and waited for the applause to subside—"I'd like to finish with a quote. This sits on my noticeboard and I read it every day to remind me of what's important. 'Systems awareness and design are important for health professionals, but they are not enough. They are enabling mechanisms only. Ultimately, the secret of quality is love. You have to love your patient and your profession. If you have love, you can then work backwards to monitor and improve the system.'[21] That's what this is all about: making the point of care the point of what we do. I can't wait to come back and tell you about our next level of evolution: this is only the beginning! Thank you very much—and goodnight."

Carol took in the applause for another few seconds before relinquishing the microphone to the session Chair to close the conference, and descending the stage stairs. As she stood in the dark, listening to his closing remarks, she felt a contented weariness descend over her. She was looking forward to a post-conference glass of wine and a celebration dinner with her colleagues and friends. But most of all, she realised, she couldn't wait for a long, blissfully white coat-free, sleep.

SOURCES AND APPENDICES

The appendices provide some of my key tools and models referred to throughout the story. They are indicated throughout the book by a superscript A# corresponding to the appendix number. Please note that any tool or method requires adapting to the local context to be successfully transplanted and applied.

SOURCES and INFLUENCES

I've been educated, informed, and influenced in my career by more researchers, authors, teachers, and mentors than I could mention. The list below relates to information in the book that is drawn from or influenced by a specific source. Detailed reference lists relating to the strategic quality system model and other tools are found in my first book, *The Strategic Quality Manager* (www.cathybalding.com).

1. Quote attributed to Joshua J. Marine.

2. P. Lencioni, *The Five Dysfunctions of a Team* (USA: John Wiley and Sons, 2006).

3. C. Balding, *The Strategic Quality Manager* (Melbourne, Australia: Arcade Custom, 2011); C. Balding, *Create a Great Quality System in Six Months Blueprint* (Melbourne, Australia: Qualityworks P/L, 2013).

4. J. Braithwaite et al., "Complexity Science in Healthcare: Aspirations, Approaches, Applications and Accomplishments: A White Paper." (Australian Institute of Health Innovation, Macquarie University, Sydney, Australia, 2017), http://aihi.mq.edu.au/ resource/ complexity-science-healthcare-white-paper

5. Safer Care Victoria, Delivering High Quality Healthcare. The Victorian Clinical Governance Framework. (State of Victoria, Department of Health and Human Services, 2017) https:// www2.health.vic.gov.au/hospitals-and-health-services/safer-care-victoria/ scv-publications

6. Institute of Medicine (IOM), Crossing the Quality Chasm: A New Health System for the 21st Century (Washington, DC: National Academy Press, 2001), https://www.ncbi.nlm. nih. gov/pubmed/25057539

7. Picker Institute, "Principles of Patient-centred Care" (Picker Institute, UK. 1987), http:// www.picker.org/

8. T. Christensen, "Rebalancing the Patient Experience: 20 Years of a Pendulum Swing," *Patient Experience Journal,* 4, no. 3, article 3 (2017) http://pxjournal.org/journal/vol4/ iss3/3

9. H. Manning and K. Bodine, *Outside In: The Power of Putting Customers at the Center of Your Business* (USA: Forrester Research, New Harvest Books, 2012).

10. "The Strength of Actions Hierarchy" (USA: Veterans Association National Centre for Patient Safety). https://www.patientsafety.va.gov/docs/joe/rca_tools_2_15.pdf

11. D. Halpern, Inside the Nudge Unit (London, UK: Penguin Random House, 2015).

12. D. Heath and C. Heath, *Switch: How to Change When Change Is Hard* (New York: Random House Business Books, 2011).

13. AIDA model attributed to E. St. Elmo Lewis, "Catch-Line and Argument," The Book-Keeper, 15 (February 1903): 124, https://en.wikipedia.org/wiki/AIDA_(marketing)

14. D.H. Pink, Drive: *The Surprising Truth about What Motivates Us* (New York: Penguin Putnam Inc, 2011).

15. M. Marshall, "Bridging the Ivory Towers and the Swampy Lowlands; Increasing the Impact of Health Services Research on Quality Improvement," *International Journal for Quality in Health Care* 26 (2014): 1–5. https://www.ncbi.nlm.nih.gov/pubmed/24141013

16. J. Juran and J. Defeo, *Juran's Quality Handbook: The Complete Guide to Performance Excellence*, 6th ed. (The McGraw-Hill Companies Ltd, 2010), https://blogs.mtu.edu/improvement/2014/02/27/the-juran-trilogy/

17. S. G. Leggat, "Editorial: The Real Business of Healthcare," Australian Health Review 32, no. 2 (May 2008), https://www.publish.csiro.au/AH/AH080203

18. B. Burchard, *The Motivation Manifesto* (California: Hay House, 2014).

19. S.G. Leggat and C. Balding, "Bridging Existing Governance Gaps: Five Evidence-based Actions That Boards Can Take to Pursue High Quality Care," *Australian Health Review Online* (2017), https://www.ncbi.nlm.nih.gov/pubmed/29127953

20. M.I. Norton, D. Mochon, and D. Ariely, The IKEA Effect. When Labour Leads to Love. Harvard business School Working Paper, 11-091. https://www.hbs.edu/faculty/Publication%20Files/11 091.pdf

21. F. Mullan, "A Founder of Quality Assessment Encounters a Troubled System Firsthand," *Health Affairs* (Jan/Feb 2001), https://www.healthaffairs.org/doi/pdf/10.1377/hlthaff.20.1.137

APPENDIX 1:
STRATEGIC QUALITY SYSTEM MODEL

STRATEGIC QUALITY SYSTEM MODEL

A GREAT CONSUMER EXPERIENCE is created by GREAT PEOPLE, supported by GREAT SYSTEMS.

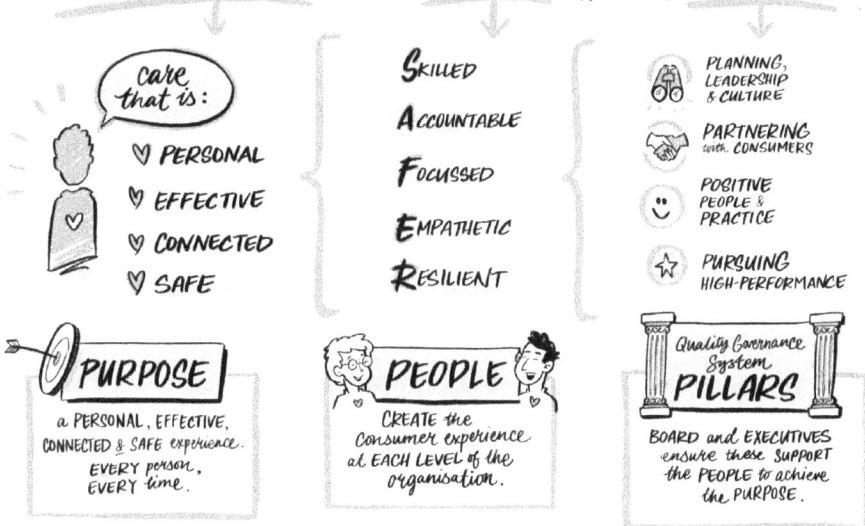

care that is:

♡ PERSONAL

♡ EFFECTIVE

♡ CONNECTED

♡ SAFE

SKILLED

ACCOUNTABLE

FOCUSSED

EMPATHETIC

RESILIENT

PLANNING, LEADERSHIP & CULTURE

PARTNERING with CONSUMERS

POSITIVE PEOPLE & PRACTICE

PURSUING HIGH-PERFORMANCE

PURPOSE

a PERSONAL, EFFECTIVE, CONNECTED & SAFE experience. EVERY person, EVERY time.

PEOPLE

CREATE the consumer experience at EACH LEVEL of the organisation.

Quality Governance System
PILLARS

BOARD and EXECUTIVES ensure these SUPPORT the PEOPLE to achieve the PURPOSE.

APPENDIX 2:
GREAT CARE GOALS AND ACTIONS

PERSONAL CARE is responsive to and focused on the individual and:

Identifies and respects individual needs

Is caring, empathic and supportive

Provides care as a partnership between consumers, carers and staff

Ensures consumers are informed and understood

Is culturally appropriate

Happens in a clean and comfortable environment

CONNECTED CARE provides a smooth, integrated pathway and:

Provides the easiest possible access to the care required

Delivers care and services when required

Is based on collaborative care planning and implementation

Strives for a smooth, coordinated journey driven by shared understanding of care pathways between staff and consumers

Avoids 'surprises' for consumers and carers by keeping everyone on the same page

EFFECTIVE CARE is the right care with the best possible results, achieved by:

Correct diagnosis based on skilled assessment and the right tests

Competent, credentialed staff working within their scope of practice

The right care and treatment based on best available evidence; and senior staff knowledge and experience

Care needs expertly met

Eliminating unnecessary tests and treatment

SAFE CARE keeps people free from harm such as:

Infection

Falls and Pressure Injuries

Medication errors

Incorrectly identified or administered blood

Incorrect consumer identification

Wrong side or site surgery and retained instruments

Unidentified deterioration

Psychological harm

Other harm risks associated with a person's condition, circumstances and care

APPENDIX 3:
STRATEGIC QUALITY SYSTEM FRAMEWORK COMPONENTS

An effective and strategic quality system comprises:	Components
A clear **PURPOSE** that paints a rich picture of the quality of care you want to provide and be known for (Great Care)	Key goals for the care to be provided to every consumer: •Personal •Effective •Connected •Safe
PEOPLE with clear roles in providing or supporting Great Care	Specific descriptions of the contribution everyone makes regardless of where they sit in the organisation
PILLARS OF GOVERNANCE and **SYSTEMS** that support the people to fulfil their roles	Governance and systems that actively support the people to create great care: •Leadership and Culture •Consumer Partnerships •Positive People and Practice •Pursuing High Performance

APPENDIX 4:
TIPS FOR LEADING GREAT CARE

1. Start Where You Really Are – not where you'd like to be. Confront the brutal facts of the situation you find yourself in. Admit vulnerability and that you don't have all the answers, because no one does. Don't sugar coat mediocrity, but don't dwell on it either. Get the real picture, develop the plan for improvement, and move, move, move.

2. Then – Start Where They Are. Work with the people who need to change to achieve great care, to define what that means to them, and how it would look and feel every day. Make the case for change based on how the current situation affects everyone. Remember that information drives understanding but feeling drive action. Don't rely only on data to make the case for change. Give it a human face.

3. Develop a set of shared, non-negotiable goals for greatness. From these conversations, develop a set of clear great care goals and map out a simple plan for achieving them. Don't over-engineer it – simplify it until everyone involved can discuss the goals and how they are to be achieved in their own way. Make achieving it part of the social fabric or the organisation, as well as part of the systems and governance. Understand that the plan may change as circumstances change, but the goals do not. Learn from wins and losses, adjust strategies as necessary, and move on.

 4. Embrace the hard yards together. Be honest about what it will take to get from where you are to where you want to go and the barriers you'll confront. People support what they help to create, so seek input and advice from everyone involved about how to get things moving in the right direction. Work together through the challenges to make it happen. Greatness is won in the tough times! Learn, take a breath and keep going.

5. Make it as easy as possible to win. Make sure everyone understands their own, specific, unique role in achieving the goals and can use their strengths and talents to progress the plan. Learn from success stories as much as from problems. Provide support, guidance and resources to make achieving the goals business as usual. Remove barriers so that it's as easy as possible for people to do the right thing. Then hold each other to account for doing the right thing.

6. Model the behaviour you want to see in the team. Leaders – lead! Be the goals and values on two legs. Get amongst it. Guide the process, pick the team up when things don't go to plan, and celebrate when they do. You don't have to be sombre to be serious. Make sure your team has some serious fun as well as hard work. And get some support for yourselves - leadership is a challenge. Take your role seriously – and enjoy every minute.

THE POINT OF CARE

APPENDIX 5:
QUALITY SUCCESS MINDSET

MOVE FROM: PROVIDING QUALITY CARE AND SERVICES IS EASY FOR US Mindset

MOVE TO: PROVIDING QUALITY CARE AND SERVICES IS AN ONGOING CHALLENGE Mindset

All services face the same challenges in providing consistently high quality care - and anyone can go backwards

We're us – so we must be good!

Everyone here knows what good care is and is out there trying hard to achieve it

'High quality care and services' must be clearly and simply defined so everyone has a common understanding of what we're trying to achieve with every consumer

Our consumers love us and would tell us if they were unhappy

We know that our consumers may feel vulnerable when in our care and may find it hard to speak up

I'm sure our staff always do the right thing and provide the best care

Our staff are busy, work under pressure and have good and bad days – and work with good and bad systems – so require ongoing training and active support to provide good care

We have all the quality governance systems in place we are required to have

We must monitor and adjust our systems to ensure they effectively support the delivery of consistently good care

We're on top of our risks

We're accredited – so we must provide high quality care

The risk situation is dynamic and changing and requires robust monitoring and management

The quality manager does a great job of looking after 'quality'

Accreditation is a snapshot in time. What are the high performing services similar to ours doing with and for their consumers to go beyond compliance?

Every person in our organisation has a specific role in and responsibility for creating a quality consumer experience at point of care

APPENDIX 6:
TURBO CHANGE MODEL OVERVIEW

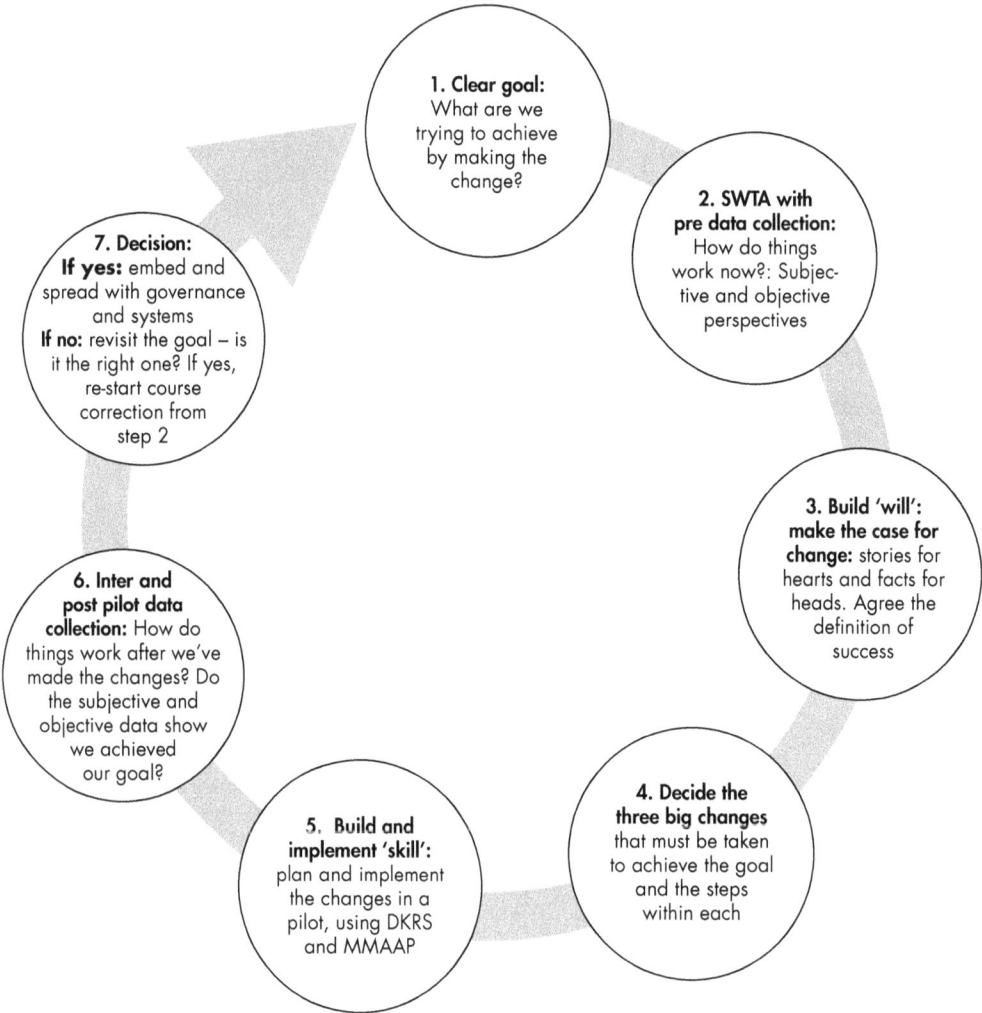

1. Clear goal: What are we trying to achieve by making the change?

2. SWTA with pre data collection: How do things work now?: Subjective and objective perspectives

3. Build 'will': make the case for change: stories for hearts and facts for heads. Agree the definition of success

4. Decide the three big changes that must be taken to achieve the goal and the steps within each

5. Build and implement 'skill': plan and implement the changes in a pilot, using DKRS and MMAAP

6. Inter and post pilot data collection: How do things work after we've made the changes? Do the subjective and objective data show we achieved our goal?

7. Decision:
If yes: embed and spread with governance and systems
If no: revisit the goal – is it the right one? If yes, re-start course correction from step 2

NOTES

Dr Cathy Balding

Cathy Balding PhD is the Director of Qualityworks, a business dedicated to making quality make sense; and Adjunct Professor, School of Psychology and Public Health, at La Trobe University. Cathy has worked in health service management, quality improvement and clinical governance for over three decades: in national and state roles, in rural and metropolitan health services, and across the community, acute and aged care sectors.

Her career has spanned a number of Australian state and national quality and clinical governance initiatives, including as inaugural manager of both the Victorian Quality Council and the Australian Council on Healthcare Standards national clinical indictor program. She has worked in, with and around health service accreditation for many years, and published articles and provided education in quality and clinical governance nationally and internationally.

Over the past decade Cathy has specialised in developing acute, community and aged care quality and clinical governance frameworks, using her strategic quality system to support aspirational, practical, whole of organisation approaches to creating great care and experiences with consumers at point of care.

Cathy also supports quality professionals and leaders to evolve their roles to be more effective and enjoyable. Her previous books: The Strategic Quality Manager Handbook and Create a Great Quality System in Six Months Blueprint are designed to help quality managers and leaders lay strong social and organisational foundations for great care. Her website is designed to further support this goal and is where you'll find her tools and training videos, the monthly QualityNews bulletin and the No Harm Done podcast; all of which delve into what it takes to create consistently good care in the complex health and human services environment.

Above all, Cathy is interested in the human side of quality. It doesn't matter how high-tech the data collection, how glossy the plan, how shiny the quality system or how complicated the spreadsheet, care is, in the end, provided by, with and for people. Helping them develop a high performance mindset and to love striving for great care is her endlessly challenging and rewarding priority. The rest is just the 'how'. She subscribes to John Cleese's observation that 'you don't have to be sombre to be serious', firmly believing that laughter is not only the best medicine, but a great way to learn and thrive.

Find out more and access Cathy's podcast, bulletin, books and tools at: **www.cathybalding.com**